Dummies 101:™ Internet Explorer 3 For Windows® 95

Your AT&T WorldNet℠ Account
CHEAT SHEET

Your AT&T WorldNet e-mail address:

_____@worldnet.att.net

First-choice phone number for connecting to AT&T WorldNet Service:

_____

Second-choice phone number:

_____

AT&T WorldNet Customer Service number:
800-400-1447

E-mail address for billing questions: wnetbill@attmail.com
E-mail address for technical support: wnettech@attmail.com
(Refer to Unit 1 for information on filling in these blanks.)

Browsing the Web

To Do This . . .	Do This . . .
Open Internet Explorer and connect to the Internet	Double-click the Internet icon on your desktop; when prompted, type your password and click OK.
Identify a link in a Web page	Text links are underlined; when you point to a text or picture link, the pointer becomes a pointing finger.
Jump where a link leads	Point to the link and click once.
Go back to the previous page	Click the Back button.
Go to your home page	Click the Home button.
Jump to a page when you know the page's address (URL)	Type the URL in the Address box (below the toolbar) and press Enter.
Add the current page to your Favorites menu	Click the Favorites button on the toolbar; choose Add To Favorites.
Jump to a page listed on your Favorites menu	Click the Favorites button on the toolbar; choose the desired page from the list.
Search the Web	Click the Search button on the toolbar; choose a Search tool.
Download a file	Click the link leading to the file.

Accessing the CD-ROM Files

Note: The CD-ROM does not contain Windows 95. You must already have Windows 95 installed on your computer.

Follow the instructions in Unit 1 and Appendix B of the book to install and access the files on the CD-ROM.

☑ Progress Check

Unit 1: Setting Up Your Account
❏ Lesson 1-1: Setting Up the AT&T WorldNet Account
❏ Lesson 1-2: Leaping Online (And Off Again!)
❏ Lesson 1-3: Moving Around in a Web Page
❏ Lesson 1-4: Creating Your Dummies 101 Folder

Unit 2: Browsing Beyond the Home Page
❏ Lesson 2-1: Clicking a Link to Jump to a New Page
❏ Lesson 2-2: Going Home, Backward, and Forward
❏ Lesson 2-3: Jumping with Quick Links

Unit 3: Entering URLs (and Smart URLs!)
❏ Lesson 3-1: Entering an URL in the Address Box
❏ Lesson 3-2: Entering an URL in the Run Dialog Box
❏ Lesson 3-3: Grabbing an URL from Anywhere

Unit 4: Building a List of Favorite Pages
❏ Lesson 4-1: Adding a Page to Your Favorites List
❏ Lesson 4-2: Jumping to a Favorite Page
❏ Lesson 4-3: Managing Your Favorites

Unit 5: Searching for Stuff
❏ Lesson 5-1: Opening a Search Tool
❏ Lesson 5-2: Clicking through Categories
❏ Lesson 5-3: Phrasing a Simple Search Term
❏ Lesson 5-4: Power Searching

Unit 6: Downloading Files
❏ Lesson 6-1: Understanding the Types of Files
❏ Lesson 6-2: Finding Files
❏ Lesson 6-3: Downloading a File
❏ Lesson 6-4: Unzipping Compressed Files

D1524823

Dummies 101:™ Internet Explorer 3 For Windows® 95

CHEAT SHEET

Unit 7: Playing Multimedia

- Lesson 7-1: Playing Inline Multimedia
- Lesson 7-2: Playing External Multimedia
- Lesson 7-3: Controlling Active Multimedia

Unit 8: Controlling Kids' Access to Web Content

- Lesson 8-1: Enabling Ratings and Choosing Types of Material to Block Out
- Lesson 8-2: Setting General Options for Content Advisor
- Lesson 8-3: Disabling Content Advisor

Unit 9: Printing Pages, Saving Pages, and Opening Pages on Disk

- Lesson 9-1: Printing the Current Web Page
- Lesson 9-2: Saving a Page to Disk
- Lesson 9-3: Opening and Printing a Saved Page

Unit 10: Making and Taking Internet Shortcuts

- Lesson 10-1: Creating a Shortcut
- Lesson 10-2: Using Shortcuts

Unit 11: Chatting "Live" with Fellow Surfers

- Lesson 11-1: Setting Up Comic Chat
- Lesson 11-2: Entering a Chat Room
- Lesson 11-3: Contributing to the Conversation

Unit 12: Messaging through E-Mail and Newsgroups

- Lesson 12-1: Sending Mail Straight from a Web Page
- Lesson 12-2: Composing a New Message
- Lesson 12-3: Sending and Receiving Messages
- Lesson 12-4: Replying to and Forwarding Messages
- Lesson 12-5: Getting Started with Internet News
- Lesson 12-6: Reading a Message
- Lesson 12-7: Posting Messages

Unit 13: Making and Taking Internet Phone Calls

- Lesson 13-1: Setting Up NetMeeting for Phone Calls
- Lesson 13-2: Making a Call
- Lesson 13-3: Taking a Call

Communicating through E-Mail, News, Phone

To Do This . . .	Do This . . .
Open Internet Mail	From the Windows 95 Start menu, choose Programs⇨Internet Mail.
Send a message from a Web page	Click the e-mail link in the Web page, type your message, and click the Send button.
Send a message when you know the e-mail address	In Internet Mail, click New Message, type the message, click the Send button, and click the Send and Receive button.
Send and receive all new mail	Click the Send and Receive button.
Open Internet News	From the Windows 95 Start menu, choose Programs⇨Internet Mail.
Subscribe to a group	Click the Newsgroups button; click a newsgroup name in the list on the All tab.
Display the list of messages for a group	Drop down the Newsgroups list (below the toolbar) and choose one of your subscribed newsgroups.
Read a message	Click the message in the message list.
Reply to a message	When viewing the message, click Reply to Group, type your reply, and click the Post button.

Chatting in a Chat Room

To Do This . . .	Do This . . .
Open Comic Chat	From the Windows 95 Start menu, choose Programs⇨Microsoft Comic Chat⇨Microsoft Comic Chat.
Connect to the chat server and display the chat room list	Click Show all available chat rooms; click OK.
Choose a nickname, character, and background	Choose View⇨Options, fill in the Personal Info, Character, and Background tabs.
Enter a chat room	Choose the room from the Chat Room list.
Contribute to the chat	Type your statement; press Enter.

IDG BOOKS WORLDWIDE™

DUMMIES 101™: INTERNET EXPLORER 3
FOR
WINDOWS® 95

by Ned Snell

IDG Books Worldwide, Inc.
An International Data Group Company

Foster City, CA ✦ Chicago, IL ✦ Indianapolis, IN ✦ Southlake, TX

Dummies 101™: Internet Explorer 3 For Windows® 95

Published by
IDG Books Worldwide, Inc.
An International Data Group Company
919 E. Hillsdale Blvd.
Suite 400
Foster City, CA 94404
www.idgbooks.com (IDG Books Worldwide Web Site)
http://www.dummies.com (Dummies Press Web Site)

Copyright © 1996 IDG Books Worldwide, Inc. All rights reserved. No part of this book, including interior design, cover design, and icons, may be reproduced or transmitted in any form, by any means (electronic, photocopying, recording, or otherwise) without the prior written permission of the publisher.

Library of Congress Catalog Card No.: 96-78134

ISBN: 0-7645-0074-0

Printed in the United States of America

10 9 8 7 6 5 4 3 2 1

1M/QX/RR/ZW/IN

Distributed in the United States by IDG Books Worldwide, Inc.

Distributed by Macmillan Canada for Canada; by Contemporanea de Ediciones for Venezuela; by Distribuidora Cuspide for Argentina; by CITEC for Brazil; by Ediciones ZETA S.C.R. Ltda. for Peru; by Editorial Limusa SA for Mexico; by Transworld Publishers Limited in the United Kingdom and Europe; by Academic Bookshop for Egypt; by Levant Distributors S.A.R.L. for Lebanon; by Al Jassim for Saudi Arabia; by Simron Pty. Ltd. for South Africa; by Pustak Mahal for India; by The Computer Bookshop for India; by Toppan Company Ltd. for Japan; by Addison Wesley Publishing Company for Korea; by Longman Singapore Publishers Ltd. for Singapore, Malaysia, Thailand, and Indonesia; by Unalis Corporation for Taiwan; by WS Computer Publishing Company, Inc. for the Philippines; by WoodsLane Pty. Ltd. for Australia; by WoodsLane Enterprises Ltd. for New Zealand. Authorized Sales Agent: Anthony Rudkin Associates for the Middle East and North Africa.

For general information on IDG Books Worldwide's books in the U.S., please call our Consumer Customer Service department at 800-762-2974. For reseller information, including discounts and premium sales, please call our Reseller Customer Service department at 800-434-3422.

For information on where to purchase IDG Books Worldwide's books outside the U.S., please contact our International Sales department at 415-655-3172 or fax 415-655-3295.

For information on foreign language translations, please contact our Foreign & Subsidiary Rights department at 415-655-3021 or fax 415-655-3281.

For sales inquiries and special prices for bulk quantities, please contact our Sales department at 415-655-3200 or write to the address above.

For information on using IDG Books Worldwide's books in the classroom or for ordering examination copies, please contact our Educational Sales department at 800-434-2086 or fax 817-251-8174.

For authorization to photocopy items for corporate, personal, or educational use, please contact Copyright Clearance Center, 222 Rosewood Drive, Danvers, MA 01923, or fax 508-750-4470.

Trademarks: All brand names and product names used in this book are trade names, service marks, trademarks, or registered trademarks of their respective owners. IDG Books Worldwide is not associated with any product or vendor mentioned in this book.

is a trademark under exclusive license to IDG Books Worldwide, Inc., from International Data Group, Inc.

About the Author

Ned Snell stayed religiously apart from computers until the mid '80s, when one of the world's largest software companies tricked him into accepting a job by telling him he'd be writing about PCs, which — the employer promised — "had no future." Before that, Ned had been an unemployed actor, a public school teacher, a writer of S.A.T. preparation courseware, and a VCR tape-changer at Bloomingdale's in Manhattan (not necessarily in that order).

Forever tainted by technology, Snell decided to make the best of it, becoming a documentation and training specialist for several major software companies, and eventually becoming an award-winning computer journalist. Snell has written hundreds of articles for *Datamation* (for which he served as a contributing editor), *Software Magazine,* and others, and he has served as editor-in-chief for several national publications, including *Edge* magazine and *Art & Design News.* He is the author of six books (including *Curious About the Internet?* and *Navigating the Internet with Windows 95,* both from Sams), and co-author of several more. Between books, Snell continues acting in regional theatre, commercials, and industrial films. He lives with his wife, an artist and translator, and their two sons in Florida.

Welcome to the world of IDG Books Worldwide.

IDG Books Worldwide, Inc., is a subsidiary of International Data Group, the world's largest publisher of computer-related information and the leading global provider of information services on information technology. IDG was founded more than 25 years ago and now employs more than 8,500 people worldwide. IDG publishes more than 270 computer publications in over 75 countries (see listing below). More than 90 million people read one or more IDG publications each month.

Launched in 1990, IDG Books Worldwide is today the #1 publisher of best-selling computer books in the United States. We are proud to have received eight awards from the Computer Press Association in recognition of editorial excellence and three from *Computer Currents'* First Annual Readers' Choice Awards. Our best-selling *...For Dummies*® series has more than 25 million copies in print with translations in 30 languages. IDG Books Worldwide, through a joint venture with IDG's Hi-Tech Beijing, became the first U.S. publisher to publish a computer book in the People's Republic of China. In record time, IDG Books Worldwide has become the first choice for millions of readers around the world who want to learn how to better manage their businesses.

Our mission is simple: Every one of our books is designed to bring extra value and skill-building instructions to the reader. Our books are written by experts who understand and care about our readers. The knowledge base of our editorial staff comes from years of experience in publishing, education, and journalism — experience which we use to produce books for the '90s. In short, we care about books, so we attract the best people. We devote special attention to details such as audience, interior design, use of icons, and illustrations. And because we use an efficient process of authoring, editing, and desktop publishing our books electronically, we can spend more time ensuring superior content and spend less time on the technicalities of making books.

You can count on our commitment to deliver high-quality books at competitive prices on topics you want to read about. At IDG Books Worldwide, we continue in the IDG tradition of delivering quality for more than 25 years. You'll find no better book on a subject than one from IDG Books Worldwide.

John J. Kilcullen

John Kilcullen
President and CEO
IDG Books Worldwide, Inc.

IDG Books Worldwide, Inc., is a subsidiary of International Data Group, the world's largest publisher of computer-related information and the leading global provider of information services on information technology. International Data Group publishes over 276 computer publications in over 75 countries. Ninety million people read one or more International Data Group publications each month. International Data Group's publications include: **ARGENTINA:** Annuario de Informatica, Computerworld Argentina, PC World Argentina; **AUSTRALIA:** Australian Macworld, Client/Server Journal, Computer Living, Computerworld, Computerworld 100, Digital News, IT Casebook, Network World, On-line World Australia, PC World, Publishing Essentials, Reseller, WebMaster; **AUSTRIA:** Computerwelt Osterreich, Networks Austria, PC Tip; **BELARUS:** PC World Belarus; **BELGIUM:** Data News; **BRAZIL:** Annuário de Informática, Computerworld Brazil, Connections, Super Game Power, Macworld, PC Player, PC World Brazil, Publish Brazil, Reseller News; **BULGARIA:** Computerworld Bulgaria, Networkworld/Bulgaria, PC & MacWorld Bulgaria; **CANADA:** CIO Canada, Client/Server World, ComputerWorld Canada, InfoCanada, Network World Canada; **CHILE:** Computerworld Chile, PC World Chile; **COLOMBIA:** Computerworld Colombia, PC World Colombia; **COSTA RICA:** PC World Centro America; **THE CZECH AND SLOVAK REPUBLICS:** Computerworld Czechoslovakia, Elektronika Czechoslovakia, Macworld Czech Republic, PC World Czechoslovakia; **DENMARK:** Communications World, Computerworld Danmark, Macworld Danmark, PC Privat Danmark, PC World Danmark, PC World Danmark Supplements, TECH World; **DOMINICAN REPUBLIC:** PC World Republica Dominicana; **ECUADOR:** PC World Ecuador; **EGYPT:** Computerworld Middle East, PC World Middle East; **EL SALVADOR:** PC World Centro America; **FINLAND:** MikroPC, Tietoverkko, Tietoviikko; **FRANCE:** Distributique, Golden, Hebdo-Distributique, Info PC, Le Guide du Monde Informatique, Le Monde Informatique, Reseaux & Telecoms; **GERMANY:** Computer Partner, Computerwoche, Computerwoche Extra, Computerwoche Focus, I/M Information Management, Macwelt, PC Welt; **GREECE:** GamePro, Multimedia World; **GUATEMALA:** PC World Centro America; **HONDURAS:** PC World Centro America; **HONG KONG:** Computerworld Hong Kong, PCWorld Hong Kong, Publish in Asia; **HUNGARY:** ABCD CD-ROM, Computerworld Szamitastechnika, PC & Mac World Hungary, PC-X Magazine; **ICELAND:** Tolvuheimur/PC World Island; **INDIA:** Information Systems Computerworld, PC World India, Publish in Asia; **INDONESIA:** InfoKomputer PC World, Komputek Computerworld, Publish in Asia; **IRELAND:** ComputerScope, PC Live!; **ISRAEL:** People & Computers; **ITALY:** Computerworld Italia, Computerworld Italia Special Editions, Macworld Italia, Networking Italia, PC Shopping, PC World Italia, PC World/Walt Disney; **JAPAN:** DTP World, HP Open World Japan, Macworld Japan, Nikkei Personal Computing, Open World Japan, OS/2 World Japan, SunWorld Japan, Windows World Japan; **KENYA:** East African Computer News; **KOREA:** Hi-Tech Information/Computerworld, Macworld Korea, PC World Korea; **MACEDONIA:** PC World Macedonia; **MALAYSIA:** Computerworld Malaysia, PC World Malaysia, Publish in Asia; **MEXICO:** Computerworld Mexico, Macworld, PC World Mexico; **MYANMAR:** PC World Myanmar; **NETHERLANDS:** Computer! Totaal, LAN Magazine, LanWorld Buyers Guide, Macworld, Net Magazine, Totaal! Beurskrant; **NEW ZEALAND:** Absolute Beginner's Guide, Computer Buyer, Computer Industry Directory, Computerworld New Zealand, MTB, Network World, PC World New Zealand; **NICARAGUA:** PC World Centro America; **NIGERIA:** PC World Nigeria; **NORWAY:** Computerworld Norge, Computerworld Privat (Datamagasinet), CW Rapport Norge, IDG's KURSGUIDE, Macworld Norge, Multimediaworld, PC World Ekspress, PC World Nettverk, PC World Norge, PC World's Produktguide, Windows World Spesial; **PAKISTAN:** Computerworld Pakistan, PC World Pakistan; **Panama:** PC World Panama; **P. R. OF CHINA:** China Computer Users, China Computerworld, China Infoworld, China Telecom World Weekly, Computer & Communication, Electronic Design China, Electronics Today, Electronics Weekly, Game Camp, Game Soft, Network World China, PC World China, Popular Computer Weekly, Software Weekly, Software World, Telecom World; **PERU:** Computerworld Peru, PC World Profesional Peru, PC World Peru; **PHILIPPINES:** Computerworld Philippines, PC World Philippines, Publish in Asia; **POLAND:** Computerworld Poland, Computerworld Special Report, Macworld, Networld, PC World Komputer; **PORTUGAL:** Cerebro/PC World, Computerworld/Correio Informático, Dealer World Portugal, MacIn/PCIn, Multimedia World Portugal; **PUERTO RICO:** PC World Puerto Rico; **ROMANIA:** Computerworld Romania, PC World Romania, Telecom Romania; **RUSSIA:** Computerworld Russia, Mir PK, Sety; **SINGAPORE:** Computerworld Singapore, PC World Singapore, Publish in Asia; **SLOVENIA:** MONITOR; **SOUTH AFRICA:** Computing S.A., InfoWorld S.A., Network World S.A., Software World; **SPAIN:** Computerworld España, COMUNICACIONES WORLD, Dealer World, Macworld España, PC World España; **SWEDEN:** CAP&Design, Computer Sweden, Corporate Computing, MacWorld, Maxi Data, MikroDatorn, Nätverk & Kommunikation, PC/Aktiv, PC World, Windows World; **SWITZERLAND:** Computerworld Schweiz, Macworld Schweiz, PCtip; **TAIWAN:** Computerworld Taiwan, Macworld Taiwan, PC World Taiwan, Publish Taiwan, Windows World; **THAILAND:** Thai Computerworld, Publish in Asia; **TURKEY:** Computerworld Turkiye, MACWORLD Turkiye, PC WORLD Turkiye; **UKRAINE:** Computerworld Kiev, Computers & Software, Multimedia World Ukraine, PC World Ukraine; **UNITED KINGDOM:** Acorn User, Amiga Action, Amiga Computing, Appletalk, Computing, GamePro, Macworld, Network News, Parents and Computers, PC Advisor, PC Home, PSX Pro UK, The WEB; **UNITED STATES:** Cable in the Classroom, CD Review, CIO Magazine, Computerworld, Computerworld Client/Server Journal, Digital Video Magazine, DOS World, Federal Computer Week, GamePro, InfoWorld, I-Way, JavaWorld, Macworld, Multimedia World, Netscape World Online, Network World, PC Entertainment, PC World, Publish, SunWorld Online, SWATPro Magazine, Video Event, WebMaster; **URUGUAY:** PC World Uruguay; **VENEZUELA:** Computerworld Venezuela, PC World Venezuela; and **VIETNAM:** PC World Vietnam. 7/16/96

Author's Acknowledgments

Many hands and minds made this book. In particular, thanks are due to Tim Gallan, Diane Giangrossi, and James Michael Stewart, who together managed this project with grace and patience, and saved me from myself on occasion.

Thanks also to Tammy Goldfeld for believing in this book and planting its seed, and to Darlene Wong for her friendly and diligent support.

Finally, I'd like to acknowledge Mary Bednarek, for opening the door.

Dedication

This book is dedicated to my family, here and far. Those far shaped me, those here put up with me. I'm grateful to both.

I also want to thank the two people most responsible for providing me with the privilege to write this stuff:

Julie — who, not knowing me, gave me my first chance

Mark — who, knowing me too well, gave me my second chance anyway

Publisher's Acknowledgments

We're proud of this book; please send us your comments about it by using the Reader Response Card at the back of the book or by e-mailing us at feedback/dummies@idgbooks.com. Some of the people who helped bring this book to market include the following:

Acquisitions, Development, and Editorial

Project Editor: Tim Gallan

Acquisitions Editor: Tammy Goldfeld

Assistant Acquisitions Editor: Gareth Hancock

Product Development Manager: Mary Bednarek

Permissions Editor: Joyce Pepple

Copy Editor: Diane L. Giangrossi

Technical Editor: James Michael Stewart

Editorial Manager: Kristin A. Cocks

Editorial Assistant: Jerelind Davis

Production

Project Coordinator: Sherry Gomoll

Layout and Graphics: E. Shawn Aylsworth, Brett Black, Cameron Booker, Linda M. Boyer, J. Tyler Connor, Dominique DeFelice, Angela F. Hunckler, Jane E. Martin, Drew R. Moore, Mark Owens, Anna Rohrer, Brent Savage, Kate Snell, Michael Sullivan

Proofreaders: Jenny Overmyer, Rachel Garvey, Nancy Price, Dwight Ramsey, Robert Springer, Carrie Voorhis, Karen York

Indexer: David Heiret

Special Help: Bryan J. Stephenson

General and Administrative

IDG Books Worldwide, Inc.: John Kilcullen, President & CEO; Steven Berkowitz, COO & Publisher

Dummies, Inc.: Milissa Koloski, Executive Vice President & Publisher

Dummies Technology Press & Dummies Editorial: Diane Graves Steele, Vice President and Associate Publisher; Judith A. Taylor, Brand Manager

Dummies Trade Press: Kathleen A. Welton, Vice President & Publisher; Stacy S. Collins, Brand Manager

IDG Books Production for Dummies Press: Beth Jenkins, Production Director; Cindy L. Phipps, Supervisor of Project Coordination; Kathie S. Schutte, Supervisor of Page Layout; Shelley Lea, Supervisor of Graphics and Design; Debbie J. Gates, Production Systems Specialist

Dummies Packaging & Book Design: Patti Sandez, Packaging Assistant; Kavish+Kavish, Cover Design

◆

The publisher would like to give special thanks to Patrick J. McGovern, without whom this book would not have been possible.

◆

Files at a Glance

ABC 123

Part I

Unit 1	Setting Up the AT&T WorldNet Account	AT&T WorldNet℠ Service
Unit 3	Grabbing an URL from Anywhere	COPYTSTTXT

Part II

| Unit 6 | Unzipping Compressed Files | WinZip |

Part IV

| Unit 11 | Setting Up Comic Chat | Comic Chat |
| Unit 13 | Setting Up NetMeeting for Phone Calls | NetMeeting |

Part V

| Appendix C | Creating Your Own Web Page | WebEdit |

Contents at a Glance

Introduction 1

Part I: Basic Browsing 9
   Unit 1: Setting Up Your Account 11
   Unit 2: Browsing Beyond the Home Page 31
   Unit 3: Entering URLs 43
   Unit 4: Building a List of Favorite Pages 53
   Part I Review 63

Part II: Big-Time Browsing 67
   Unit 5: Searching for Stuff 69
   Unit 6: Downloading Files 85
   Unit 7: Playing Multimedia 99
   Part II Review 113

Part III: Housekeeping 117
   Unit 8: Controlling Kids' Access to Web Content 119
   Unit 9: Printing Pages, Saving Pages, and Opening Pages on Disk 129
   Unit 10: Making and Taking Internet Shortcuts 139
   Part III Review 147

Part IV: Chat, Mail, and Other Extracurricular Activities 151
   Unit 11: Chatting "Live" with Fellow Surfers 153
   Unit 12: Messaging through E-Mail and Newsgroups 169
   Unit 13: Making and Taking Internet Phone Calls 187
   Part IV Review 197

Part V: Appendixes 203
   Appendix A: Answers 205
   Appendix B: Dummies 101 CD-ROM Installation Instructions 213
   Appendix C: Creating Your Own Web Page 217

Index 229

IDG BOOKS WORLDWIDE, INC. END-USER LICENSE AGREEMENT 252

Dummies 101 CD-ROM Installation Instructions 254

Table of Contents

Introduction 1

   Who Needs an Internet Explorer, Anyhow? 1

   OK, So Who Needs this Book? 2

   What (If Anything) Do You Need to Start? 2

      Stuff you need to have 3

      Stuff you need to know 3

   About the CD-ROM 4

   How to Use This Book 4

      The gray boxes 5

      Stuff in the margins 5

      The quizzes & tests 5

      A few conventions 6

   How This Book Is Organized 6

      Part I: Basic Browsing 6

      Part II: Big-Time Browsing 7

      Part III: Housekeeping 7

      Part IV: Chat, Mail, and Other Extracurricular Activities 7

      Part V: Appendixes 7

   Icons Used in This Book 7

   Where to Go from Here 8

Part I: Basic Browsing 9

   Unit 1: Setting Up Your Account 11

   Lesson 1-1: Setting Up the AT&T WorldNet Account 13

      Starting the setup Wizard 14

      Setting up your modem 15

      Registering with AT&T 16

      Installing Internet Explorer 20

   Lesson 1-2: Leaping Online (And Off Again!) 21

      Opening Internet Explorer and the Internet 21

      Signing off the Internet 23

   Lesson 1-3: Moving Around in a Web Page 25

   Lesson 1-4: Creating Your Dummies 101 Folder 27

      Recess 28

   Unit 1 Quiz 28

   Unit 1 Exercise 29

Unit 2: Browsing Beyond the Home Page 31
   Lesson 2-1: Clicking a Link to Jump to a New Page 32
      Identifying a link 33
      Clicking links 34
   Lesson 2-2: Going Home, Backward, and Forward 35
      Jumping home 35
      Jumping backward and forward 36
   Lesson 2-3: Jumping with Quick Links 38
      Recess 39
   Unit 2 Quiz 40
   Unit 2 Exercise 41
Unit 3: Entering URLs 43
   Lesson 3-1: Entering an URL in the Address Box 44
      Entering an URL 44
      Editing an URL 46
   Lesson 3-2: Entering an URL in the Run Dialog Box 47
   Lesson 3-3: Grabbing an URL from Anywhere 49
      Recess 50
   Unit 3 Quiz 51
   Unit 3 Exercise 52
Unit 4: Building a List of Favorite Pages 53
   Lesson 4-1: Adding a Page to Your Favorites List 54
      Creating a Favorite for the current page 54
      Creating a Favorite from a link 55
   Lesson 4-2: Jumping to a Favorite Page 56
   Lesson 4-3: Managing Your Favorites 57
      Organizing Favorites 58
      Organizing Favorites as you go along 60
      Recess 60
   Unit 4 Quiz 61
   Unit 4 Exercise 62
Part I Review 63
   Unit 1 Summary 63
   Unit 2 Summary 63
   Unit 3 Summary 63
   Unit 4 Summary 63
   Part I Test 64
   Part I Lab Assignment 66

Part II: Big-Time Browsing 67
Unit 5: Searching for Stuff 69
   Lesson 5-1: Opening a Search Tool 71
      Using the Search button 71
      Entering a search tool's URL 73
   Lesson 5-2: Clicking through Categories 74
      Wandering aimlessly — why not? 74
      Browsing aimfully 76
   Lesson 5-3: Phrasing a Simple Search Term 77
      Understanding search terms 77
      Using a search term 78
   Lesson 5-4: Power Searching 80
      Phrasing the perfect search term 80
      Tips for using multiple words 80
      Searching without a search tool 82
      Recess 83

Unit 5 Quiz 83
Unit 5 Exercise 84
Unit 6: Downloading Files **85**
Lesson 6-1: Understanding the Types of Files 86
Lesson 6-2: Finding Files 89
Lesson 6-3: Downloading a File 90
Retrieving the file 90
Opening a downloaded file 92
Lesson 6-4: Unzipping Compressed Files 94
Unit 6 Quiz 96
Unit 6 Exercise 97
Unit 7: Playing Multimedia **99**
Lesson 7-1: Playing Inline Multimedia 101
Lesson 7-2: Playing External Multimedia 103
Finding an external media file 103
Dealing with Internet Explorer's unpredictable behavior 105
Displaying a picture 105
Playing a clip 106
Lesson 7-3: Controlling Active Multimedia 108
Recess 109
Unit 7 Quiz 110
Unit 7 Exercise 111
Part II Review **113**
Unit 5 Summary 113
Unit 6 Summary 113
Unit 7 Summary 113
Part II Test 114
Part II Lab Assignment 116

Part III: Housekeeping **117**
Unit 8: Controlling Kids' Access to Web Content **119**
About the Web content controversy 120
Understanding the ratings 121
Lesson 8-1: Enabling Ratings and Choosing Types of Material to Block Out 122
Lesson 8-2: Setting General Options for Content Advisor ... 124
Lesson 8-3: Disabling Content Advisor 126
Recess 126
Unit 8 Quiz 127
Unit 8 Exercise 128
Unit 9: Printing Pages, Saving Pages, and Opening Pages on Disk **129**
Lesson 9-1: Printing the Current Web Page 130
Lesson 9-2: Saving a Page to Disk 132
Lesson 9-3: Opening and Printing a Saved Page 133
Opening a saved page from Windows 133
Opening a saved page from within Internet Explorer 134
Printing a saved page 135
Recess 136
Unit 9 Quiz 136
Unit 9 Exercise 137
Unit 10: Making and Taking Internet Shortcuts **139**
Lesson 10-1: Creating a Shortcut 140
Making an Internet shortcut from a page 140
Making a shortcut from a link 141

Lesson 10-2: Using Shortcuts 142
    Opening a shortcut 142
    Copying shortcuts from Favorites 144
    Recess 145
Unit 10 Quiz 145
Unit 10 Exercise 146
Part III Review **147**
Unit 8 Summary 147
Unit 9 Summary 147
Unit 10 Summary 147
Part III Test 148
Part III Lab Assignment 150

Part IV: Chat, Mail, and Other Extracurricular Activities **151**
Unit 11: Chatting "Live" with Fellow Surfers **153**
Lesson 11-1: Setting Up Comic Chat 155
Lesson 11-2: Entering a Chat Room 156
    Opening Comic Chat and connecting to the server 156
    Choosing a nickname, character, and background 157
    Entering a room 159
    Understanding the chat display 160
Lesson 11-3: Contributing to the Conversation 161
    Adding your two cents' worth 162
    Changing expressions 163
    Making gestures 164
    Switching rooms 165
    Recess 166
Unit 11 Quiz 166
Unit 11 Exercise 167
Unit 12: Messaging through E-Mail and Newsgroups **169**
Lesson 12-1: Sending Mail Straight from a Web Page 170
Lesson 12-2: Composing a New Message 171
Lesson 12-3: Sending and Receiving Messages 173
Lesson 12-4: Replying to and Forwarding Messages 174
    Replying to a message 174
    Forwarding a message 176
Lesson 12-5: Getting Started with Internet News 176
    Opening a newsgroup from a Web page 177
    Opening Internet News 178
    Downloading the newsgroup list 178
    Subscribing to newsgroups 178
Lesson 12-6: Reading a Message 180
Lesson 12-7: Posting Messages 181
    Understanding netiquette 181
    Replying to a message 182
    Posting a new message 184
    Recess 184
Unit 12 Quiz 184
Unit 12 Exercise 185
Unit 13: Making and Taking Internet Phone Calls **187**
Lesson 13-1: Setting Up NetMeeting for Phone Calls 188
    Installing NetMeeting 189
    Opening and configuring NetMeeting 189
Lesson 13-2: Making a Call 191

Lesson 13-3: Taking a Call 193
    Recess 194
  Unit 13 Quiz 194
  Unit 13 Exercise 195
Part IV Review 197
  Unit 11 Summary 197
  Unit 12 Summary 197
  Unit 13 Summary 198
  Part IV Test 199
  Part IV Lab Assignment 201

Part V: Appendixes **203**
  Appendix A: Answers **205**
    Unit 1 Quiz Answers 205
    Unit 2 Quiz Answers 205
    Unit 3 Quiz Answers 206
    Unit 4 Quiz Answers 206
    Part I Test Answers 206
    Unit 5 Quiz Answers 207
    Unit 6 Quiz Answers 207
    Unit 7 Quiz Answers 208
    Part II Test Answers 208
    Unit 8 Quiz Answers 209
    Unit 9 Quiz Answers 209
    Unit 10 Quiz Answers 209
    Part III Test Answers 210
    Unit 11 Quiz Answers 210
    Unit 12 Quiz Answers 211
    Unit 13 Quiz Answers 211
    Part IV Test Answers 211
  Appendix B: Dummies 101 CD-ROM Installation Instructions **213**
    Installing the CD-ROM 213
    Installing Programs and Files 214
      Units 1 and 12: Using the AT&T WorldNetSM Software 214
      Unit 3: Using the COPYTST.DOC file 214
      Unit 6: Setting up WinZip 215
      Unit 11: Using Comic Chat 215
      Unit 13: Using NetMeeting 215
      Appendix C: Creating Your Own Web Page 216
  Appendix C: Creating Your Own Web Page **217**
    What's an HTML File, Anyway? 217
    Creating a Page in WebEdit 220
      Opening WebEdit 221
      Using the Home Page Wizard 221
      Viewing a page you've created 223
      Composing a page 223
      Using a template 224
    Publishing Your Web Page 225
    Learning More about Authoring 226

Index **229**

IDG BOOKS WORLDWIDE, INC. END-USER LICENSE AGREEMENT **252**

Dummies 101 CD-ROM Installation Instructions **254**

Reader Response Card .... Back of Book

Introduction

Welcome to *Dummies 101: Internet Explorer 3 For Windows 95,* the textbook that answers the popular question: "How can I enjoy and exploit the wonders of the Internet without listening to some geek explain it like it was nuclear fusion?"

You know you're no dummy. But when discussing the Internet, the Net-knowledgeable have a way of describing things that makes IRS Form 1040-Long seem simple, by comparison. To learn what you need to explore the Internet — and *just* what you need to know, without a lot of extraneous technobabble about how things work — you want someone to lay things out *as if* you were a dummy. "Go ahead," you say. "Insult my intelligence. Just make sense, okay?" Okay. It's a deal.

In this book, you discover how to cruise the Net using Internet Explorer. You learn through a series of simple, fear-free, hands-on examples and exercises — and from the very first lesson, you'll be on the Net.

You won't learn much about anything that doesn't pertain directly to *using* Internet Explorer and the Net — if you want to know the details of the Internet's 30-year evolution, the names of all of the programmers who have made important contributions, the principles of binary math, or Bill Gates' shoe size, you've come to the wrong place. But if you just want to know how to operate all of the important features of Internet Explorer and apply those features in traveling to any and all corners of the Net, you're where you belong.

Who Needs an Internet Explorer, Anyhow?

Actually, nobody needs Internet Explorer. Nobody needs the Internet. Nobody needs $100 sneakers, or electric rice steamers, or car phones, or a lot of other stuff we're happily force-fed by Madison Avenue and Silicon Valley. But since you've picked up this book, you apparently *want* the Internet. And on the Internet, Internet Explorer can be pretty darn useful.

You see, while many talk about "The Internet" as if it were one thing, the Net actually hosts a variety of different services, some of which you've probably already heard of. E-mail, newsgroups, interactive chats, and Internet phone calls are all part of the Internet family. (Don't worry if you're not yet familiar with these terms — you'll discover them as you go.)

But by far, the segment of the Internet that draws the most newcomers (dubbed *newbies*) is the World Wide Web, that part of the Internet in which users view colorful screens featuring pictures, sound, video, and more. When CNN or your local nightly news does either of the only two stories ever broadcast about the Internet ("The Internet: Best Invention Since Penicillin?" and "The Internet: Minion of Satan?"), they always show computer users viewing pretty screens with pictures of the White House or maps of Czecho-slovakia or whatever. Those folks are "surfing the Web."

Surfing the Web (about which you'll learn much more, beginning with Unit 1) requires a *browser*, a software program that shows you those pretty Web pictures and enables you to get from place to place on the Web. There are many browsers, and Microsoft Internet Explorer is one of the best, perhaps *the* best. While it is as capable a browser as you can get, it's also an ideal browser for dummies like us. It's powerful *and* easy to use — an unlikely combination, yes, but true.

But Internet Explorer does not stand alone. Microsoft supplies a family of companion programs for Internet Explorer. These companions enable you to do unWebby things, like sending e-mail and browsing newsgroups. No tutorial about the Internet or Internet Explorer would be complete without some instruction in the non-Web parts of the Internet and how Internet Explorer and its companions get you there. So this book is more than an Internet Explorer tutorial; it's a complete Internet tutorial in which the Internet Explorer family appears as the complete Net toolbox.

Okay, So Who Needs This Book?

It's cheap, it can't hurt you, and it's fully recyclable, so I heartily recommend this book to everybody. At the very least, it'll keep you from blowing that $25 on the lottery.

Who needs it *most*? Folks who possess all of the following:

- A sense of humor
- A yen for the Internet
- A yen to use Internet Explorer
- A low tolerance for computer books
- No inclination to mingle with the lonely singles that frequent evening computer classes
- A desire to know just enough about the subject to do what you want to do without acquiring excess information that could displace brain space you're saving up in case you ever get on *Jeopardy!*

What (If Anything) Do You Need to Start?

If you were drawn to picking up this book, odds are that you already have most of the prerequisite hardware, software, and minor knowledge required to dive right into this book. But just to be sure, here's everything you'll need to have, know, and do before you can use this tutorial productively.

Stuff you need to have

Surfing the Net with Internet Explorer requires, at minimum, three things:

A PC with Windows 95: Microsoft developed Internet Explorer chiefly for Windows 95 (and Windows NT) systems. Microsoft makes versions of the program available for other systems, such as Windows 3.1 and Macintosh. Other versions notwithstanding, Internet Explorer really is a Windows 95 program and performs best in Windows 95. All of the examples and steps in this book are based on the Windows 95 version. If you use another version, much of what appears in this book still applies, but some of it won't.

While Windows 95 can run (albeit badly) in a PC with a 386 processor and 4MB of memory, the minimum configuration for Internet Explorer is a 486 (or Pentium) PC with at least 8MB of memory. For best performance, I recommend 12 to 16 MB of RAM. Also, you'll need a CD-ROM drive to use the programs on the CD-ROM bundled with this book, a graphics card capable of displaying 256 colors (or more), and a modem with a speed of 14.4 kbps (kilobits per second) or faster. Finally, while a sound card is not required, you'll miss out on some great sound-related Internet stuff if you don't have one.

An Internet account: The software included on the CD-ROM with this book can sign you up, if you choose, for AT&T WorldNet^{SM} Service (you'll learn how in Unit 1). You can also get an Internet account in a lot of other ways. As you know if your mailbox has been clogged with free disks, the major online services — America Online, CompuServe, Prodigy, and The Microsoft Network — all offer Internet access. You may use Internet Explorer with any of these services, or with an Internet account from an Internet Service Provider (ISP).

The Internet Explorer software (and its companions): This is the easy one — all of the software you need is included on the CD-ROM at the back of this book.

Stuff you need to know

First off, please be reassured that this book assumes you know absolutely nothing about the Internet — *nada,* zip, zero — except maybe that it's this big worldwide computer network that you can sign up for, you connect to it through a modem and your phone line, and you can do stuff on it that may be valuable and/or fun. Beyond that, the book will fill you in with as much info as you need to accomplish the job at hand. (Of course, if you already know a lot about the Internet, you can still benefit from this book's coverage of Internet Explorer's bells and whistles.)

True to its name, this book assumes not only that its readers may be "dummies" where Internet Explorer and the Internet are concerned, but also that they're no geniuses when it comes to using Windows 95. In that spirit, I'll show you exactly what to do in Windows 95 as we go along. I'll assume only that you already know how to do the following six simple things:

- ◆ Turn on your PC and start up Windows 95 (if it does not start up by itself).

- ◆ Point to objects on the screen (icons, menu items, toolbar buttons, and so on) with your mouse.

  ◆ Click the object you're pointing to (click your left mouse button once) or double-click it (click the left mouse button twice, quickly).

  ◆ Open your Start menu and choose other menus or items from it.

  ◆ Choose items from an application's menus (File, Edit, and so on).

  ◆ Click your way around in Windows by opening and closing folders.

Note that you can learn how to do all of these things (except for the first one) by taking the Windows 95 built-in tour.

When you need to know how to do anything other than these six things, I'll show you how, step by step.

About the CD-ROM

The CD-ROM that comes in the back if this book contains all the programs and files you need to do the lesson and exercises in this book. The most important programs on the CD-ROM are Internet Explorer and the AT&T WorldNet Service, which you can install (if you don't already have an Internet Service Provider) by following the directions in Unit 1. The CD-ROM contains a handy installation program that copies the files to your hard drive in a very simple process, so installation will be a breeze.

Note: The CD-ROM does *not* contain Windows 95. You must already have Windows 95 installed on your computer.

How to Use This Book

Unlike many current computer books, this one is not a reference work designed to let you jump around, willy-nilly. Each unit builds on skills you learn in the unit that precedes it; within each unit, lessons proceed in a logical order. Each unit begins with a short list of prerequisites, the stuff you need to know before you begin. But if you follow the order of the book, you can ignore the prerequisites — the only real prerequisite for any unit is that you've completed most of the units that came before it.

To make the most of this book, start at the beginning (which, obviously, you already have) and work in order until you reach the end, or at least until you have acquired all the skills you came for. If you already have some Internet or Internet Explorer experience, you may want to skim through the early units first. Then, if you feel confident jumping ahead, go for it. Another good way to judge whether you can skip a lesson is to read the lesson's Progress Check (described later in this introduction). If you already know how to do every-thing listed in the Progress Check, you can skip ahead. To find out whether you can skip a whole unit, take the quiz at the unit's end. If you ace it, move on. If not, go back and take a lesson.

As you work through the units and lessons, keep in mind that there's no time pressure — you can work at your own pace. The first two things you learn in this book are (1) How to get on the Internet with Internet Explorer and (2) How to get off. With just those two skills, you're equipped to get on the Internet, do as much of a unit or units as you wish, and then quit. (Not all lessons require connecting to the Internet, but most do.) After quitting, you can go cook a tuna casserole or get some sunshine or change a diaper; then return later to pick up where you left off.

Note: Some of the lessons in the book have you visit various Web pages on the Internet so that you can practice using the many features of Internet Explorer. Unfortunately, this method of hands-on learning doesn't always work with the Internet. Web pages change and even disappear over time, which is a situation I cannot control. By the time you begin working on these lessons in the book, however, you will already be proficient with Internet Explorer, and you'll know how to search for other Web pages with similar content. So if a lesson mentions a Web page that has changed or disappeared, think of it as a challenge for you to either maneuver through the new Web page or find a different one.

The gray boxes

Here and there throughout the book, you'll see stuff set off in gray, shaded boxes called *sidebars*. These boxes all supply information that's interesting and useful, if not altogether essential to the task at hand.

Some gray boxes simply supply additional, useful information as it comes up. But other gray boxes come in either of two special types:

- **Q/A Session:** These Question/Answer boxes supply a question, related to the topic at hand, that may or may not be forming in your mind, and then answer it.

- **Extra Credit:** Identified by a little apple icon, Extra Credit boxes supply fun, surprising, powerful, or otherwise valuable information that's great to know but not required.

Stuff in the margins

The Notes text in the margin labels a good spot to jot some notes about what you're learning as you go along. (Between you and me, it's your book, so you can scribble notes anywhere you bloody well feel like it.) I also provide the occasional note in the margin to highlight an important point.

a note in the margin summarizes an important point

The Pencil graphic identifies a Progress Check. A Progress Check appears at the end of each lesson. If you can do everything listed in the Progress Check, you've mastered the lesson. If not, you may want to go back and review.

The quizzes & tests

Yeah, we got quizzes and tests. This book is a tutorial, so quizzes and tests go with the territory. Be thankful there's no essay.

- At the end of each unit, a quiz checks your mastery of the material in that unit. Following the quiz, an optional exercise provides practice in the skills you picked up in the unit.

♦ At the end of each part is a test (a big quiz) that checks your understanding of the entire part. Following the test is a lab assignment (a big
exercise). Note that lab assignments do not actually require any sort of
lab — it's just an expression.

Now, let's be brutally frank: You don't have to take the quizzes and tests, and
nobody can make you. And as a matter of fact, if you read most of the book in
order, you'll do fine without these exams, anyhow. (Although, if you really did
follow the book, you'd ace the quizzes and tests. So there.)

So why have tests? Well, tests can be a handy way of making sure you
understand a unit or part before moving forward. If you miss a question or
two, you may want to make a quick review of related lessons, paying special
attention to any material tagged with the on the test icon.

A few conventions

In the text, stuff you need to type appears in **boldface**. When you have to
press more that one key at a time, I indicate this key combination by connecting the keys with a plus sign. For example, Ctrl+P means hold down the Ctrl
key and then press P.

When I want to indicate a menu command, I use an arrow to separate the
menu name from the command. For example, File⇨Save means that in order
to choose the Save command, you should click on the word File in the menu
bar and then click the word Save in the menu (the File menu, in this case) that
appears. The underlined characters in the menu and command names are *hot
keys,* which allow you quickly access menu commands when used in combination with the Alt key. To access the Save command, you hold down the Alt
key, press the F key, and then press the S key.

How This Book Is Organized

Consistent with standard publishing practices, the contents of this book
appear on paper pages conveniently sandwiched within a laminated cardboard
cover; the cover provides a durable surface on which to place your coffee cup
without staining the pages, and it also serves nicely as an emergency mouse
pad when yours gets lost under old newspapers.

Following this Introduction, the pages are divided into four parts, each made
up of units covering a different aspect of using Internet Explorer and its
companions:

Part I: Basic Browsing

Believe it or not, all by itself this first part equips you to perform all of the
basic browsing activities, including opening Internet Explorer and connecting
to the Internet, jumping from one place to another by clicking links, going
directly to an Internet resource by using its Internet address, and even creating
and managing a list of "favorite" Internet resources so that you can jump
quickly to them any time you want. Many thousands of happy, productive
Internet users know nothing more than what you'll find in Part I.

Part II: Big-Time Browsing

But dummy or not, you're not content just to flop around the Internet like an amateur. So in Part II, you learn to exploit all of the cutting-edge features of the Web, including searching the Web for specific information, downloading files, and playing multimedia — video clips, sound, animation, and more.

Part III: Housekeeping

Part III imparts time-saving techniques such as creating "Internet shortcuts" that take you quickly to anywhere on the Net, printing Web pages, and saving Web information on your hard disk. You also discover in Part III how to deploy and control Internet Explorer's built-in capability to shield you or your loved ones from online material you may consider unfit for family viewing.

Part IV: Chat, Mail, and Other Extracurricular Activities

In Part IV, you move beyond the Internet Explorer Web browser and into the realm of its companion products. Using these free Microsoft programs (which are integrated with Internet Explorer and are included on the CD-ROM with this book), you can send and receive e-mail, browse newsgroups (also known as discussion groups), have a long-distance telephone conversation through your PC (for the price of a local call), and even participate in online, interactive conversations and conferences.

Part V: Appendixes

In Appendix A, you'll find the answers to all the quizzes and tests (no peeking!) and cross-references to the lesson where you can review if you get an answer wrong. In Appendix B, you'll learn all about the *Dummies 101: Internet Explorer 3 For Windows 95* CD-ROM bundled with this book — what's on it, how to set it up on your PC, and so on. Appendix C is for the adventurous reader. Here, I show as simply as I can how you can create your own Web page. This task is definitely not for everyone (which is why I cover it in an appendix and not in a unit), but I'm sure that many readers, especially kids, want to give Web publishing a try.

Icons Used in This Book

You'll see several icons lurking in the margins. These icons identify items or areas of special interest.

on the CD

This icon tells you when you need to use a file or program that comes on the *Dummies 101: Internet Explorer 3 For Windows 95* CD-ROM.

heads up

This icon tags an important idea or point, just to make sure you don't miss it.

on the test

This icon appears beside information that will be on the quiz that appears at the end of each unit. The icons help you either (A) pay special attention to that information, or (B) cheat. Either way, you'll learn something.

extra credit

Identified by a little apple icon, Extra Credit boxes supply fun, surprising, powerful, or otherwise valuable information that's great to know but not required.

Where to Go from Here

If you already have an Internet account set up on your computer, you'll need a copy of Internet Explorer 3.0 installed on your machine. Internet Explorer 3 is available free from Microsoft's web site at `http://www.microsoft.com/ie/`. You may need to contact your Internet service provider to get your copy of Internet Explorer configured properly.

If you don't have an Internet account, we've provided setup software on the CD-ROM to connect to AT&T WorldNet Service. Bundled with the AT&T WorldNet setup software is a customized version of Internet Explorer that you can use.

Before beginning, set up the CD-ROM as described in Appendix B. Doing so won't actually install any of the programs from the CD-ROM — setting up the CD-ROM simply prepares your PC for using the CD-ROM, when necessary, as you work your way through the tutorial. After setting up the CD-ROM, start off with Unit 1. Whenever a unit requires the use of a program or file that's on the CD-ROM, the unit tells you exactly what to do to install the required file or program.

If you already have some Internet or Internet Explorer experience, you may want to skim through the book first, locating lessons that offer something you don't yet know how to do.

All set? Move ahead. I think you'll have fun.

Basic Browsing

In this part . . .

There's learning to drive and then there's learning to *drive*. In an hour, anybody can learn how to back out of the driveway, pull through Dairy Queen, and then loop back home — that's driving. Given more time, anybody can build upon that skill to learn how to shift a five-speed, parallel park, control a skid, and follow a map cross-country. That's *driving*.

In this part of the tutorial, you get to Dairy Queen and back. You learn how to get set up for cruising the Net, jump onto the Web and move around in any page, get from any page to any other, and build a list of your "favorite" Web pages so you can revisit them in a flash.

Those four, simple skills are the basis of all happy Web browsing. They get you on, off, and around the Web, and help you get back again to the parts you like. They also form the foundation for the serious browsing (the *driving*) that you discover in Part II.

Setting Up Your Account

Objectives for This Unit

✓ Setting up your Internet connection

✓ Opening Internet Explorer and connecting to the Internet

✓ Moving around in a Web page

✓ Quitting Internet Explorer and the Internet

✓ Creating your Dummies 101 folder

Prerequisites

▶ The Introduction that precedes this unit

▶ The CD-ROM at the back of this book installed (Appendix B)

▶ The AT&T WorldNet℠/ Internet Explorer software copied to your PC (Appendix B)

*Q*uick gratification is what attracts folks to the Internet and to Internet Explorer, so quick gratification you shall have. All by itself, this unit gets your Internet account set up and shows you how to get on and off the Net. All that's really left after that is getting from place to place on the Net, which you discover in Units 2 and 3.

Before you get started, though, you need to understand just four simple ideas: *Web, server, browser,* and *page.*

on the test

Although to many people the World Wide Web (or just the Web) and the Internet seem synonymous, they're really not; the Web is a specific group of computers that happen to use the Internet to communicate with one another. But there is more to the Internet than the Web — the Web is a *part* of the Internet, but not all of it. The Web just gets all the good press because it's the cool, colorful, graphical part of the Internet that everybody wants to get into.

Computers called *Web servers* contain all of that cool Web stuff — news, gossip, catalogs, pictures, video clips, research data, and so on. The Web address (those cryptic-looking lines, like http://www.disney.com) that you see in a magazine article or an ad is the Internet address of a particular Web server, the address that any other computer needs in order to communicate with the server through the Internet. (Don't worry about the addresses for now — you'll learn more about them as you go along.)

Web = group of computers on Internet; one part of Internet

Web server = computer at specific Web address, with all info contained at that address; need to connect to Web server to reach Web stuff

Notes:

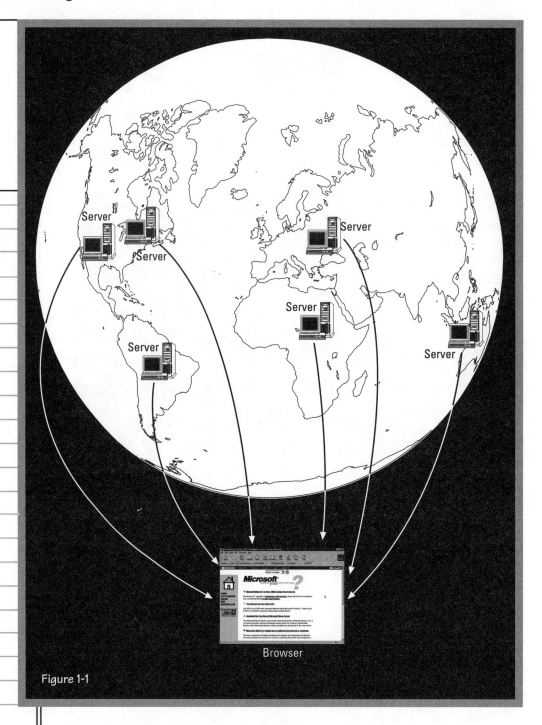

Figure 1-1

Web browser =
program (like
Internet Explorer)
needed for
communicating with
Web servers

The only way anybody can see the stuff stored on Web servers is through a computer (such as a PC) running a program called a *browser*. A Web browser knows how to contact a Web server through the Internet, retrieve information from the server, and display that information on the computer screen. In case you didn't already know, Internet Explorer is a Web browser. Other Web browsers you may have heard of include Netscape Navigator and Mosaic. With Internet Explorer, an Internet account, and a modem, your PC is equipped to access any Web server in the world and show you the information that the server contains. Figure 1-1 illustrates how information travels through the Internet from Web servers to Web browsers.

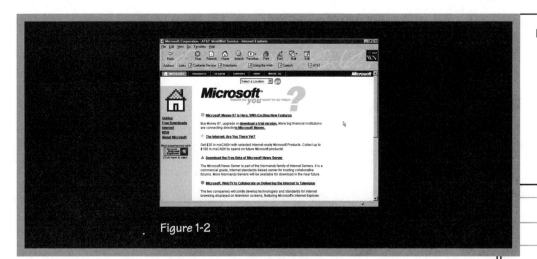

Figure 1-2

Finally, when you're looking through your browser at a screenful of information retrieved from a Web server, you're looking at a Web *page*. Figure 1-2 shows a typical Web page, displayed by the Internet Explorer browser. A *page* is a single file of information retrieved from the server, just as your resume may be a single word-processing file stored on your PC. Some people refer to a page (or a set of related pages) as a *Web site*; that same term also sometimes describes a whole Web server.

> Web page = screen of info on Web server

Okay, all clear on *Web, server, browser,* and *page?* If so, it's time to hit the water. If not, come along anyway — I promise that you can't drown online, and if these ideas seem fuzzy now, they'll come into focus as you go.

Remember: When you're actually on the Internet doing something, you're *online.* When you're not connected — that is, your modem is not using your phone line — you're *offline.*

Setting Up the AT&T WorldNet Account

Lesson 1-1

Before you can surf the Net, you need an account with an Internet Service Provider. There are thousands of Internet Service Providers, from the little local operations you may see advertised in your local newspaper to big providers like America Online, CompuServe, Microsoft Network, and AT&T WorldNet Service. Choose whichever you like, or whichever offers you the best deal — because in general, once you're on, the Net is the Net.

If you already have an Internet account, a copy of the Internet Explorer, and mail and news software, you have to contact your Internet Service provider for specific instructions on how to set it all up. Every provider is a little bit different, so I can't give "one size fits all" instructions here.

If you don't yet have an Internet account, the CD-ROM bundled with this book contains a file you may wish to use. That file contains Internet Explorer (and its companion programs, Internet Mail and Internet News, which you learn about in Unit 12), plus a Windows 95 Wizard that leads you step by step through signing up for AT&T's WorldNet Service.

This lesson describes how to set up the AT&T WorldNet software, including Internet Explorer, Mail, and News. When you're done, you'll have an account with AT&T WorldNet Service, and you'll have all the software you need to get started set up and ready to go.

heads up

While this Unit cannot provide exact setup instructions for providers other than AT&T WorldNet Sevice, note that you do not have to use this service in order to learn Internet Explorer through this tutorial. With a few small exceptions — which I carefully explain when they come up — Internet Explorer works the same, regardless of the Internet provider you choose. Once you have your account and Internet Explorer set up — whether with AT&T WorldNet Service or another provider — you can use every lesson in this book productively, beginning with Lesson 1-2. In fact, nearly all of the niggling little differences between different Internet Explorer implementations come up in this unit — so if you can deal with the problem here, it won't faze you a bit in later units.

heads up

Before beginning, you must

- Have already installed the CD-ROM (as described in Appendix B).

- Have on hand a major credit card to which you want your AT&T WorldNet charges billed.

- Have installed a modem in your PC and configured it for use by Windows 95.

- Have connected your modem to a telephone line.

Starting the setup Wizard

To begin setting up your AT&T account, you need to have loaded the CD-ROM into your drive and opened up the Installer program. These steps are covered in Appendix B. When the Installer window is on your screen, take the following steps:

1 From the Installer window, click the AT&T WorldNet Service button.

A dialog opens, giving you a chance to change the name of the folder in which the AT&T WordNet files will be stored. Unless you happen to know of some really good reason to change the folder, do nothing in this dialog box except what Step 2 says to do.

2 Click OK.

A box appears for a few moments to report that the software is "Installing." Then the AT&T WorldNet Service setup opens, as shown in Figure 1-3.

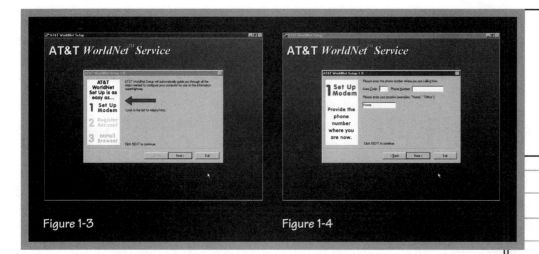

Figure 1-3

Figure 1-4

Figure 1-3: The first dialog of the AT&T WorldNet Service Setup describes the three phases of setting up your account and software.

Figure 1-4: Tell the Wizard your telephone number.

Notes:

This dialog describes the three steps you are about to perform to complete the installation:

1. Set Up Modem: You'll verify your modem speed, the phone number you're calling from, and other information required to set up your modem to dial the Internet.

2. Register Account: You'll supply AT&T with your identification and billing information.

3. Install Browser: You'll install the Internet Explorer software.

Setting up your modem

To complete the modem setup phase of setting up your account, follow these steps:

1 Click Next and verify that the modem listed in Installed Modems is the modem you will use to connect to the Internet.

If the modem listed is correct, click Next. If not, click the down arrow on the drop-down list of Installed Modems to open the list; then choose from the list and click Next.

After you click Next, a dialog like the one in Figure 1-4 appears.

Note: If your modem does not appear in the list of Installed Modems, you probably have not yet configured it in Windows. Consult your PC's or modem's manuals, or consult *Windows 95 For Dummies* by Andy Rathbone (from IDG Books).

2 Enter your Area Code, Phone Number, and location description; then click Next.

To enter each item, click in the box and type. (Use the telephone number from which you will be dialing the Internet.) Note that it doesn't matter how you format the seven-digit Phone Number — **555-5555**, **555 5555** or **5555555** are all the same as far as the Wizard is concerned. Type only your three-digit area code and seven-digit number, and do not attempt to include any "dial out" numbers or other special dialing instructions — that comes later.

The location description allows you (at a later time) to set up multiple dialing configurations on your PC for dialing AT&T WorldNet Service from different locations.

Figure 1-5: Tell the Wizard any special dialing instructions for your phone line.

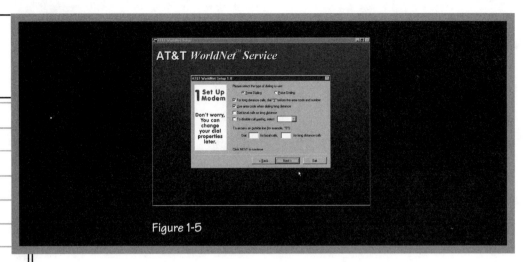

Figure 1-5

Notes:

After you click Next, a dialog like the one in Figure 1-5 appears.

3 Adjust your dialing properties, if necessary.

The dialog shown in Figure 1-5 reports the Wizard's best guesses about how you want your PC to dial the Internet — you must make sure its assumptions are correct. For example, if you have call waiting and wish to disable it while on the Internet, click in the box next to To disable call waiting... to insert a checkmark there; then drop down the adjacent list (click the down arrow on the list box) and choose the code you must dial to disable call waiting. (If you don't know the code, contact your local phone company's customer service department.)

If the phone line from which you will dial the Internet requires you to dial a number to get an outside line, enter that number under To access an outside line.

4 When your dialing properties appear as you wish, click Next.

The first Register Account dialog appears. Move on to Registering with AT&T.

Registering with AT&T

To complete the registration phase of setting up your account, do the following:

1 On the first Register Account dialog, make sure that the radio button next to Create a new account is selected and click Next.

A dialog reports that your PC is about to make a toll-free (1-800) call to AT&T to continue the setup and registration.

2 Click Next.

Your PC dials AT&T WorldNet Service. After a few moments and the appearance of a few quick status messages, a dialog like the one in Figure 1-6 appears.

3 Click the number you want to use to connect to AT&T WorldNet Service and then click Next.

Typically, the dialog shown in Figure 1-6 offers you one or more local numbers to choose from and an 800 number. Always choose the local number if one is offered because AT&T WorldNet Service charges a higher rate for your Internet account when you use the 800 number.

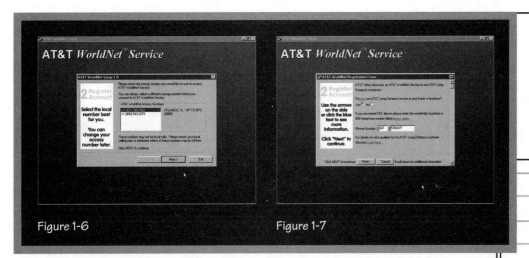

Figure 1-6
Figure 1-7

Figure 1-6: Choose the primary phone number your modem will dial to connect to the Internet.

Figure 1-7: Select Yes or No to tell AT&T whether you use its long-distance service.

After you choose a local number and click Next, a dialog pops up to warn you that just because a number is local doesn't mean it's toll-free. Even if the number you select is a local call, it may be a number outside your local calling plan, in which case your local phone company may charge extra for all of your time on the Internet. The dialog advises you to contact your phone company's customer service number to verify that the call is within your local calling area.

4 Click OK to clear the message.

A status message appears while the Wizard retrieves registration information it requires to complete your setup. After a few moments, a new dialog prompts for your Registration Code.

5 Type your Registration Code and click Next.

The Registration codes differs depending on whether you are already an AT&T long-distance customer:

If you *are* an AT&T long-distance customer, the code is **L5SQIM361**

If you *are not* an AT&T long-distance customer, the code is **L5SQIM362**

After you click Next, the Service Agreement and Operating Policies dialog box appears.

6 Read the Service Agreement and Operating Policies; then click the radio button next to Yes and click Next.

To read the whole agreement, you'll need to press PgDn. After reading, press PgUp repeatedly to return to the top of the dialog so you can choose Yes. (Note that if you do not accept the agreement by selecting Yes, you cannot use AT&T WorldNet Service.)

After you click Next, a status message appears. Then the dialog shown in Figure 1-7 opens.

7 Select Yes or No to indicate whether you are already an AT&T long distance customer.

AT&T collects this information because it offers discounted pricing for AT&T WorldNet Service if you are also an AT&T long-distance telephone customer. If you choose Yes, you must also enter the phone number (area code and number) from which you are an AT&T long-distance customer.

After you click Next, a dialog opens describing the available pricing plans.

8 Review the pricing plans, click the radio button to the left of the plan you want to use, and click Next.

Figure 1-8: Tell AT&T about yourself.

Figure 1-9: Tell AT&T about your credit card.

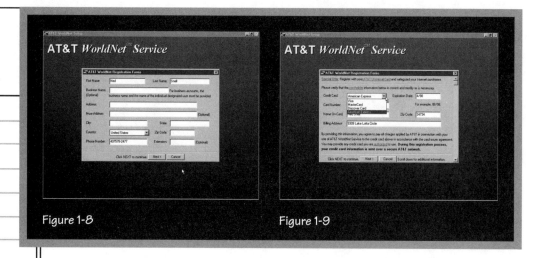

Figure 1-8   Figure 1-9

Notes:

After a status message appears for a moment, the AT&T WorldNet Registration Forms dialog appears, as shown in Figure 1-8.

9 Click in each box on the Registration form, enter the information, and click Next.

You do not have to supply a More Address line (if your whole street address fits in one line). You must enter a Business Name if you're setting up a business account (leave it blank otherwise). If an extension must be dialed to reach you at the Phone Number you entered, be sure to enter it in Extension.

After you click Next, a second form appears, as shown in Figure 1-9.

10 In the list box next to Credit Card, click the down arrow to drop down the list; then select the type of card (VISA, MasterCard, and so on) to which your Internet charges should be billed.

11 Click in the Card Number box and type your credit card number.

Don't worry about how to break up the numbers. For example, if your credit card number is 5555 6666 666 8888, just type **555566666668888**.

12 Click in the Expiration Date box and type the expiration date that appears on your credit card.

Be sure to include a slash in the middle of the date (for example, **11/98**), and always use two digits for the month. If your card expires in March of 1999, type **03/99**, not **3/99**.

13 Review the information in Name on Card, Zip Code, and Billing Address, and change it if necessary.

The Wizard has filled in these boxes automatically with information you supplied in earlier steps. But if any of it is incorrect for billing purposes, make any changes necessary.

When your registration information appears correctly, click Next. The dialog shown in Figure 1-10 appears.

14 Click in E-Mail Name and type the name you wish to use as your identity on the Internet.

The e-mail name you type will be used as the first part of your e-mail address. Many people use cute names (SuperBoy), while others prefer simpler, professional-sounding names (Nsnell, NedS). Note that you cannot use any spaces or punctuation (other than periods, hyphens, and underscores), and that capitalization is not important (NEDs, nedS, and NEDS are all the same). You can use up to 46 characters for your name, but shorter is better. Also, you must be the only person on AT&T WorldNet Service to use your name. If you select a name that's already being used by another AT&T WorldNet customer, a box will pop up to tell you that you must choose a different name.

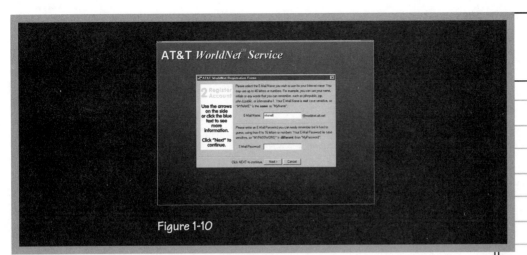

Figure 1-10: Choose an
e-mail name and
password.

Figure 1-10

heads up

Tip: In the dialog in Figure 1-10, look to the right of your e-mail name — what
you see is the *rest* of your e-mail address, `@worldnet.att.net`. For
example, if you enter CindyL as your e-mail name, your full Internet e-mail
address is `CindyL@worldnet.att.net`. This is the address you will give
to your friends and associates who may wish to contact you by e-mail.

To keep your password and account security word secret, make sure that no
one can see your screen while you perform Steps 15 through 18.

15 **Click in E-Mail Password and type a password you will use for your
Internet account.**

You password can be anything, from six to 16 characters in length (no spaces
or punctuation). Try to use a word, words, or numbers that you will find easy
to remember — but avoid choosing something easy to guess. Family names,
birthdates, and social security numbers, for example, are poor choices because
they're the first things that might be tried by someone attempting to use your
account without your authorization.

Be sure to remember exactly how you capitalized your password because
passwords are case-sensitive. If your password is "Godfather" and you are
required by some Internet activity to type your password, only **Godfather**
does the trick — **GODFATHER**, **godfather** and **GodFather** would not be
recognized as your valid password.

When your e-mail name and password appear as you wish, click Next. A dialog
opens, prompting you for an Account Security Word.

16 **Enter an Account Security Word and click Next.**

Your account security word can be up to 16 characters long. You use it to
prove to AT&T's customer service line that you're you. For example, if you
forget your e-mail password, you can call AT&T WorldNet customer service
and say your Account Security Word when asked for it (proving you're you) so
that customer service will tell you your password. Again, choose something
that's easy for you to remember but hard for someone else to guess.

17 **To avoid being listed in the AT&T Member Directory, click No and
then click Next. To be listed, simply click Next without clicking No.**

The member directory is a searchable database that includes your name, e-mail
address, and other information about you. Leaving the Yes in this dialog gives
AT&T permission to list you not only in the AT&T WorldNet directory but in
"other directories" as well. Unless you really want the whole world (including
purveyors of junk mail and dinner-time telemarketing calls) to know everything
about you, choose No.

After you click Next, a dialog appears reporting your earlier choices for e-mail
name, password, and security word.

Notes:

☑ **Progress Check**

If you can do the following, you've mastered this lesson:

❏ Locate the AT&T WorldNet software icon.

❏ Set up your AT&T WorldNet account.

❏ Install Internet Explorer, Mail, and News.

18   **Verify your name and password information.**

If you want to change your mind about any of these choices, you can do so now simply by editing the information shown.

19   **Click Register Now.**

A dialog appears, giving you a chance to save your account information (e-mail name and passwords) on a diskette for safe-keeping. To save this info on a diskette, check the checkbox, insert a diskette in your A: drive, and click Next. (When finished, removed the diskette, label it, and store it in a safe place.)

After you click Next, the first Install Browser dialog box appears. Move on to the final phase of setting up your account: Installing Internet Explorer.

Installing Internet Explorer

To complete the final phase of setting up your account:

1   **On the first Install Browser dialog box, click Next.**

The Internet Explorer license agreement appears.

2   **Read the license agreement and click Yes to accept its terms.**

To scroll the agreement, press PgDn and PgUp.

After you click Yes, a series of status messages appears while Internet Explorer sets up.

When setup is complete, a dialog prompts you that you must restart your computer for the changes made during setup to take effect.

3   **Click Yes.**

Windows 95 shuts down and then restarts. You may notice that Windows takes a little longer to start up than usual. That's only a temporary problem; Windows takes extra time, just this once, to update configuration information. The next time you start up Windows, it will open as quickly as it ever did.

Shortly after Windows opens, the AT&T WorldNet Setup program reopens to report that you are finished, as shown in Figure 1-11.

4   **Click the checkbox next to Connect to AT&T WorldNet Service to remove the checkmark; then click Finish.**

If you left the checkmark in place, you'd connect automatically to WorldNet. But since you're about to learn how to connect in the day-to-day way (in Lesson 1-2), you needn't leap online just yet.

Q/A Session

Question: If Internet Explorer comes out in an updated version, how do I get it?

Answer: The best way to keep up with developments in Internet Explorer — including new versions and new companion products — is to visit Microsoft's Web site from time to time. An easy way to do that is built into the menu bar of every copy of Internet Explorer (regardless of who supplied it to you). Just go online and open Internet Explorer (as described in the next lesson). Then choose Help⇨Microsoft on the Web⇨Microsoft Home Page. (But don't go there yet — at least not until you've learned how to get around, as you will in Unit 2.)

If you want a peek at the Microsoft Home Page, look back at Figure 1-2.

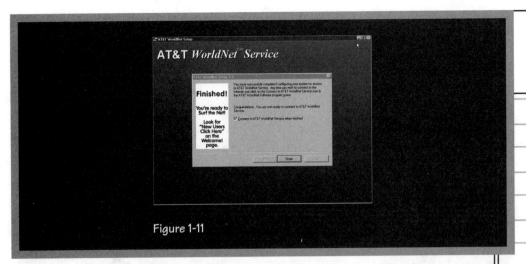

Figure 1-11

Figure 1-11: Click the
checkbox to remove the
checkmark — you'll go
online soon enough.

Leaping Online (And Off Again!)

Lesson 1-2

After you finish Lesson 1-1, you'll see two new icons on your desktop:

- The Internet (a little globe)
- Connect to the AT&T WorldNet Service (the AT&T logo)

Truth be told, both icons do the same thing: They connect you to the Internet
and open Internet Explorer. Because most people who don't use AT&T
WorldNet will nevertheless see the globe icon (that's Internet Explorer's
default icon), I favor that one as your jumping-off point for the Internet.

Opening Internet Explorer and the Internet

Time to go online. Here's how:

1 **On your Windows 95 desktop, locate the globe icon labeled The
Internet.**

2 **Double-click the icon.**

A connection dialog opens for dialing your Internet provider. What happens
next depends upon who your Internet provider is. If it's AT&T WorldNet
Service, the dialog looks like the one in Figure 1-12, and there's nothing left for
you to do. All by itself, the dialog dials AT&T WorldNet Service and connects to
the Internet.

The Connect dialogs from other Internet providers may work the same way
AT&T WorldNet Service does. Some, like the dialog shown in Figure 1-13,
require that you type your password and click Connect before dialing begins.

Whichever type of Connect dialog you see, once the connection is established,
Internet Explorer opens automatically, as shown in Figure 1-14.

Note: If the Connect dialog can't get connected (which may happen because
all the lines are busy or a server is down at your Internet Provider), a message
usually appears, advising you to try again later. Some connect routines,
including AT&T WorldNet's, also present you with a list of alternate phone
numbers to try when you can't get through on your primary number.

double-click
Internet icon on
Windows 95 desktop
to connect to
Internet

Figure 1-12: When AT&T WorldNet's Connect dialog opens, there's nothing for you to do — it automatically connects you to the Internet and opens Internet Explorer.

Figure 1-13: The connection dialog boxes used by some Internet providers may require you to type your password and click a Connect button, after which the software connects you to the Internet and opens Internet Explorer.

Figure 1-14: As soon as your Internet connection and Internet Explorer are both open, Internet Explorer automatically jumps to your home page (whatever your home page may be).

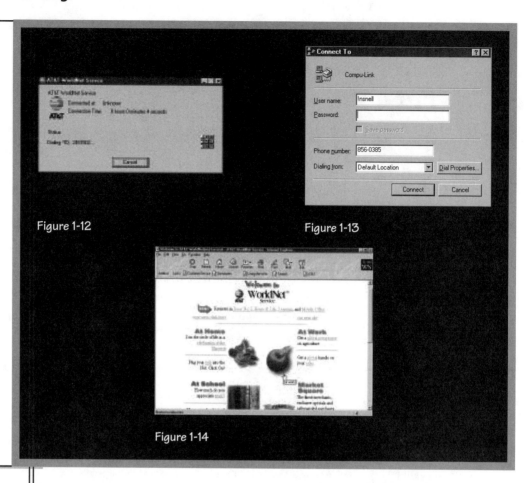

Figure 1-12

Figure 1-13

Figure 1-14

on the test

As soon as Internet Explorer opens, it jumps to your *home page* on the Web. The home page is the page that always appears first, automatically, each time you connect to the Internet. Your home page is your jumping-off point for most Web activities. Most home pages contain a range of handy activities, so they really serve as an effective home base.

heads up

Exactly which Web page serves as each user's home page differs. AT&T WorldNet customers see the Welcome to the AT&T WorldNet Service page shown in Figure 1-14. Users of other services will see a different home page. The chosen home page is programmed into your copy of Internet Explorer, so whoever supplied your copy chooses what your home page will be. While home pages differ, keep the following in mind:

▶ The home page does not affect your ability to perform all of the activities in all of the units that follow in this tutorial. No matter what your home page happens to be, you'll be able to follow the lesson just fine.

▶ After you've gained some experience, you may decide you'd like to change your home page to a page other than the one that's been chosen for you. You learn how to change your home page in Unit 2.

heads up

Hey, you're on the Internet! Cool. I'm sure I don't have to remind you (but I will anyway) that you're probably paying for the time you spend online (exactly how much depends on your provider and your payment plan). In this book, you'll find that several exercises are usually strung together for one online session. Of course, you can choose to disconnect before I tell you to (you'll learn how in a moment) and then get back online later to continue.

What you may want to do is skim through the exercises *before* you connect so that you don't spend a lot of time reading while racking up the online time. Remember though, that trying to reconnect can sometimes be a bigger hassle than just staying online.

Q&A session

Question: How come it takes so long for some pages to appear?

Answer: A browser shows you a Web page by first copying the whole thing from the server (through the Internet, of course) to your PC and then showing it to you. The delay you often experience between clicking a link and seeing the page is made up of two parts:

- The time the browser takes to contact the Web server that the link points to
- The time required to transfer the page file from the server to your PC

Because computer graphics are made up of a lot of data, the more pictures a page contains, the more time the page requires to travel through the Internet. So the slickest, most graphical pages are often the ones you have to wait for, while simple pages containing mostly text appear relatively quickly.

To minimize the wait, Internet Explorer retrieves just the text of a page first and displays it to you with little boxes standing in for the pictures that haven't yet arrived from the server. You can begin reading the text while waiting for the graphics to materialize — which they do, little by little, as they come in from the server.

---

extra credit

There's no place like home . . . except another home

The notion of a "home" page confuses many a Net neophyte. The problem is that the term *home page* has two meanings.

A *home page* can be the page that a browser accesses automatically each time you start up the browser. Known also as the *startup page,* that home page is not only the one that appears automatically at startup but also the page that you can jump to from anywhere on the Web simply by clicking the little house icon on your Internet Explorer toolbar (house = home, get it?), as you learn in Unit 2. However, *home page* is also used sometimes to describe a page that's the main location for information about a person or company. Companies publish home pages about themselves, as do people, to present Web surfers with a place to learn more about them.

Signing off the Internet

Yes, I know. You just got online and now I'm already having you get off. It's not some cheap, cruel tease because after quitting, you can jump back online again any time you want. But maybe you don't intend to complete the remaining lessons in this unit all at once. Maybe the doorbell will ring. Maybe it's time for *Seinfeld.* Maybe your muffins are burning. Maybe your significant

closing Internet
Explorer alone
doesn't disconnect
from Internet; have
to quit Internet
separately

on the test

File→Close or X
button closes
Internet Explorer

heads up

if modem icon
appears in taskbar,
you're still online

✎

☑ **Progress Check**

If you can do the following,
you've mastered this lesson:

❑ Open Internet Explorer
from the Internet icon on
your desktop.

❑ Connect to the Internet.

❑ Close Internet Explorer
and disconnect from the
Internet.

other, parents, or kids are about to walk in, and you haven't yet confessed to him/her/them that you've signed up for an Internet account and plan to start hogging the phone line. In any event, learning here and now how to get offline makes sense. That way, you can complete the lessons in this book at your own sweet pace.

Quitting Internet Explorer and quitting the Internet are two separate, if related, activities. Remember that a Web browser like Internet Explorer is used to browse the Web, but browsing the Web is not the only thing you can do on the Internet. So depending upon your Internet provider, when you close Internet Explorer, Windows may or may not automatically hang up the modem to disconnect you from the Internet — it may leave the connection open in case you want to do something else on the Internet, like send some e-mail. Also, as you'll learn in upcoming units, you can use Internet Explorer to perform a variety of activities offline, with your Internet connection closed. So if you disconnect from the Internet while Internet Explorer is open, Internet Explorer may not close automatically.

Tip: When you decide to get off the Internet, you do not have to go to any particular page first. You can quit right from wherever you are, no matter what you may have been doing. The next time you connect to the Internet, you still begin at your home page, just like always.

To close Internet Explorer and get off the Internet, do the following:

1 **Choose File▷Close. (Or click the X button in the extreme upper-right corner of Internet Explorer.)**

Internet Explorer closes. Depending on your configuration, one of three things happens next:

- You're automatically disconnected from the Internet (this is what happens on AT&T WorldNet Service).

- A dialog box pops up, asking you to click Yes to disconnect or No to stay online.

- No dialog pops up and you remain online.

Tip: To check whether Windows has hung up your modem (disconnecting you from the Internet), check your Windows 95 taskbar. If a modem icon appears at the right end of the taskbar (near the spot where the time appears), you're still online.

2 **If you see that Yes/No dialog box, click Yes to disconnect from the Internet.**

3 **If no dialog box appears and you're still online, disconnect manually.**

Look in your Windows 95 taskbar for a button that appears related to your Internet connection. Click it and a dialog box should open that reports the number of minutes you've been online and also shows a Disconnect button (it might instead be labeled "Sign Out" or "Hang Up."). Click the button to go offline.

Q&A session

Question: Can I just switch off my PC to disconnect from the Internet?

Answer: Yes and no. Technically, turning off your PC should automatically "hang up" (disconnect) your modem, which would disconnect you from the Internet. However, in some cases, your modem could leave the phone line "open" even after you switch off your PC, which would have the same effect as leaving a phone off the hook. Also, Windows 95 automatically performs a number of important housekeeping chores when you choose the Shut Down command on the Start menu before turning off your PC. So it's never a good idea to simply switch off your PC when Windows 95 is running. Always quit any open applications (including your Internet connection), click your Start button (on the taskbar), choose Shut Down, and press Enter. Then switch off your PC only when Windows says it's okay to do so.

don't just shut off PC to disconnect

Moving Around in a Web Page   Lesson 1-3

Some Web pages take up just one screenful of information, so you can see the whole page at once. But many Web pages are too big to be viewed all at once through the Internet Explorer window. To see the whole page, you have to *scroll* to the parts of the page that don't appear.

If you've used any Windows-based word processor, you've scrolled before. You operate *scroll bars* to move hidden parts of the page into view within the Internet Explorer window. Figure 1-15 shows what a scroll bar looks like.

use scroll bars to move up and down or left and right on Web page

Of course, if Internet Explorer covers less than your full screen, you won't see as much of the page as you could. If Internet Explorer appears in a window instead of filling the entire screen, double-click Internet Explorer's *title bar* (the bar along the very top of the window). Double-clicking the title bar *maximizes* Internet Explorer to make it fill your whole screen.

double-click Internet Explorer's title bar to fill entire screen

Scroll bars appear automatically in Internet Explorer whenever a Web page stretches beyond its borders. Sometimes the page is wider (side to side) than Internet Explorer can display; when a page is too wide, a horizontal scroll bar appears along the page bottom so that you can scroll to the right or the left to see the sides of the page. But more often, a Web page is too long (top to bottom) for Internet Explorer, and a vertical scroll bar appears (on the right edge of the page) so that you can scroll down to the bottom of the page or scroll back up to the top. Occasionally, a Web page is too long *and* too wide, and both horizontal and vertical scroll bars appear.

If you take a look back at Figure 1-14 (in Lesson 1-2), you can see a vertical scroll bar along the right side of the Internet Explorer window. This bar tells you that there's more page to be seen below the part you're looking at. No horizontal scroll bar appears, so you know that the full width of the page fits within the Internet Explorer window — there's nothing else to see on the sides.

Remember: When you see no scroll bars, there's nowhere to scroll to. The whole page is visible in the window.

Figure 1-15: Click the arrow at either end of a scroll bar to scroll in that direction, or drag the slider between the arrows in the direction in which you want to scroll.

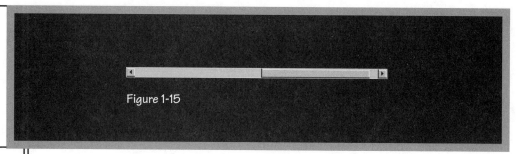

Figure 1-15

A scroll bar has two (well, three, if you count the arrows separately) parts, as shown in Figure 1-15:

♦ At each end of the scroll bar, an arrow appears. Clicking an arrow once scrolls the page a tiny bit in the direction of the arrow. Clicking and dragging (that is, holding the mouse button down while you move the mouse) an arrow scrolls continuously in the arrow's direction until you release the mouse button.

♦ Between the arrows, a small rectangle appears. The rectangle is a *slider* control. To operate the slider, point to it and then click and drag the slider in the direction in which you want to scroll the page; then release the mouse button.

slider = rectangle in scroll bar

Most home pages (probably yours) are longer than Internet Explorer can show. To see all of your home page, try the following:

1 Open Internet Explorer and connect to the Internet, as described in Lesson 1-2.

Shortly after your connection and Internet Explorer are open, your home page appears. If it's too long for the window, a vertical scroll bar appears along its right side.

2 Find the downward-pointing arrow on the bottom of the scroll bar.

3 Click and drag the arrow until the page stops moving and the slider has reached the bottom of the scroll bar.

The bottom of your home page appears.

4 Now click and drag the up arrow until the page stops moving and the slider has reached the top of the scroll bar.

The top of your home page appears.

5 Click and drag the slider to the center of the scroll bar and then release the mouse button.

The general center of your home page appears.

☑ **Progress Check**

If you can do the following, you've mastered this lesson:

❑ Recognize horizontal and vertical scroll bars.

❑ Display hidden areas of a Web page by scrolling left and right or up and down.

Tip: Instead of using scroll bars, you can use your PgUp and PgDn keys to move up and down in a long Web page, although using the scroll bars is more precise.

extra credit

Watch the moving logo

How can you tell when Internet Explorer is busy getting a page and when it's done? You'll know when Internet Explorer is busy retrieving a page from the server: The little logo to the right of the toolbar becomes animated in some way.

What that logo looks like and how it's animated, depends upon who supplied your copy of Internet Explorer. Most users see an "e" (for *explorer,* presumably) that spins during page retrieval. AT&T WorldNet users see the AT&T logo phasing in and out, as if lit by a spinning searchlight. When the logo is still, page retrieval is complete.

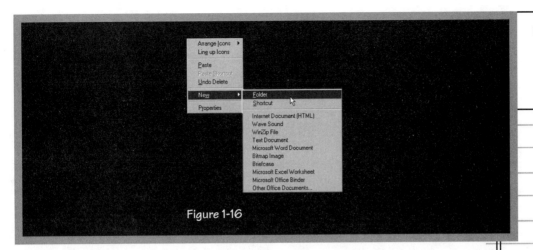

Figure 1-16

Figure 1-16: Right-click almost anything in Windows 95 to display a context menu for the item you clicked.

Creating Your Dummies 101 Folder

Lesson 1-4

A number of lessons in upcoming units require you to save stuff on your PC — usually files you picked up somewhere on the Internet. Just so you have a place to put that stuff, set up a Dummies 101 folder on your desktop right now.

To set up a folder on your desktop, you need to do something new: *Right-clicking*. To right-click, you simply point to an object in Windows and then click your right mouse button (not the left mouse button, the one you usually click). Right-clicking an object in Windows 95 usually opens a *context menu*, a list of activities related to the item you right-clicked.

heads up

If you're left-handed, you may have adjusted your mouse's settings so that what I refer to as your "right mouse button" (the secondary button) is actually your *left* mouse button and the "left mouse button" (the primary button) is actually your *right* mouse button. If you don't know what I'm talking about, then never mind — this situation doesn't affect you.

To create your Dummies 101 desktop folder, take these steps:

1 Point to any empty area of your Windows 95 desktop.

Take care not to point to a folder, icon, or other object.

2 Right-click.

A content menu opens.

3 In the context menu, choose New⇨Folder, as shown in Figure 1-16.

A new folder appears on the desktop, waiting for its name.

4 Type Dummies 101 and press Enter.

Your Dummies 101 folder waits on your desktop, ready to go.

on the test

Internet Explorer makes great use of Windows 95's context menus. For example, you can open Internet Explorer (and connect to the Internet) by right-clicking the Internet icon and then choosing Open from the context menu. As you move through the units in this tutorial, you'll discover other great right-clicking tips.

right-click = click
with your right
mouse button

context menu =
menu that right-
clicking brings up

☑ **Progress Check**

If you can do the following, you've mastered this lesson:

❑ Right-click an object to open a context menu.

❑ Create a Dummies 101 folder on your desktop.

Recess

Wow — you're all set up, and you can get on and off the Internet. Take a break, have a cookie, and call a friend to say, "I'm on the Net!" When you're relaxed and refreshed, take the quiz to see how much you remember. (It's easy, I swear!)

Unit 1 Quiz

Notes:

For each question, circle the letter of the correct answer.

1. **Are the Web and the Internet the same thing?**

    A. Yes, absolutely.

    B. Not exactly — the Internet is just one part of the Web.

    C. Not exactly — the Web is just one part of the Internet.

    D. No, the Web and the Internet are distinct fruits — apples and oranges.

2. **The home page is . . .**

    A. The same for every Internet Explorer user, regardless of Internet provider.

    B. The page that appears first every time you connect to the Internet.

    C. The only page where they really understand you.

    D. Any page where you may hang your hat.

3. **Web pages often appear slowly on your screen because . . .**

    A. Internet Explorer processes graphical information slowly.

    B. Your neighbors are monopolizing the available high-speed lines in your circuit.

    C. You're just impatient, so you *think* the pages are appearing slowly.

    D. The large amount of data contained in some Web pages requires a long time to travel from the Web server to your PC.

4. **Which tools can help you see more of a Web page?**

    A. Scroll bars and the PgUp and PgDn keys.

    B. The screen-stretching cursor.

    C. A bigger monitor.

    D. An open mind.

5. **You display the context menu for an object by . . .**

    A. Passing the pointer over it.

    B. Pointing to it and then pressing Ctrl+Shift+Esc+P+Alt+End+Home+NumLock+F12.

    C. Clicking it three times quickly.

    D. Clicking it once with the right (not left) mouse button.

Unit 1 Exercise

1. Connect to the Internet and open Internet Explorer, as described in Lesson 1-2.

2. Using the scroll bars, explore your home page. Read all of it and look at every part of it.

3. Select items on your home page you'd like to explore further, once you learn about using *links* in Unit 2.

4. Close Internet Explorer and disconnect from the Internet, as described in Lesson 1-2.

Notes:

Browsing Beyond the Home Page

Objectives for This Unit

✓ Jumping from page to page by clicking *links*

✓ Returning to your home page from anywhere else

✓ Retracing your steps with the Back button

✓ Jumping to preprogrammed destinations with Quick Links

Prerequisites

▶ The Introduction

▶ Internet Explorer installed on your PC (Lesson 1-1)

▶ Opening and closing Internet Explorer and your Internet connection (Lesson 1-2)

Okay, you're on the Internet and you're looking at your home page. Where to now? Just how *does* one move from one Web page to another?

Well, in fact, there are two basic ways to move beyond your home page to other pages on the Web:

▶ **The ridiculously easy way:** Jump from page to page by clicking *links* you find on each page you visit.

▶ **The still easy, but a little harder, way:** Supply Internet Explorer with the Internet address of a page you want to visit.

In this Unit, you learn all about the ridiculously easy way to get around the Web, including not only jumping from page to page through links, but also getting back to where you started after a Web excursion. Link navigation is the one essential skill in Web browsing, and by the time you complete this simple unit, you'll be clicking around like a pro.

Getting around by entering addresses is a little trickier and best saved until after you've gained some experience with links. You discover how to use Internet addresses in Unit 3.

Note: All of the examples in this Unit begin at your home page. The exact home page you see may differ depending on who your Internet provider is and where you obtained your copy of Internet Explorer. Readers who use the copy of Internet Explorer included on the CD-ROM with this book (and set it up using the lessons in Unit 1) will see the AT&T WorldNet^{SM} Service home page as their home page. But to complete the examples in this Unit, you needn't have any particular home page — all you need is a home page that has links on it, which all home pages do.

Lesson 2-1   Clicking a Link to Jump to a New Page

A *link* is a spot in a Web page that you click to make something happen. Most of the time, clicking a link takes you to another Web page or to another part of the Web page that you're looking at. It's these links that truly enable Web browsing — using links and links alone, you can click your way all over the Web. Links are easy and fun, and they insulate you from having to fiddle with the addresses of Web pages — when you click a link, the link tells Internet Explorer where to go.

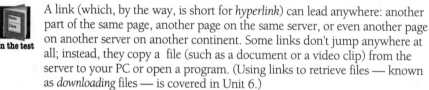

on the test

A link (which, by the way, is short for *hyperlink*) can lead anywhere: another part of the same page, another page on the same server, or even another page on another server on another continent. Some links don't jump anywhere at all; instead, they copy a file (such as a document or a video clip) from the server to your PC or open a program. (Using links to retrieve files — known as *downloading* files — is covered in Unit 6.)

link = jumps to another page or another part of same page or downloads file

Tip: Some links look like underlined e-mail addresses. Clicking one of these *e-mail links* doesn't take you to a Web page but rather opens Internet Mail so that you can compose an e-mail message. You learn about using e-mail links in Unit 12.

Most links deal with pages, though, so for now, just focus on using links to jump among pages. But keep in mind, in case you suddenly become inspired to start clicking around the Web on your own (and you will!), that some links have these non-page purposes. The text leading to and surrounding such links usually describes exactly what the link will do, so you needn't worry about accidentally clicking a link that does something you don't want it to. And in the unlikely event that you do inadvertently click such a link, just remember that

- Nothing dire can happen. You cannot click a link on the Web that will erase your hard disk, vacuum your bank account, or start a Global Thermonuclear War. If the link will download a file and you don't *want* to download a file, a Cancel button always appears on a dialog before any downloading begins, so you can bail out.

- You can easily stop a link from doing whatever it's doing, as you'll learn later in this lesson. (**Hint:** Find the Stop button on Internet Explorer's toolbar.)

heads up

There is one unusual event you should be made aware of when you begin journeying beyond the home page: *Certificates* appearing. Some Web pages have the ability to actually reprogram Internet Explorer in subtle ways to enable it to do something special that the page provides. Any time you go to such a page, a certificate appears to identify the company who made the program and to give you a chance to accept the program or reject it. The idea behind certificates is that you should be able to tell, from looking at the

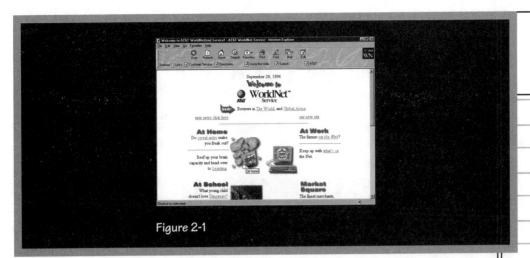

Figure 2-1

certificate, whether the company supplying the program is one you accept or fear — and if you fear it, you have a chance to reject the program. Of course, the flaw in that logic is that, as a new Web surfer, you have no idea whether a company is a good one or not. As a rule, unless you're skittish, just accept the code any time you see a certificate, and have fun.

Identifying a link

Any text that you see in a Web page may serve as a link. A single letter, a word or phrase, or even a whole paragraph may be a link that you can click. Also, any picture that you see may be a link. In fact, a single picture may contain several links; clicking different parts of the picture takes you to different places.

In a well-designed Web page, the links are pretty obvious — a word or picture stands out as if to say "click me," and the text on the page describes where to click and what happens when you do. However, in many Web pages, the links may not be all that obvious, especially to a new Web surfer. Sometimes you open a Web page only to see a company logo staring back at you, with no text telling you what the heck to do next. (In such cases, invoke my Web-surfing motto: "When in doubt, click something and see what happens.")

on the test

In fact, you can find any and all of the links on a page easily. In Internet Explorer, links made out of words or letters always appear <u>underlined</u>. (Text links are also usually blue, but that's not as reliable an indicator as the underlining.) Also, when you move the mouse pointer to text that serves as a link, your regular mouse pointer changes to a pointing finger (shown in Figure 2-1). That finger means you're pointing to a link, and if you click, something's gonna happen.

heads up

Links in pictures are a little trickier to spot: Pictures have their own colors and can't be underlined. Again, pictures that serve as links are usually self-explanatory; a company logo, for example, naturally leads to information about the company. You can always tell whether a picture is a link by moving the mouse pointer to it and seeing whether the finger appears.

When a single picture contains several links, the finger appears over certain areas of the picture and reverts to the regular mouse pointer over others. Such pictures are usually drawn so that you can easily spot how they're divided up into separate links.

link usually appears as underlined text or as picture

mouse pointer turning into pointing finger indicates link

single picture can contain several links

Notes:

Some pages show every link twice

Most Web pages that use pictures as links repeat the same links somewhere else on the page as text links. Some Web browsers can display only text, not pictures, and can't use the picture links, so the authors of the Web pages supply text-based duplicates of any picture links.

For example, next to the picture-links in the AT&T WorldNet Service home page (shown in Figure 2-1), you may notice descriptions in which some of the words are underlined. These underlined words are text links that go the same places the pictures do. In many pages, all of the text links that duplicate picture links are grouped together at the very bottom of the page so that they don't intrude on the page's design.

Find the links on your home page:

1 If you're not still online, open Internet Explorer and connect to the Internet, as described in Lesson 1-2.

After a few moments, your home page appears.

2 Move the pointer to any picture you see on your home page. (Don't click; just point.)

Does the pointer become a pointing finger? If so, the picture is a link. If not, the picture is just decoration — move the pointer to another picture to see if you can find a link. If you see an ad on the page, try pointing to it — an ad is almost always a link to a page containing more information about the product or service advertised.

Tip: If you let the pointer rest on a link for a moment, a brief description of where the link leads appears near the pointer (see Figure 2-1).

3 Locate any underlined words in the page and point to them (don't click . . . just point).

The pointer becomes a pointing finger — the words are a text link.

4 Move the pointer around the screen, pointing to any text or pictures and watching for any change in the pointer.

How many links can you find?

Clicking links

Now that you know how to spot links, you're ready to work 'em. From your home page, follow these steps:

1 Locate any link that looks interesting to you.

2 Move the pointer to the link.

The pointer turns into a pointing finger as it hits the link.

3 Click once.

A single click does the job — there's no need to double-click a link, although doing so doesn't hurt anything and activates the link just the same.

When you click a link, the logo at the far right end of Internet Explorer's toolbar begins to move to indicate that Internet Explorer is busy trying to get what you've requested. Sometimes, retrieving a page from a server takes a while — even a minute or more. So be patient. While the logo moves, Internet Explorer is hard at work. Give it a chance to do its job.

After a few moments, the page the link leads to appears.

4 **Examine the page that appears and look for any links on it.**

5 **Click another link. Where are you now?**

After clicking a second link in Step 5, stay where you are — you want to be a few steps off the home page for Lesson 2-2. If you choose to go offline before doing Lesson 2-2, just remember to go back online and then click a couple of links before performing the steps in Lesson 2-2.

extra credit

Changing your mind (Stop!)

Clicking around the Web mesmerizes people. The experience is so dynamic and stimulating that folks often get ahead of themselves — their fingers click a link before their brains realize that the link is not what they wanted. Such mistakes are no big deal; any time you journey down a wrong path, getting back is a cinch, as you learn in the next lesson.

But clicking some links initiates activities that may take a long time, like copying a video clip to your PC. Also, sometimes a Web server gets overloaded or experiences technical problems. When Internet Explorer attempts to access a page on such a server, it may try for a very long time to get through. After waiting a while, you may decide that you no longer want to see that page — at least not now. You can instruct Internet Explorer to quit trying and to try another page instead. You can try to access the slow page again in an hour or two, by which time the problem at the server may have been fixed.

When you click a link that starts something you don't want to finish, just click the Stop button on Internet Explorer's toolbar. Internet Explorer immediately stops what it's doing. You can then jump wherever you want to.

☑ Progress Check

If you can do the following, you've mastered this lesson:

❑ Recognize a link made of text or in a picture.

❑ Click links to jump from page to page.

Going Home, Backward, and Forward   Lesson 2-2

In clicking your way out through the Internet, you may find yourself somewhere you'd rather not be. When that happens, you can do either of two things instantly from Internet Explorer's toolbar:

▶ Use the Home button to jump to your home page.

▶ Use the Back button to backtrack to familiar territory.

You discover both techniques, plus the Forward button, in this lesson.

Jumping home

When you're lost, out on a limb, or simply someplace you don't want to be, the Home button is your parachute, your eject button, your emergency beamout. The Home button takes you from wherever you are on the Web — no matter where you may be — and takes you to your home page, where you can forget the whole sorry episode in comfortable surroundings.

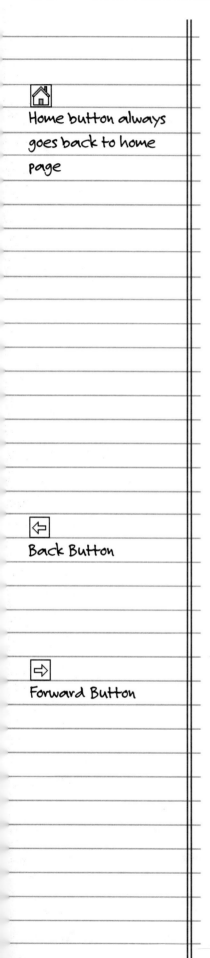

Home button always goes back to home page

Back Button

Forward Button

To go Home:

1 **Connect to the Internet, if you're not already, and click through as many links as you want to, getting as many pages removed from your home page as you want.**

If you've just finished Lesson 2-1, you should already be a link or two away from your home page. If you've gone offline since completing Lesson 2-1, open Internet Explorer and connect to the Internet, click a link on your home page, and then click another link on the page that appears, if one is available.

To establish the proper spirit for this example, try as hard as you can to get completely lost.

2 **Click the Home button.**

Internet Explorer returns to your home page. You are now home, safe and fully forgiven.

3 **Repeat Steps 1 and 2.**

For practice, for reassurance, and for the heck of it.

Stay online for the next example.

Jumping backward and forward

Internet Explorer remembers the address of each page that you visit in an online journey, and it also remembers the order in which you visited the pages. Because of this feature, you can use the Back button to maneuver back (to pages you've visited earlier in the current session), and the Forward button to move forward again after "Back-tracking."

When you're on your Home page, the Back button is grayed out — it's unavailable. And that makes perfect sense. You're at the starting point, so there's nowhere to go back to. As soon as you jump from the home page to a new page, the Back button becomes available. Each time you click it, it takes you back one page. If you've journeyed through five pages since your home page, clicking Back five times takes you home. (Obviously, if home is where you want to go, using the Home button is easier. Back is most useful when you want to backtrack a few pages to try a new direction but don't need to go all the way home.)

The Forward button merely reverses the action of the Back button. The Forward button remains grayed out until you've used the Back button — because there can be no forward without backward. After you've gone back at least once, you can use the Forward button to *re*-retrace your steps.

on the test

As you click back and forward in the next example, observe any text links you've used along the way. You may notice that all of the text links you've clicked have changed color. To help you keep track of where you've been, Internet Explorer changes the color of any link you've already used (the exact color may vary — all that matters is that the color changes). After the link changes color, it still works the same — the color change just helps you remember that you've already visited the page that the link leads to. Links that have changed color are called *visited* links.

Try your Back and Forward buttons.

1 Journey three links away from your home page.

To get three links away from home: Click a link on your home page. On the page that appears, click a link. On the next page, click a link. If, before you've clicked three links, you hit a page that has no links in it, click Home and start over. Also, as you click, avoid clicking any links that take you back to the home page or a page you've already visited.

Note: To avoid confusion in the next steps, I'll call the three pages you've visited Page 1, Page 2 and Page 3. In other words, from the home page, you clicked a link to go to Page 1, then another to go to Page 2, and a third to go to Page 3.

2 While viewing Page 3, click the Back button once.

Page 2 appears.

3 Click the Back button again.

Page 1 appears.

4 Click the Back button once more.

The home page appears. The Back button goes grey — there's no more back. However, the Forward button is available.

5 Click the Forward button once.

Page 1 appears.

6 Click the Forward button again.

Page 2 appears.

7 Click the Forward button once more.

Page 3 appears, and the Forward button goes gray — there's no place left to go forward to, until you use Back again.

Stay online for the next lesson. You can stay at Page 3 or go back home — for what you'll do in Lesson 2-3, it makes no difference where you start!

extra credit

Suddenly, the pages appear so *fast!*

When you use the Home, Back and Forward buttons, you may notice that the pages seem to display much more quickly than they did the first time you visited them. That's because Internet Explorer stores on your hard disk a copy of each page you visit. When you first jump to a page, Internet Explorer must copy the whole thing from the server. When you go back to the same page later, Internet Explorer doesn't get the page from the server again; it just retrieves it from your hard disk, which it can do much more quickly.

☑ Progress Check

If you can do the following, you've mastered this lesson:

❏ Click the Home button to return to your home page from anywhere on the Web.

❏ Click the Back button to move backward through pages you've viewed.

❏ Click the Forward button to reverse the action of the Back button.

Figure 2-2: The Quick Links go to pre-programmed destinations (if you don't see the Quick Links, click the word Links that appears next to the Address box).

Figure 2-2

Lesson 2-3   Jumping with Quick Links

By now, you've probably noticed the row of icons, labeled "Links," that appears directly beneath your Internet Explorer toolbar (see Figure 2-2). These icons are called *Quick Links*, and each works just like a link on a page — click it and you go somewhere.

on the test

Note: If you don't see the Quick Links beneath the toolbar, but instead see the Address box, click the word Links that appears next to the Address box to display the Quick Links. To redisplay the Address box and hide the Quick Links, click the word Address next to the Quick Links.

Where the Quick Links lead depends upon where you got your copy of Internet Explorer. If you use the AT&T WorldNet Sevice version of Internet Explorer, each Quick Link is pre-programmed to go someplace AT&T thinks you may be interested in. If you got your copy of Internet Explorer another way, the Quick Links are pre-programmed differently — usually to pages at Microsoft (such as a page where you can download Internet software) or to pages set up for your use by your Internet provider. Labels on the Quick Links (see Figure 2-2) describe where each Quick Link leads.

To use a Quick Link, just click it. The Quick Link takes you to its pre-programmed page no matter where you are when you click it — at your home page or anywhere else on the Web. After visiting a page through a Quick Link, you can click Back to go back where you were, Home to go home, or even click another Quick Link.

Give your Quick Links a try:

1 Open Internet Explorer and connect to the Internet, if you have not already done so.

2 Find the Quick Links below the toolbar.

(If you don't see the Quick Links, display them as described in the Note near the beginning of this lesson.)

3 Click the Quick Link that appears farthest to the left.

You jump where that Quick Link leads. Check out what you find there.

4 One at a time, click the other Quick Links to see where they go.

After checking out your Quick Links, you can go home, go offline, or go anywhere else — it's your Internet Account, and you know how to get home and back if you get lost.

Notes:

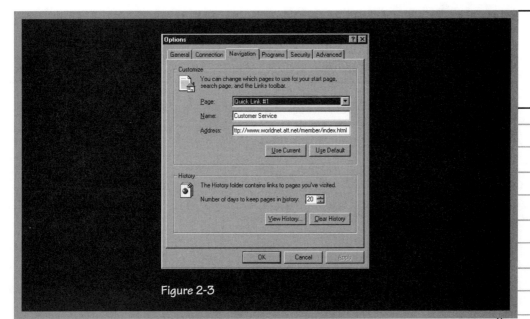

Figure 2-3

Figure 2-3: Change your Home (start) page and Quick Links on the Navigation tab of the Options dialog.

Recess

And that's all there is to navigating the Web with links — click, click, click, and you're all over the place. If you want to try some alternative methods of moving around, go on to the next lesson. Or you can shut down Internet Explorer and your Internet connection and take a well-deserved break.

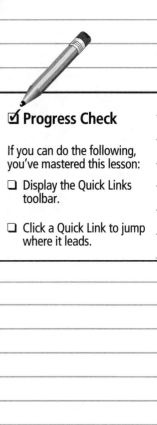

☑ Progress Check

If you can do the following, you've mastered this lesson:

❏ Display the Quick Links toolbar.

❏ Click a Quick Link to jump where it leads.

extra credit

Customizing your Quick Links and Home page

In your copy of Internet Explorer, you can change the home page Internet Explorer goes to when you connect to the Internet and when you click the Home button. You can also change the pages the Quick Links jump to, as well.

Note that to change these, you must know the Internet address, or *URL*, of the page you want to use as a Quick Link or Home page. If you don't yet know about URLs, you'll learn all about them in Unit 3.

To change your Home page or Quick Links:

1. Open Internet Explorer and choose <u>V</u>iew⇨<u>O</u>ptions⇨<u>N</u>avigation.

   The Navigation tab of the Options dialog opens, as shown in Figure 2-3.

2. Drop down the list next to <u>P</u>age and select Start Page or the Quick Link you want to change.

   The Quick Links are listed by number; Quick Link #1 is the icon farthest to the left in the Quick Links toolbar, and Quick Link #5 is the one farthest to the right. (Notice that "Search Page" is also listed in the Page drop-down list. The Search Page is the page that Internet Explorer jumps to when you click the Search button on the toolbar. You learn about the Search Page — including changing the Search Page — in Unit 5.)

3. If changing a Quick Link, double-click in the <u>N</u>ame box and type a name for the Quick Link. (If changing the Start Page, skip to Step 4.)

4. Double-click in the <u>A</u>ddress box, and type the complete URL of the page you want to use.

5. Click OK.

Unit 2 Quiz

For each question, circle the letter of the correct answer.

1. **Clicking a link can . . .**
    A. Take you to another page.
    B. Copy a file to your PC (*download* a file).
    C. Take you to a new spot in the same page.
    D. Any of the above.

2. **You can tell that the pointer is on a link when . . .**
    A. The pointer turns into a pointing finger.
    B. The Internet Explorer window flashes bright green.
    C. Your PC beeps.
    D. The pointer disappears.

3. **Which of the following actions jump(s) you to a different page than the one you're on?**
    A. Clicking a link.
    B. Clicking the Back button (if available).
    C. Clicking Home (when the current page is not the home page).
    D. All of the above, plus clicking a Quick Link.

4. **To switch between your Quick Links toolbar and Address box . . .**
    A. Type **Links** in the Address box, or choose the Address Quick Link.
    B. In the bar below the regular toolbar, click Links to show the Quick Links, or click Address to show the Address box.
    C. Do nothing — the item you want appears automatically when required.
    D. Choose File⇨Show Links or File⇨Show Address.

5. **Many pages show the same link twice — once as a picture, once as text — because . . .**
    A. The authors want to be sure you see the link.
    B. Picture links work only in the presence of an identical text link.
    C. The author was sloppy.
    D. Some browsers can't show pictures, so their users wouldn't see picture links.

Unit 2 Exercise

1. Get connected to the Internet.

2. By clicking links and using the Back button only, start from your home page, progress through four consecutive pages, and then return to the home page.

3. Now start from the home page, progress through six consecutive pages, then work backward to revisit one of the pages you just visited.

4. Disconnect from the Internet and from Internet Explorer.

Entering URLs

Objectives for This Unit

✓ Opening a Web page by typing its URL in the Address box

✓ Opening a page by entering an URL through the Run dialog box

✓ Opening a page by copying an URL from another document and pasting it into Internet Explorer

Prerequisites

▸ Opening Internet Explorer and connecting to the Internet (Lesson 2-1)

▸ Clicking a link (Lesson 2-2)

▸ Jumping back (Lesson 2-3)

Ideally, you should never have to type a Web page address directly into Internet Explorer — after all, hopping from page to page is what links are for, right? No doubt one reason for the Web's popularity is that it is (or can be) a virtually typing-free experience. Nevertheless, you'll sometimes want to pry your fingers from the mouse, crack your knuckles, and try to remember where they put the H key.

Suppose you're flipping through the latest *Redbook* or *National Geographic* and you see an ad for this sexy little Toyota — just what you've been looking for. You see Toyota's Web site address right there in the ad: `http://www.toyota.com`. Now, if you did a Web search (as described in Unit 5) using **toyota** as your search term, you'd probably wind up with a link to Toyota's Web page among your search hits. But why search? You've got the key already. All you have to do is turn it, and you zip straight to your automotive fantasies.

on the test

Internet addresses come in several types. But only one type is ever used in a Web browser such as Internet Explorer: a Uniform Resource Locator, or *URL*. ("URL" is pronounced either "earl" or "you-are-el," all depending on who's talking. I like "earl.") That `http://` part at the front of the address is the tip-off; whenever an address has a short beginning part separated from the rest of the address by a colon (:) and, usually, a double slash (//), it's an URL. In this unit, you discover how simple using URLs is, even if they do look complicated.

Note that entering an URL directly into Internet Explorer does not always require typing. You'll often see URLs lurking in the text of e-mail messages and in other Windows-based documents. In this unit, you learn how to grab an URL from anywhere and copy it into Internet Explorer so that you can jump straight to where the URL points — without once letting go of your mouse.

URL = Uniform Resource Locator; address type used in Web browsers

Figure 3-1: To go straight to any page, type its URL in the Address box (below the toolbar).

Figure 3-1

Lesson 3-1 — Entering an URL in the Address Box

Address box shows complete URL of current page

must use exact punctuation and capitalization when typing URLs

add ending slash only if URL includes it

The easiest place to enter an URL in Internet Explorer is the Address box, which appears directly beneath the toolbar (see Figure 3-1). (If you don't see the Address box, look for the word Address somewhere on the toolbar. Click the word Address, and the Address box appears.)

The Address box always shows the complete URL of the page you're viewing. Whenever you jump to a new page, the URL of the new page appears in the Address box. (You may have noticed that happening when you were browsing around the Web in Unit 2.) By entering a new URL in the Address box, you instruct Internet Explorer to jump to that page. The process is really that simple.

on the test

Of course, entering URLs has its rules. (You *knew* there would be rules, didn't you?) Carefully examine the URL you want to enter, and when typing it, be sure that you type it exactly as it appears where you found it (book, magazine, or whatever). That means *exactly* — letter for letter, punctuation-perfect. Watch out for making capital letter Os into zeroes or 1s into ls, and vice versa.

heads up

Follow the precise capitalization (pattern of UPPERCASE and lowercase letters). If the URL is `http://FREDO/Friends.HTM`, typing the same letters capitalized differently (`http://fredO/friends.HTM`, for example) may fail to take you where you want to go — or, in fact, anywhere at all.

If the URL ends in a slash (/), include the slash. If the URL does not end in a slash, don't add one.

Entering an URL

In this exercise, you jump to the Centre for the Easily Amused, a page that defies description.

To begin, open Internet Explorer and connect to the Internet, as described in Unit 1.

1 **Click once in the Address box.**

Your click highlights the URL already in the Address box. The current URL will be replaced by whatever you type next.

Remember: When typing your URL, follow the *rules* — match spelling, capitalization, and punctuation exactly as they appear where you found the URL.

2 **Type the following URL:**

```
http://www.amused.com/
```

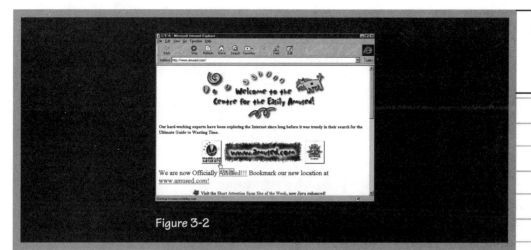

Figure 3-2

Following your first keystroke, the old URL in the Address box vanishes. As you type, you may use your Backspace, Insert, and Delete keys to fix mistakes. Double-check your typing before moving on to Step 3.

3 Press Enter.

If you've typed the URL correctly, the Centre for the Easily Amused Web page appears (see Figure 3-2).

You can amuse yourself at this page for a while, if you like — but get back to your home page for the next exercise.

Q&A session

Question: What if I enter an URL and Internet Explorer shows a message saying that it can't find the page I've requested?

Answer: When you see that message, Internet Explorer can't find a Web page whose URL matches the one you typed. That's usually because

- You made an error when typing the URL.

- You got an inaccurate URL from whatever source gave it to you.

- The page that the URL points to is no longer on the Web.

There's nothing you can do about the last two. But just in case the problem is the first one, try the following fixes:

- Triple-check your typing. If you find a mistake, fix it as described in the "Editing an URL" section of this lesson.

- If the URL ends in a slash (/), remove the slash and press Enter again. If the URL does not end in a slash and does not end in the letters .HTM or .HTML, add a slash to the very end of the URL and press Enter again. (Yes, the rules say to type the URL — slash or no slash — exactly as you find it. But Web servers can be goofy about when and whether they want slashes, and publishers can be sloppy about slashes when showing URLs in books, in magazines, and even online.)

- Delete everything in the URL following the first single slash. For example, if the URL that failed was `http://www.toyota.com/tercel.htm`, trim the URL to `http://www.toyota.com`. Trimming the URL in this way may take you to a default home page on the Web server that was supposed to contain the page you wanted. You may find that you can get to what you want by clicking through the links presented on that default page.

- Perform a Web search as described in Unit 5.

if URL doesn't work, try removing or adding end slash

deleting everything past first slash usually leaves default home page address

Editing an URL

If the URL that appears in the Address box is similar to the URL you want to enter, you don't have to erase the URL that's there and start over — you can just edit the URL already in the Address box.

For example, suppose you're visiting the Microsoft Network (MSN) home page. That page is a great place to check out new Internet Explorer developments, and it also shows you how to build a "custom start page," a personalized home page that reports sports scrores you follow, TV listings, and more. When you visit the MSN home page, the URL you type in the Address box is

```
http://www.msn.com
```

But suppose that, while at the MSN home page, you decide to jump to Microsoft's home page (which is different from the MSN page), another great spot for Internet Explorer info. Microsoft's home is at:

```
http://www.microsoft.com
```

To jump from the MSN home page to the Microsoft home page by editing the URL in the Address box:

1 **Go to the MSN home page by entering the URL**

```
http://www.msn.com
```

2 **Point to the Address box.**

3 **In the URL in the Address box, point to the spot between** msn **and the period that follows it.**

4 **Double-click.**

The edit cursor appears at the spot between msn and the period that follows it.

5 **Press Backspace twice to delete two letters. The URL now appears as**

```
http://www.m.com
```

6 **Type** icrosoft.

The correct URL for Microsoft's home now appears.

7 **Press Enter to jump to the page that the URL in the Address box now describes.**

When editing an URL, use the right and left arrow keys to move the edit cursor within the URL, and use Backspace or Delete to delete unwanted characters.

If you're going right on to the next lesson, stay online.

can edit URL in Address box by double-clicking and using arrow keys and Delete/ Backspace

extra credit

Fly the friendly URL

Internet Explorer adds to Windows 95 a capability that Microsoft calls friendly URLs. A friendly URL is just a regular URL with the `http://` part left off. For example, instead of typing `http://www.microsoft.com` in the Address box, you can just type `www.microsoft.com`.

You can enter any URL as a friendly URL, and you can use friendly URLs anywhere you would use a regular URL — in the Address box or in the Run dialog box.

So why do I show complete URLs (including the `http://` part) throughout this book, and why did I just teach you to type complete URLs? First, friendly URLs are not 100% reliable. There are circumstances under which Internet Explorer may incorrectly interpret an URL entered as a friendly URL and take you to the wrong place or nowhere. Second, friendly URLs are supported only by Internet Explorer, not by any other browser. If you get in the habit of using friendly URLs, you're teaching yourself a nonstandard way of working with the Web. Should you one day use a browser other than Internet Explorer, you could have trouble remembering how to phrase full URLs properly.

Of course, friendly URLs usually work, and they save you seven keystrokes — so if you wanna use 'em, use 'em. Just use full URLs from time to time as well to keep your Internet skills sharp.

☑ **Progress Check**

If you can do the following, you've mastered this lesson:

❑ Open a Web page by entering an URL in Internet Explorer's Address box.

❑ Edit an URL in Internet Explorer's Address box.

Entering an URL in the Run Dialog Box   Lesson 3-2

on the test

The Address Box is not the only home for your typed URLs. As an alternative, you can type an URL in the Run dialog box.

The Run dialog box isn't in Internet Explorer — it's part of Windows 95. But the Run dialog box does offer one neat advantage over using the Address box: If Internet Explorer is not already open before you enter your URL in the Run dialog box, the Run dialog box opens Internet Explorer automatically. Using Run, you open Internet Explorer *and* jump directly to your desired page all by turning on your PC, choosing one item from the Start menu, typing an URL, and pressing Enter. Slick.

on the test

Before you enter an URL in the Windows 95 Run dialog box, Internet Explorer can be open or closed. If it's open, it jumps to the URL you entered. If it's closed, Windows 95 opens Internet Explorer automatically, and then Internet Explorer jumps directly to the URL you entered (bypassing the home page).

To see how using the Run dialog box opens Internet Explorer for you, start this exercise with Internet Explorer and your Internet connection both shut off.

Here's how to use the Run dialog box to jump to the CheeseNet page:

1 **Choose Run from the Windows 95 Start menu.**

The Run dialog box appears, as shown in Figure 3-3.

2 **Type this URL:**

`http://www.wgx.com/cheesenet/`

gotta type URL exactly as it appears here!

Figure 3-3: You can open a Web page *and* Internet Explorer together by typing an URL in the Run dialog box.

Figure 3-4: Hungry? Check out CheeseNet, "The Internet's Cheese Information Resource."

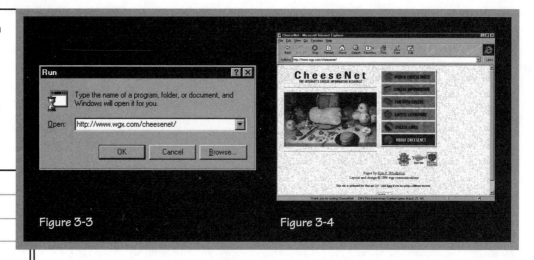

Figure 3-3   Figure 3-4

As you type, use your Backspace, Insert, and Delete keys to fix mistakes. Double-check your typing before moving on to Step 3.

3 **Press Enter.**

The Run dialog box closes, Internet Explorer opens, and Internet Explorer jumps to CheeseNet (shown in Figure 3-4).

Stay online if you're going straight into the next lesson.

URL ending in .HTM or .HTML points to specific file; text before slash is server name

☑ Progress Check

If you can do the following, you've mastered this lesson:

❏ Open a Web page by entering an URL in the Windows 95 Run dialog box.

❏ Edit an URL in the Run dialog box.

Q&A session

Question: How come some URLs end in a slash but others don't?

Answer: Some URLs point to an actual file. When the URL ends in .HTM or .HTML, it's pointing to a specific file on a specific Web server. The text following the last slash in the URL is a filename. For example, the URL `http://acme.com/gadgets.htm` points to a file called `gadgets.htm` on a server called `acme.com`. No slash is ever used after a filename.

However, some URLs don't point directly to a file. Instead, they just point to a server or to a directory on a server. The server is configured so that it automatically knows what file to show you when you access the server; no filename is required in the URL. For example, the URL `http://www.microsoft.com` points to Microsoft's Web server but doesn't identify a file to display. That's okay — Microsoft's server automatically shows the Microsoft home page file to any visitor who arrives at its server without naming a file.

When the URL doesn't end in a filename, some types of Web servers require a slash at the end and some don't. That's why you see such variation in the use of this "trailing slash." And historically, leaving off a required trailing slash (or adding one that's not required) is one of the most common mistakes in typing URLs.

Grabbing an URL from Anywhere

Believe it or not, on the Web you frequently find URLs that aren't also links — they're just text in an online document, and clicking them does absolutely *nada*. In other words, a Web page may tell you the URL of another Web page, but it doesn't set up that URL as a link — the address is just text and isn't underlined or displayed in blue, as links usually are.

Although such URLs aren't links, you can use them to jump to the pages they describe. In fact, you can use any URL you see in a document in Windows as a link. That includes URLs mentioned in e-mail messages or in word-processing documents.

The secret is the Windows 95 copy-and-paste facility. All you need to do is copy the complete text of the URL from where you find it and then paste it into any of the places Internet Explorer can accept an URL: the Address box (see Lesson 3-1) or the Run dialog box (see Lesson 3-2).

can copy and paste URL from another document into Address box

heads up

The steps required to paste the URL into Internet Explorer are always the same, regardless of where the URL comes from. The steps for copying the URL, however, can vary depending on the application in which the URL appears. The problem is highlighting: To copy something, you have to highlight it first. Usually, you can highlight a block of text — such as an URL — in a Windows-based document by clicking and holding at the text's beginning, dragging to its end, and then releasing — but not always. Sometimes, double-clicking the URL does the trick to highlight it. If neither of those techniques works, ask your coworker in the next cubicle or look through the application's Help menu under "highlighting" or "selecting" text.

In the following example, you jump to the Britannica's Lives page by copying its URL from an ordinary word processing document. On the Britannica's Lives page, you can find short biographies of everyone who was born on your birthday. For example, I share a birthday (October 24) with actor Kevin Kline and with Trujillo, the brutal (and eventually assassinated) dictator of the Dominican Republic. Top that.

Note: Before beginning, you must first have set up the CD-ROM as described in Appendix B.

1 **From the Start Menu, choose Programs⇨Dummies 101⇨Dummies 101 - Internet Explorer 3 Installer to open the CD-ROM Installer. Click the Install Exercise Files button and then close the Installer.**

2 **In My Computer (or in Windows Explorer), navigate to the folder C:\My Documents\Dummies 101 - Internet Explorer 3 and double-click the file COPYTST.DOC.**

The file COPYTST.DOC opens in Microsoft Word (if you have Word) or Windows WordPad if you don't have Word (WordPad is built into Windows 95). If you have another Windows word processor installed on your PC, the file may open in that program instead.

3 **Locate the URL text** `http://www.eb.com/bio.html` **and highlight it.**

Highlight the text by clicking at its beginning, dragging to its end, and releasing. Be sure to highlight the entire URL and nothing but the URL. Figure 3-5 shows the URL in COPYTST.DOC.

Copy button (Edit⇨Copy does the same thing)

Figure 3-5: You can usually highlight an URL that you see in the text of an online document by clicking and dragging from the beginning of the URL to its end and then releasing. You can then copy and paste it into Internet Explorer.

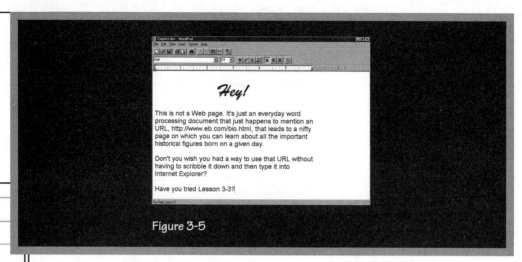

Figure 3-5

Paste button
(Edit⇨Paste does
the same thing)

☑ Progress Check

If you can do the following, you've mastered this lesson:

❑ Copy the text of an URL from a Windows-based document.

❑ Paste that URL into Internet Explorer's Address box or Run dialog box.

4 **Click the Copy button on the toolbar (Word's or Wordpad's) to copy the URL text.**

Most Windows-based applications have a Copy button, which looks like two tiny pages. If you don't see a Copy button, choose Edit⇨Copy from the application's menu bar or press and hold the Ctrl key, press the C key, and then release both keys.

5 **Switch to Internet Explorer (or open it if it's closed).**

You may close the word processor that you copied the URL from or leave it open — doesn't matter.

6 **Click in the Address box.**

Your click highlights the URL already in the Address box (if there is one). That means that the current URL will be replaced by what you paste.

7 **Click the Paste button on Internet Explorer's toolbar.**

The URL appears in the Address box.

If you don't like toolbars, you can paste the URL into Internet Explorer by choosing Edit⇨Paste from the menu bar or by pressing and holding the Ctrl key, pressing the V key, then releasing both keys.

8 **Press Enter.**

Internet Explorer jumps to the page that the URL identifies, provided the URL was typed correctly in the document from which you copied it.

To copy and paste an URL by using the Run dialog box, first copy the URL text by performing Steps 2 and 3 of the preceding exercise. Then, from the Windows 95 Start menu, choose Run. Press and hold the Ctrl key, press the V key, and then release both keys. Finish by pressing Enter. Internet Explorer opens (if it's not already open) and jumps to the page that the URL identifies.

Recess

See, using URLs isn't difficult at all. Let out that sigh of relief and go pop a cold one. Oh, and you can close Internet Explorer and disconnect from the Internet. You won't need to go online again until the next unit.

Unit 3 Quiz

For each question, circle the letter of the correct answer.

1. **URL stands for . . .**

    A. Unanimous Research Library.

    B. Uniform Resource Locator.

    C. Nothing — Net geeks made it up 'cause it's easy to remember, like Kodak.

    D. Upton Randolph Lancaster, father of the Web.

2. **Where can you type an URL to jump to the Web page that the URL stands for?**

    A. In the Windows 95 Run dialog box.

    B. In the Internet Explorer Address box.

    C. In Solitaire.

    D. A or B.

3. **Which of the following is the correct typing of the URL** `http://www.snellco.com/Prices/SALE.htm`**?**

    A. `http://WWW.SNELLCO.COM/PRICES/SALE.HTM`

    B. `http://www.snellco.com/Prices/SALE.htm`

    C. `http://www.snellco.com/prices/sale.htm`

    D. `http://www.snell.co/Price/SALE.htm`

4. **Precisely what does the URL** `http://www.apple.com/fruit/orange.htm` **describe?**

    A. A Web page with the filename `www.apple.com/fruit/orange.htm`.

    B. A Web page file called orange.htm, which is stored in the fruit directory on a Web server called `www.apple.com`.

    C. Nothing — an URL is a purely abstract representation with no literal connection to any tangible object.

    D. A Web page called fruit, stored in the orange directory.

5. **True or false: You must open Internet Explorer *before* entering an URL in the Windows 95 Run dialog box.**

    A. True

    B. False

Unit 3 Exercise

Enter URLs to navigate to the following fun and funky Web pages:

1. All about "Sporks": `http://www.spork.org/`

2. Academic writings and analysis, all on the subject of Wile E. Coyote: `http://www.uoknor.edu/scs/WILE/`

3. Fun explanations of the science underlying the day's news stories: `http://whyfiles.news.wisc.edu/`

4. A random lightbulb joke: `http://www.crc.ricoh.com/ ~marcush/lightbulb/random.cgi`

5. Vegetarian recipes: `http://www.vegweb.com/`

6. A regularly updated estimate of Microsoft Chairman Bill Gates's personal wealth and the prorated contribution of every U.S. citizen to it: `http://www.webho.com/WealthClock`

7. A dumbed-down condensation of James Joyce's *Ulysses*: `http:// www.bway.net/~hunger/ulysses.html`

Building a List of Favorite Pages

Prerequisites
▶ Opening Internet Explorer and connecting to the Internet (Unit 1)
▶ Browsing through links (Unit 2)
▶ Understanding URLs (Unit 3)

Objectives for This Unit

✓ Adding favorite pages to an easy-access list

✓ Using your Favorites list to jump to a favorite page

✓ Organizing and managing your Favorites

Millions and millions and millions (and millions!) of pages make up the Web. Nobody visits 'em all. And while your Web travels may take you far, you'll soon settle into a pattern of visiting certain pages regularly. A page may contain regular updates about your favorite TV show, author, or political controversy — so you'll visit it often to see what's new. Or a page may contain your preferred search tool or a list of links you like to browse often. Whatever the reason, a page you keep coming back to might be called a "favorite" of yours.

After you have a few favorites, wouldn't you like to be able to get to them quickly, any time you want to? Especially if a page has a long URL (too much typing!), or you found the page through a search (as you'll learn to do in Unit 5).

Internet Explorer offers a great way to solve this problem: Favorites. Favorites is a menu that you create — quite easily, as it turns out — listing your favorite Web pages. To jump straight to any of your Favorites, you need only choose it from the menu — no links, no URLs, no fuss or muss. Best of all, if you have many Favorites (most people do), you can group them and organize them into folders, so you can find any Favorite in a snap. Figure 4-1 shows a Favorites menu.

jump straight to frequently visited page by putting it on Favorites menu

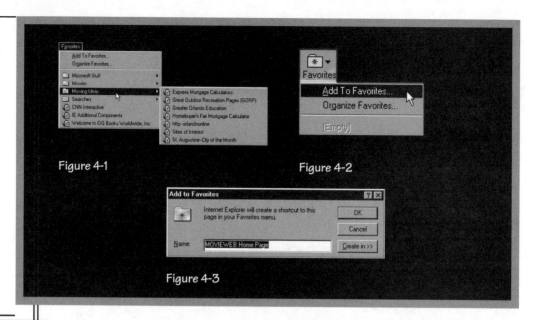

Figure 4-1: By building a menu of Favorite pages, you gain instant access to pages you visit often.

Figure 4-2: To make the page you see into a Favorite, click the Favorites button and then choose Add To Favorites.

Figure 4-3: The page's title appears automatically in the Add to Favorites dialog box, to serve as the page's name in the Favorites menu — but you can change it if you want to.

Figure 4-1

Figure 4-2

Figure 4-3

Lesson 4-1

Adding a Page to Your Favorites List

Before you can begin building your list of Favorites, you need to have chosen one or more pages that you'd like to put there. Obviously, I don't know what your tastes are, and the pages that I've picked out as Favorites won't please everyone. But you gotta start somewhere, so just go ahead and use the Favorites I've chosen (you can replace them later, as you'll learn in Lesson 4-3).

Creating a Favorite for the current page

Make the MovieWEB page a Favorite in the traditional way: while looking at it (there's another way, too — more about that later). MovieWEB is a great place to learn more about upcoming films.

Favorites→Add To Favorites to put current page on Favorites list

1 **Start up Internet Explorer and your Internet connection. In the Address box, type the following URL:**

```
http://movieweb.com/
```

The MovieWEB page appears.

2 **Click the Favorites button on the toolbar or choose Favorites from the menu bar.**

You get the same menu either way, and it looks like the one shown in Figure 4-2. You haven't created any Favorites yet, so your menu says (Empty) where the list of Favorites will appear. (If you use AT&T WorldNet Service, some Favorites have been provided.)

what appears in Name box shows up on Favorites menu; can keep page's title as name or can type new name

3 **Choose Add To Favorites.**

on the test

A dialog box like the one in Figure 4-3 appears. In the Add to Favorites dialog box, the title of the page appears in the Name box. The Name is what you'll see listed in your Favorites menu when you finish, so make sure that the Name

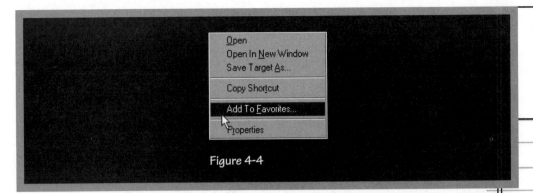

Figure 4-4

Figure 4-4: Right-clicking a link brings up a context menu from which you can make a Favorite of the page that the link points to.

describes the page in a way that helps you remember what's on the page. Usually, the title does the trick, so all you need to do in the Add to Favorites dialog box is click OK. However, if you'd prefer another Name for the listing, type one before clicking OK.

4 **When the <u>N</u>ame box shows what you want, click OK.**

Internet Explorer adds the page to your Favorites menu. (To see the menu, click the Favorites button on the toolbar.)

In the next exercise, you create a Favorite from a link, so stay online.

Creating a Favorite from a link

on the test

Creating a Favorite while viewing the page that you intend to make Favorite makes sense, but you can also create a Favorite from a link to a page. When you create a Favorite in this way, choosing the Favorite later doesn't go to where you found the link — it goes to the page or other resource that the link points to.

Why create a Favorite from a link? I can think of at least two reasons:

▶ The link appears to lead to something you'll like, but for some reason, the link isn't working properly — maybe the server storing the page is having problems. By making a Favorite from the link, you can easily try to access the page later by choosing its Favorites entry.

▶ The link leads not to a page but to a file for downloading — perhaps a large file that will take a long time to download (you learn about downloading files in Unit 6). By saving the link as a Favorite, you can download the file later, at a more convenient time, simply by choosing it from your Favorites menu.

For example, in Unit 5 you learn all about searching. One way to search is to use the category listings at a Web site called Yahoo!. You learn much more about Yahoo! in Unit 5, but just to get your feet wet, you'll browse to a Yahoo! category here and make it a Favorite.

1 **From any Web page, move to Yahoo! by typing** http://www.yahoo.com **in the Address box and pressing Enter.**

2 **In the Yahoo! page, point to the <u>Arts</u> link.**

The Arts link leads to the Yahoo! Arts page, a listing of Arts-related links.

3 **Click the right mouse button (not the left, the usual clicker).**

Favorite created from link goes to what link points to, not to page that link is on

can create Favorite for link to file for downloading later

search tool category can be added to Favorites list

right-click link and choose Add To Favorites from context menu

A Windows 95 context menu opens, as shown in Figure 4-4. All the items on the context menu are actions that you can take regarding the link you're pointing to.

☑ Progress Check

If you can do the following, you've mastered this lesson:

❏ Open your Favorites menu.

❏ Add the current page to your Favorites menu.

❏ Add to your Favorites menu from a link.

4 **Choose Add To Favorites from the context menu.**

A dialog box like the one shown earlier in Figure 4-3 appears. You can type a new name for the Favorite or leave the name as is, if it's sufficiently descriptive.

5 **Click OK.**

Internet Explorer adds the Yahoo! Arts category page to your Favorites menu.

In the next lesson, you learn how to use the Favorites menu from any Web page.

Lesson 4-2

Jumping to a Favorite Page

If you completed Lesson 4-1, you now have at least two items in your Favorites menu: the Yahoo! Arts directory and MovieWEB. Try 'em out. . . .

1 **Go to any page on the Web (other than the two you just chose as Favorites).**

Your home page serves fine for this example.

click Favorites button and choose page to go to that page

2 **Click the Favorites button on your toolbar.**

The Favorites menu drops down, just as it did in the preceding exercise. Only now, as you can see in Figure 4-5, two additional items appear at the bottom of the menu — the Favorites you just created. Observe that the Favorites are listed in alphabetical order.

3 **Choose either of the two Favorites (your choice!).**

The Favorites menu closes, and Internet Explorer jumps to the page you selected.

You can be on any Web page for the next lesson, so go ahead and explore those links you've been curious about before moving on.

☑ Progress Check

If you can do the following, you've mastered this lesson:

❏ Open your Favorites menu.

❏ Select an entry from your Favorites menu.

Favorites work anytime

If you are working in Internet Explorer but aren't connected to the Internet (a situation you'll face in upcoming units), you can still pick a Favorite from the menu. When you do, Internet Explorer opens your connection dialog box. After you connect, Internet Explorer jumps directly to the Favorites page you requested.

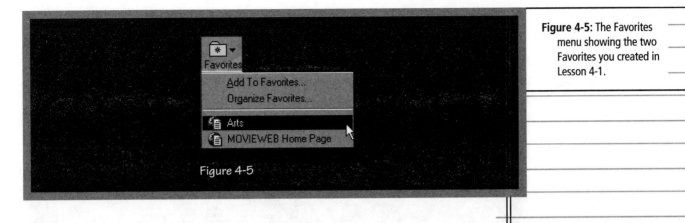

Managing Your Favorites

Lesson 4-3

Over time, as you discover new adventures on the Web and save the best as Favorites, you may make a disheartening discovery: Your Favorites have multiplied like nail salons. Having a list of 10 to 20 Favorite sites is useful; having a list of 50 to 100 is a little nuts.

For one thing, the Favorites menu has space for only about 25 entries (the exact number may vary depending on such factors as your display resolution settings and screen fonts). You may save as many Favorites as you like, but only the first 25 will fit on the menu; to get to the rest, you must choose More Favorites from the bottom of the Favorites menu and then choose from the Favorites folder (as shown in Figures 4-6 and 4-7). That's an extra step, which cuts into the convenience of Favorites.

on the test

Perhaps more important, having too many Favorites makes finding the Favorite you want time-consuming. After all, few people really have more than about 20 or 30 true *favorites* — people with more entries than that have probably just neglected to organize their Favorites and clean out old, rarely used Favorites entries.

Internet Explorer enables you to manage your Favorites in three important ways. You can

- ▶ **Group Favorites in folders:** To keep them organized for easy location and to fit more of them on the Favorites menu
- ▶ **Delete Favorites:** To remove entries that have fallen out of favor
- ▶ **Rename Favorites:** To make a name more descriptive or to give an old Favorite a new name so that you can use the old name for a new Favorite

keep number of Favorites manageable

can group Favorites in folders, delete Favorites, or rename Favorites

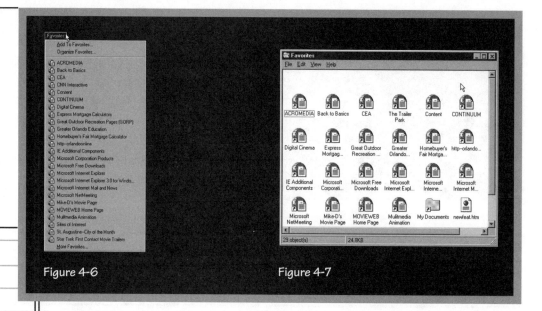

Figure 4-6

Figure 4-7

Figure 4-6: When you have more than about 25 Favorites entries, a More Favorites option appears at the bottom of the menu.

Figure 4-7: Choosing More Favorites opens the whole Favorites folder, from which you can select any of your Favorites by double-clicking it.

---

extra credit

What are "Favorites" *really?*

Each Favorite is actually an *Internet shortcut,* a special kind of file with the file extension .URL. You can do a lot more with an Internet shortcut than just stick it in your Favorites folder. For example, you can put Internet shortcuts right on your desktop to go quickly to anywhere on the Net. You learn how to use Internet shortcuts in Unit 10.

Organizing Favorites

To organize your Favorites:

1 From any Web page, click the Favorites button on the toolbar.

2 Choose Organize Favorites.

The Organize Favorites dialog box opens, as shown in Figure 4-8. You can click any Favorite and then click one of the buttons to act on it, as follows:

- **Move button:** Moves the selected Favorite into a folder

- **Rename button:** Allows you to change the Favorite's name

- **Delete button:** Deletes the Favorite (moves it to your Windows 95 Recycle Bin)

- **Create Folder button:** Creates a new folder

3 Click the Create Folder button on the toolbar of Organize Favorites.

A new folder appears in the window, with the name New Folder.

4 Type Searches.

The folder is now named Searches.

5 Press Enter.

The Searches folder now appears within the Organize Favorites dialog box, as shown in Figure 4-9.

Margin notes:

Favorite = Internet shortcut

click Favorite and click button to delete, rename, or move Favorite or add new folder

Move...
Move button

Rename
Rename button

Delete
Delete button

Create Folder [icon]
button

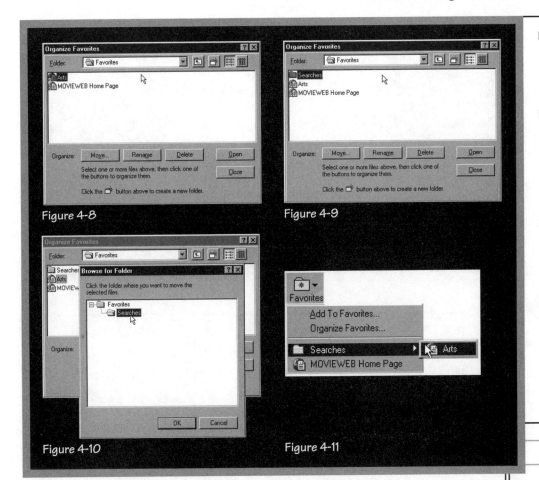

Figure 4-8

Figure 4-9

Figure 4-10

Figure 4-11

Figure 4-8: To manage your list of Favorites, click the Favorites button and then choose Organize Favorites.

Figure 4-9: Click the Create Folder button on the Organize Favorites toolbar to create a new folder into which you can move as many Favorites as you want.

Figure 4-10: To move a Favorite into a folder, select the Favorite, click Move, and then select the folder in the Browse for Folder dialog box.

Figure 4-11: To use the Favorites in a folder, click the folder on the Favorites menu. The contents of the folder appear on a submenu to the right of the folder.

6 **Select your Arts Favorite.**

7 **Click the Move button.**

A Browse for Folder dialog box opens, showing any folders you've created, including the new Searches (as shown in Figure 4-10).

8 **Select the Searches folder by clicking it.**

9 **Click OK.**

The Organize Favorites dialog box returns, and Arts is gone (it's now inside the Searches folder).

10 **Click Close.**

Organize Favorites closes, and you return to Internet Explorer.

11 **Click the Favorites button.**

Two items now appear on your Favorites menu: MovieWEB and the Searches folder.

on the test

12 **Select the Searches folder.**

Your Arts Favorite appears on a submenu, from which you can select it (see Figure 4-11).

That's the last online exercise for this unit, so you can go ahead and shut down your Internet connection. You may want to keep Internet Explorer open, though, in case you want to try out what you learn in the next section.

Notes:

Figure 4-12: In the Add to Favorites dialog box, click the Create in button to put a new Favorite in a folder.

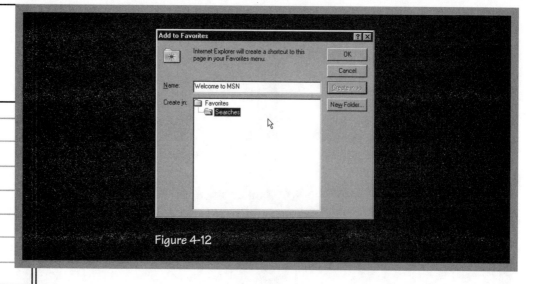

Figure 4-12

Notes:

when adding page
to Favorites menu,
click Create in
button to put page
in existing or new
folder

☑ Progress Check

If you can do the following, you've mastered this lesson:

❑ Create Favorites folders and move items into folders.

❑ Make your Favorites list more manageable by organizing similar items into folders and deleting items that you're tired of.

❑ Put a Favorite into a new or existing folder as you're creating the Favorite.

Q&A session

Question: In my Favorites menu, can I create folders within folders (within folders, within folders . . .)?

Answer: Sure! This is Windows 95, and folders is folders. To put a folder within a folder, follow Steps 1 through 3 for organizing Favorites. Then click one of the existing folders before typing a name for your new folder. The new folder is created inside the folder you clicked.

In the Browse for Folder dialog box that appears when you click Move (see Figure 4-10), your new folder appears beneath the folder that contains it. Click your new folder to move a Favorite into it.

Organizing Favorites as you go along

Just to keep things simple, I didn't tell you about putting Favorites in folders until this lesson. But now that you understand how Favorites in folders work, I should point out that you can insert a Favorite in a folder — and even create a new folder to put it in — when you create the Favorite.

When you choose the Add To Favorites command, the Add to Favorites dialog box opens so that you can accept (or change) the Favorite's name. That dialog box contains a button called Create in. When you click Create in, the Add to Favorites dialog box expands, as shown in Figure 4-12. You can click a folder to choose the folder into which the new Favorite goes, or click the Create Folder button to make a new folder for the Favorite.

Recess

The seeming anarchy of the Web can be daunting. With your Favorites folder, you have at least a sense of control and stability (but remember that the Web changes all the time, so a Favorite that you created just yesterday may not function when you click it today).

So now you know all about browsing the Web. But what do you do when you find a page, besides just read it? Ponder that thought over a cup of java and then move on to Part II.

Unit 4 Quiz

For each question, circle the letter of the correct answer.

1. **To add a page to your Favorites menu, you can . . .**

   A. Jump to the page, click the Favorites button, and choose Add To Favorites.

   B. Find a link that leads to the page, right-click it, and choose Add To Favorites.

   C. Jump to the page and tell the page that you really, really like it.

   D. A and B

2. **To jump to any page listed in your Favorites menu . . .**

   A. Click Home and then choose the Favorites link on your home page.

   B. Enter the URL `http://www.myfavorites.com`.

   C. Click the Favorites button on the toolbar and then choose a Favorite from it.

   D. All of the above

3. **A good number of Favorites to have is . . .**

   A. No more than 12.

   B. At least 40.

   C. No Favorites at all — why play that childish game?

   D. As many as you use regularly, organized into manageable folders.

4. **When you choose a folder from the Favorites menu . . .**

   A. A submenu opens, showing a group of Favorites and/or more folders.

   B. The Favorites folder opens.

   C. Internet Explorer jumps to the Microsoft Favorites Folders page.

   D. Nothing happens — folders are not supported on menus.

5. **The name you give to a Favorite when creating it . . .**

   A. Must match the page's title.

   B. Should be a descriptive name that helps you remember what's on the page.

   C. Cannot be more than 11 characters long.

   D. Must contain the secret password "sparky" somewhere within it, for security purposes.

Unit 4 Exercise

1. Browse the Web through a half-dozen or so pages and save every page you see as a Favorite, even if it's really boring or stupid. Observe the default names given to the Favorites and be sure to rename any whose names are not sufficiently descriptive.

2. After you've accumulated these Favorites, go to Organize Favorites, create a folder called Ned Made Me Do This, and move all your new Favorites into it.

3. Open your Favorites menu and observe the way the items are organized on it.

4. Return to your browsing and create a few new Favorites, saving them directly into the Ned Made Me Do This folder.

5. Next time you think of it, return to Organize Favorites, delete any of the Favorites you don't want to keep, move others to more descriptive folders, and delete the Ned Made Me Do This folder.

Part I Review

Unit 1 Summary

▶ **Installing the AT&T WorldNet℠ software:** From the Start Menu, choose Programs⇨ Dummies 101⇨Dummies 101 - Internet Explorer 3 Installer to open the CD-ROM Installer. Click the AT&T WorldNet Service with Internet Explorer 3 button; then follow the prompts.

▶ **Connecting to the Internet:** To open Internet Explorer and connect to the Internet, double-click the Internet icon on your desktop.

▶ **Disconnecting from the Internet:** To go offline and close Internet Explorer, choose File⇨Close.

▶ **Moving around in a page:** When a page is too large to fit within the Internet Explorer window, operate the scroll bars to scroll to unseen parts of the page.

Unit 2 Summary

▶ **Finding a link:** Pictures and text may serve as links. Whenever the mouse pointer is on a link, it changes to a pointing finger. Also, text links usually appear underlined and in a different color from the surrounding text.

▶ **Jumping to another page:** To jump to another page or to another part of the same page, click a link once with the left mouse button.

▶ **Jumping home:** To return to your home page from anywhere on the Web, click the Home button on the toolbar.

▶ **Jumping backward or forward:** To jump backward through pages you've visited, click the Back button. To reverse the action of back, click Forward.

▶ **Using a Quick Link to jump to a preselected page:** Display the Quick Links (click Links on the toolbar) and click the desired Quick Link.

Unit 3 Summary

▶ **Entering an URL in the Address box:** To jump to a page, type its URL in the Address box on Internet Explorer's toolbar and press Enter.

▶ **Entering an URL in the Run dialog:** If you enter an URL in Windows 95's Run dialog (choose Run from the Start menu), Internet Explorer opens, connects to the Internet, and jumps to the page.

▶ **Editing an URL:** To edit an URL in the Address box or Run dialog, click in the spot you wish to change and edit with your Del and Backspace keys.

▶ **Copying an URL from any Windows document:** Using Windows 95's cut and paste techniques, copy the text of an URL from any windows document and then paste that text into the Address box or Run dialog to jump to that page in Internet Explorer.

Unit 4 Summary

▶ **Adding to your Favorites menu:** To add a page to your list of Favorites (so that you can return to it easily), go to the page, click the Favorites button, and choose Add To Favorites.

▶ **Creating a Favorite from a link:** Create a Favorite entry for a page by finding a link to the page, right-clicking the link, and choosing Add To Favorites from the context menu.

▶ **Using a Favorite to jump quickly to a favorite page:** To jump to a favorite page, click the Favorites button and then choose the Favorite from the menu.

▶ **Managing your Favorites:** Click the Favorites button and then choose Organize Favorites to open a dialog on which you can delete or rename Favorites or organize them in folders.

Part I Test

The questions on this test cover all the material presented in Part I, Unit 1 through Unit 4.

True False

Each statement is either true or false.

T   F   1. The precise steps required to connect to, or disconnect from, the Internet depend on who supplies your Internet connection.

T   F   2. You can recognize a link because it appears in flashing, bold letters.

T   F   3. When it is on a link, the pointer changes to a closed fist.

T   F   4. To jump to a particular Web page, you can enter its URL in the Address box.

T   F   5. The Home button takes you to your home page, no matter where you are when you click it.

T   F   6. Quick Links cannot be changed.

T   F   7. When you type an URL, capitalization doesn't matter.

T   F   8. The Back button takes you to the page you visited before the one you're on.

T   F   9. Web pages appear slowly because of the inferior copper that contaminates sections of the world's telecommunications networks.

T   F   10. The logo on the right side of the toolbar is animated when Internet Explorer is busy retrieving information from a server.

Multiple Choice

For each of the following questions, circle the correct answer.

11. An URL is . . .

A. The name of a Web page.

B. The name of a Favorite.

C. A form of Internet address you enter in a Web browser.

D. A form of address you use to connect to the Internet.

12. The Web pages you view are stored on a computer called a . . .

A. WebIntosh.

B. IBM PCjr (Web Edition).

C. Web server.

D. Web browser.

13. The Forward button works . . .

A. Only after you've used Back.

B. Anytime.

C. Only for shops that are union signatories.

D. Poorly.

14. After you use a text link, the next time you see that link it will have . . .

A. Disappeared.

B. Changed color.

C. Turned fuzzy.

D. Drifted to the right.

Part I Test

15. **As in any Windows 95 program, the X button in the upper-right corner of Internet Explorer . . .**

    A. Maximizes Internet Explorer.

    B. Activates Internet Explorer.

    C. Invigorates Internet Explorer.

    D. Closes Internet Explorer.

16. **Your connection dialog establishes the connection between . . .**

    A. Your modem and the Internet.

    B. Your PC and your modem.

    C. Your modem and your local phone company.

    D. Your PC and another PC.

Matching

17. **Match up each button with the action it takes:**

    A.

    1. Jumps to the page you always see first when you connect to the Internet.

    B.

    2. Jumps you to a page you viewed earlier.

    C.

    3. Jumps you to a page of search tools.

    D.

    4. Shows a menu of pages you visit often and lets you jump to one of the pages and/or add another page to the menu.

Part I Lab Assignment

This lab assignment helps you to find new and interesting Web pages by entering URLs into Internet Explorer.

Step 1

Offline, browse print magazines and newspapers, keeping an eye out for interesting Web pages described there.

Step 2

Whenever you come upon an interesting Web page, jot down its URL in a notebook.

Step 3

When you have accumulated about a dozen URLs to try, connect to the Internet and visit each one.

Explore not just the page but other interesting pages accessible through links on the page.

Step 4

Add a Favorite for anything that pays off.

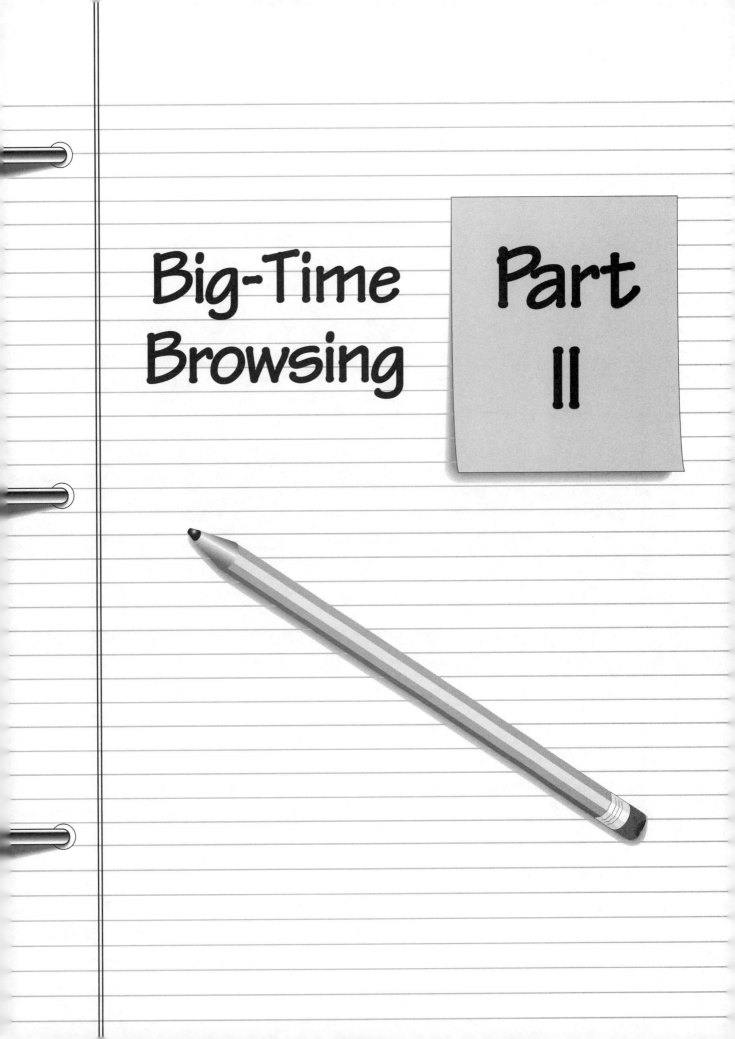

Big-Time Browsing

Part II

In this part . . .

Clicking your way around the Web with nothing more than what you discovered in Part I, you can do mucho-plenty. You can visit any page, anywhere, and enjoy whatever goodies the page chooses to show you.

But by interacting a little more deliberately with Internet Explorer and the Web, you can do so much more. You can pick up free files containing everything from programs to movie trailers to Shakespeare. You can look at video clips and play music. Most importantly, you can apply powerful search techniques to bullseye just the pages containing information you want to see.

While remaining well within the reach of us Dummies, these activities nonetheless require a little more skill and experience than the basic browsing you've tried so far. I think you'll find the new material simpler than you'd expect and more rewarding than you'd imagine.

Searching for Stuff

Objectives for This Unit

✓ Finding and jumping to pages where you can search for stuff

✓ Finding stuff by clicking through lists

✓ Using an automated search program to find stuff

✓ Finding stuff in creative, funky ways

Prerequisites

▶ Opening Internet Explorer and connecting to the Internet (Unit 1)

▶ Scrolling a Web page (Unit 1)

▶ Clicking links (Unit 2)

▶ Jumping backward and forward (Unit 2)

▶ Entering URLs (Unit 3)

If you're like most folks, the giddy high of your first Web browsings soon gives way to the inevitable, sobering crash. At first, you're tantalized by the seemingly limitless range of information available on the Web. Soon after, you're frustrated by the difficulty of locating any particular needle in the Web haystack. Browsing around is fun, but when you want to see something about the Beatles or Borneo or Bob Dole, that's what you want to see, darn it! And you don't want to have to click crazily around the Web for a week to find it.

I'd like to assure you that there is a single, comprehensive, up-to-date, all-encompassing master index to the entire contents of the Web in which you can look up pages related to any topic. I'd *like* to assure you of that . . . but I'd be lying. There's no such thing. No master index exists because the Web isn't really just one thing; it's millions of independent people publishing billions of words and pictures on thousands of servers, and nobody can control — or, in fact, keep up with — everything that's published on every server everywhere. (A few of the *Fortune 500* companies are desperately trying to seize control of the Web, but they haven't figured out how to do it yet. If they ever succeed, we may get a master index — but we'll also lose everything else that makes the Web worthwhile.)

no master index to Web exists

In lieu of a master index, the Web offers an assortment of pages from which you can search for other pages related to a topic you're interested in. For lack of a better description, I call the services offered by these pages *search tools*. In this chapter, you learn how to use search tools to locate Web pages that contain the information you want.

search tools = Web pages for searching Web for specific topics

heads up

While the examples in this unit show exactly how to use a few of the popular search tools, note that other tools — and any new tools to come — are used in essentially the same way. Note, too, that I do not endorse or otherwise recommend any particular search tool over any other. Like a lot of things on the Web, search tools are a matter of personal preference. Try 'em all and then return to the ones you like and ignore the rest. But leave me out of it. I have my own problems.

On the Web, search tools come in two basic types:

directory = listing of Web pages organized by topic

▶ **Directories:** Listings of Web pages organized and categorized by topic, like an index. These listings are painstakingly created and kept up-to-date by the folks who started the list. Thousands of other Web users help the list-keepers keep the directory current by sending information about new Web pages and updates about older pages that have disappeared or have changed addresses. Most directories let you add an entry to the listings yourself, so if you know about a Web page that's not included in the directory, you can add it for the benefit of everyone who uses the directory.

To use a directory, you click category headings and their subheadings until you find what you want, as described later in this unit. Most directories give you an alternative to clicking the supplied category headings: You can type in a specific topic, and the directory uses a *search engine* to dig through the entire directory and find the related pages for you — giving you near-instant access to a page that you would normally have to click through heading after subheading to find.

crawler (or worm or spider) = program that periodically scans all Web servers and creates directories

▶ **Crawlers:** Also known by various other crawly names, such as *worms* and *spiders.* Programs that systematically contact every server on the Web (at regular intervals), scan the contents of the server, and add information about the contents of the server to a directory that the crawler actually writes and updates as it crawls its way around the Web.

crawlers' listings more complete and up-to-date; traditional directories more organized and descriptive

The important difference between traditional directories and those created by crawlers is that the crawlers' listings tend to be more complete and up-to-date, while traditional directories tend to contain more meaningful categorization and more useful, descriptive information. Also, few of the crawlers provide a way to browse the categories in their directories — to use a crawler-based directory, you almost always must use the search engine provided on the crawler's Web page rather than click through headings as you can do with a traditional directory.

That said, the truth is that Web searching is very much a trial-and-error activity. Any of the search tools may locate a page or pages that meet your needs; any of them may not. In practice, you'll probably try your favorite search tool first. If you don't find what you want, you'll move on to the other search tools until you hit pay dirt.

different search tools come up with different results

on the test

But keep in mind that no search tool actually searches the entire contents of the Web — even crawlers, which may contact every server, cannot catalog absolutely everything stored there in a timely manner. The contents of the directories that are compiled and searched by each tool differ. All search tools try to be as comprehensive as possible, but ultimately, each will catalog stuff that some or all of the others miss. So if you can't find what you want through one search tool, try another.

on the test

Like the patch of fungus that it is, the Web constantly grows and mutates. All the time, new pages are added and older ones deleted, and pages that remain may have their addresses or filenames changed. Because of this constant change, no Web searching tool is ever completely up-to-date. From time to time, a search will turn up an out-of-date entry. Nothing terrible happens when you try that entry — Internet Explorer simply reports that it can't find the page you've requested. But when searching, don't be surprised if you hit a dead end from time to time. Just try another entry or another search.

So remember that when you go through the lessons and do the searches, your screen won't look exactly like what you see in the figures, at least with respect to what pages come up.

Opening a Search Tool   Lesson 5-1

A half-dozen or so major Web search tools are out there at this writing. You can reach any of them simply by supplying Internet Explorer with the URL of the page that serves as the search tool's home. Alternatively, you can use the Search button on Internet Explorer's toolbar. You'll test out both techniques in the following examples.

Using the Search button

The Search button on Internet Explorer's toolbar opens a "Search page," a Web page that combines several different search tools into one, easy-to-use page — call it an *all-in-one* search page. The exact page the Search button opens varies, depending upon who supplied your copy of Internet Explorer.

For example, when users of AT&T WorldNet℠ Service (such as those using the version of Internet Explorer supplied with this book) click Search, the AT&T WorldNet Service Search page appears (see Figure 5-1). When users of most other Internet providers click Search, Microsoft's Internet Searches page appears (see Figure 5-2). If you compare the two figures, you'll notice a number of words in common: Yahoo!, Excite, AltaVista, and so on. Each of these is a search tool in its own right. The all-in-one pages pull the various tools together so that you can operate them from one spot.

Generally, you can do either of two things on either of the two all-in-one search pages:

- By clicking the radio button next to the name of a search tool and then typing a key word in the box, you can perform a search using the selected tool's *search engine* (you learn about search engines in Lesson 5-3). Even though you're really using the selected search tool, you can perform your search straight from AT&T's or Microsoft's search page — you needn't jump to the tool's own Web page.

- By clicking a search tool's link on an all-in-one page, you can jump directly to a search tool's own Web page. For example, if you click the picture-link called Excite in the AT&T WorldNet Search page, you jump to Excite's Web page. This capability is useful when you want to browse a search tool's directory (as you learn to do in Lesson 5-2), or when you need to apply the search tool's optional features.

Figure 5-1: If you use AT&T WorldNet Service, clicking the Search button opens the Search page.

Figure 5-2: If you use an Internet provider other than AT&T WorldNet, clicking the Search button most likely opens Microsoft's Internet Searches page.

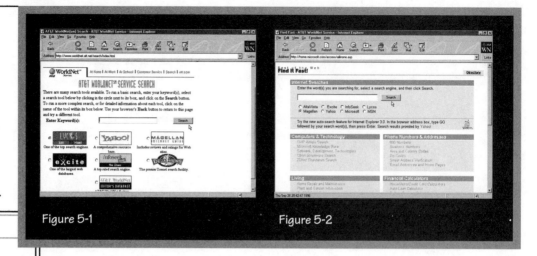

Figure 5-1   Figure 5-2

Notes:

Find out where your search button leads:

1 Open Internet Explorer and connect to the Internet.

heads up

The Search button works the same no matter what page you're looking at when you use it: It always goes to your all-in-one search page, no matter which page — the home page or any other page — you see when you click Search.

2 Click the Search button on the toolbar.

The all-in-one search page configured in your copy of Internet Explorer opens. Scroll around the page and examine what it has to offer. In the next two lessons, you learn the specifics of using any of the search tools you see on the page.

3 Visit the *other* all-in-one search page and examine what it has to offer.

If your Search button took you to the AT&T WorldNet Search page, check out Microsoft's Internet Searches page at

`http://home.microsoft.com/access/allinone.asp`

If your Search button took you to Microsoft's Internet Searches page, check out the AT&T WorldNet Search page at

`http://www.worldnet.att.net/search/index.html`

heads up

As you can see, different readers of this book will go to different places when they click Search. Also, the design and operation of these all-in-one search pages tends to change quite often. Finally, links in these pages that appear to lead to a search tool's page sometimes don't lead to the *real* page of the search tool, but to a customized version of it. Because of all of these variables, I cannot provide reliable instructions in this unit that lead from clicking the Search button to using a specific search tool. Instead, in the remaining activities in this Unit, you are instructed to jump to search tools by entering their URLs, not by using your Search button. Of course, after you complete this unit, you'll understand the general operation of search tools well enough that, on your own, you can easily explore and operate whatever page your Search button leads to.

extra credit

Changing your search page

In Unit 2, you discovered that you can change the home page that Internet Explorer goes to when you connect to the Internet and when you click the Home button, and that you can change the pages the Quick Links jump to as well. So it probably comes as no surprise that you can also change the page that Internet Explorer jumps to when you click Search.

If, after some practice, you have a favorite search tool, you can reconfigure Internet Explorer so that the Search button goes there. (Of course, you can also add any search tool to your Favorites list, as you learned to do in Unit 4. But clicking the search button will take you to a favorite tool faster than clicking Favorites and then choosing a tool from the list.)

To change the page where the Search button takes you, try these steps:

1. **Open Internet Explorer and choose <u>V</u>iew⇨<u>O</u>ptions⇨<u>N</u>avigation.**

   The Navigation tab of the Options dialog opens.

2. **Drop down the list next to <u>P</u>age and select Search Page.**

3. **Double-click in the A<u>d</u>dress box and type the complete URL of the page you want to use.**

4. **Click OK.**

Clicking the Search button now opens the page you entered in A<u>d</u>dress.

Entering a search tool's URL

The other way (and, for the purposes of this unit, the recommended way) to jump to a search tool is to enter that search tool's URL. Table 5-1 shows the URLs of the most popular Internet search tools. You'll visit several of these in coming examples, but feel free to visit any others you like. In addition to showing the URL for each tool, the table describes what the tool offers — search engine, directory, or both.

Table 5-1	URLs of Popular Search Tools	
Tool	*URL*	*Search Methods Supported*
Yahoo!	http://www.yahoo.com	Directory, search engine
Excite	http://www.excite.com	Search engine
Lycos	http://www.lycos.com	Directory, search engine
AltaVista	http://www.altavista.digital.com	Search engine
Magellan	http://www.mckinley.com	Directory, search engine
InfoSeek	http://www.infoseek.com	Directory, search engine
Microsoft's Search Page	http://home.microsoft.com/access/allinone.asp	Search engines, links to search tool pages
AT&T WorldNet Search Page	http://www.worldnet.att.net/search/index.html	Search engines, links to search tool pages

☑ **Progress Check**

If you can do the following, you've mastered this lesson:

❑ Click the Search button to go to the all-in-one searches page configured in your copy of Internet Explorer.

❑ Go to a search tool by entering its URL.

Lesson 5-2

Clicking through Categories

use categories instead of search terms when desired topic is general

As a rule, using a search term (described in Lesson 5-3) is the quickest way to find pages related to a certain topic. After they discover search terms, most Web surfers use nothing else. Too bad.

on the test

When you're first becoming familiar with the Web, foregoing the search engines and instead clicking through a directory's categories is not only an effective way to find stuff but also a great way to become more familiar with what's available on the Web. As you browse through categories, you inevitably discover detours to interesting topics and pages that you never set out to find. Exploring directories is an important part of learning how the Web works and what's on it.

Also, the less specific your topic, the more useful categories become. For example, if you want information about a broad subject area, you may find greater satisfaction browsing a directory than using a search engine. For example, suppose you're generally interested in dogs and want to explore what the Web has to offer. By clicking through a few category headings, you may locate an entire subdirectory about dogs, which you may then explore to your heart's content. If you applied a search engine to as broad a search term as "dogs," you'd more than likely wind up with thousands of pages to sift through, some about dogs, but many others about "hot dogs," "Snoop Doggy Dogg," or the "dog days of summer."

The most popular directory on the Web is the one you've already heard of before: Yahoo! (You created a Favorite to Yahoo!'s Arts directory in Unit 4). The best way to learn how to browse through Yahoo!'s categories is to get started. In the following two examples, I take you wandering aimlessly through a few Yahoo! categories (true "browsing") and then show how you can purposefully work down through a directory's categories to find pages about a specific topic.

heads up

I know you — as soon as you start clicking around the directories, you'll deviate from the tutorial and go looking for your own stuff. That's okay — you have my permission to conduct a one-credit-hour session of Dummies 101: Independent Study. Just be sure that you read through the examples to pick up any techniques you don't discover on your own. And as always, rely on the Back and Home buttons to keep your bearing.

Wandering aimlessly — why not?

1 **While connected to the Internet, go to the Yahoo! page by entering this URL:**

```
http://www.yahoo.com
```

Yahoo! opens, as shown in Figure 5-3.

2 **Click Education.**

A list of subcategories under Education appears, as shown in Figure 5-4.

3 **Click Languages.**

A list of Education subcategories under Languages appears, as shown in Figure 5-5. Under the subcategories, some actual pages are listed. (You may need to scroll down to see the whole list.) These pages are general Language

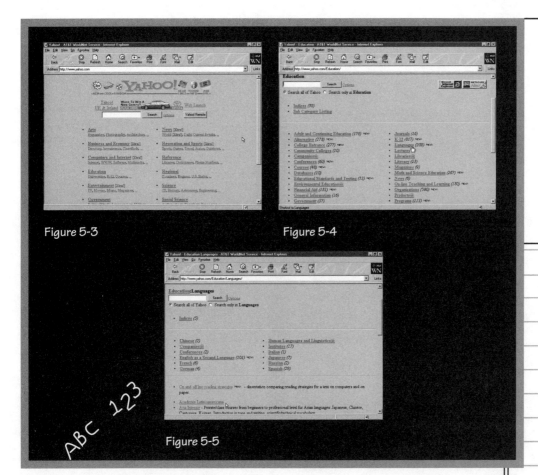

Figure 5-3

Figure 5-4

Figure 5-5

Figure 5-3: You can browse to what you're looking for by clicking through Yahoo!'s categories.

Figure 5-4: Each entry on this page is a link to further subcategories narrowing the topic.

Figure 5-5: This listing appears when you choose Languages from the Education listing.

Education pages that don't fit neatly within any of the subcategories above them. You may choose one of the subcategories to move to more specific groupings of pages, or you can check out the more general Language Education pages by clicking a page's link.

4 Scroll down the list of pages and select one that looks interesting to you.

The page you selected appears. Congratulations! You've made your way from the top of Yahoo! to a specific page by choosing a category, then a subcategory, and then a page. Note that the number of levels of categories you might have to pass through to arrive at any particular page may vary by what you're looking for. This time, you arrived at a page in three steps. For other topics, you may work down through four, five, six, or more levels of Yahoo! before you get to a page.

5 Click Back twice to return to the Education subdirectory shown in Figure 5-4.

Observe that you can try any path or page and then back out by as many levels as you want to so that you can try a different path.

6 Now click any Education link you want — and see what happens.

7 Explore, clicking down through the directory and back up again with Back.

click Back button to retrace steps

Figure 5-6: Like Yahoo!, Magellan offers optional categories to browse through, in addition to offering a search engine.

Figure 5-7: This listing appears when you choose <u>Science</u> from Magellan's BROWSE TOPICS.

Figure 5-8: This listing appears when you choose <u>Archaeology</u> from the Science listing.

Figure 5-9: I found this page in the Archaeology listing.

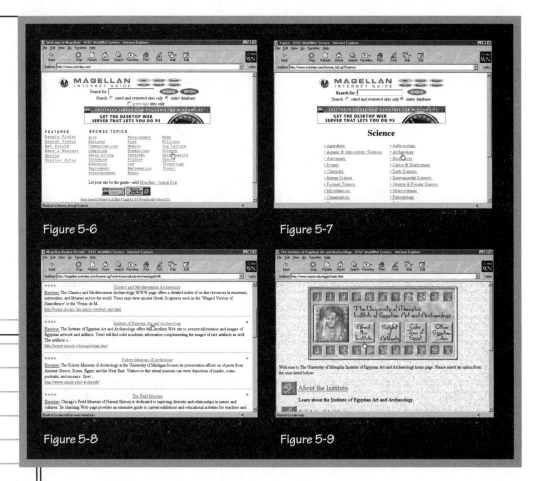

Figure 5-6

Figure 5-7

Figure 5-8

Figure 5-9

Notes:

Magellan is another popular directory

☑ **Progress Check**

If you can do the following, you've mastered this lesson:

❏ Open a search tool directory.

❏ Browse from top-level category headings to a particular Web page by clicking category, subcategory, and page links.

Browsing aimfully

Now that you know how easy clicking around Yahoo! is, it's time to get serious. You're already familiar with Yahoo!, so the next example explores another popular directory: Magellan.

This time, the object is specific: You want to find a page about Egyptian archaeology.

1 **While connected to the Internet, go to the Magellan page by entering this URL:**

```
http://www.mckinley.com
```

Magellan opens, as shown in Figure 5-6. The categories appear under BROWSE TOPICS. Archaeology is a science, so the first category to try is Science.

2 **Click <u>Science</u>.**

A list of science-related subcategories appears, as shown in Figure 5-7. <u>Archaeology</u> appears as a subcategory. You're getting warmer.

3 **Click <u>Archaeology</u>.**

A list of Archaeology–related pages appears, as shown in Figure 5-8. On the list, a link appears for the <u>Institute of Egyptian Art and Archaeology</u>.

4 **Click the link for <u>Institute of Egyptian Art and Archaeology</u>.**

The page appears, as shown in Figure 5-9. You've found what you went looking for.

Go ahead and explore the other archaeology pages.

Phrasing a Simple Search Term
Lesson 5-3

Throughout this unit, little text boxes have appeared in the figures, often accompanied by a button labeled Search (refer to Figures 5-1 and 5-2). In all these boxes, you do the same thing: Type a partial word, a full word, or a phrase as a *search term* to describe what you're looking for; then click the Search button (which may also be labeled Submit, or some other searchy name).

The act of typing a search term and then clicking a button to send it to the search tool is known as *submitting a search term.*

submitting a search term = typing text and clicking Search button

Understanding search terms

When you submit a search term, the search engine searches through its directory to find every page that contains information matching the term. For example, if you submit the search term *artichoke,* the search engine finds every entry in its directory in which the word *artichoke* appears.

When it has found all the entries that match the search term, the search tool displays its findings as a list of links, usually accompanied by brief descriptions. From this list, you can choose any link that looks like it may hold what you're looking for. After viewing any page in the list, you can press Back to return to the search results and choose another link in the list.

Often, a search term turns up hundreds or even thousands of pages from a single search term, which is too many to use productively. Some search engines try to make smart guesses about which pages best match what you're looking for. For example, if your search term is *dog,* the list produced by the search engine may begin with pages that feature the word *dog* in the title of the page and then afterward show pages that simply mention *dog.* That way, the pages at the top of the list are the one most likely to be all about dogs, while pages later in the list may merely mention dogs.

some search engines list most promising pages first

heads up

Despite the search engines' smartness, you may wind up with more pages on the list than you can make sense of. When that happens, you need to narrow your search by rephrasing your search term to make it more specific. For example, the search term *dog* would surely produce thousands of hits (a *hit* is a found page). A search on *Airedale* would find far fewer hits.

Q&A session

Question: Can I use multiple words in a search term? Like *Irish Setter*?

Answer: Absolutely — in fact, the more specific you can be, the more likely the search engine is to turn up what you want, and being specific often demands a few words. For now, just understand that you can use multiple words, and feel free to try it if you want. But be aware that search engines have special ways of dealing with multiple words, and you may need to consider that in the phrasing of your search term. In Lesson 5-4, you learn more about how search engines handle multiword terms.

Notes:

Using a search term

All the popular search tools feature a search engine, so if you jump to the page of any search tool, you'll find a little text box waiting for your search term. A good place to start is AltaVista, since it's a great search tool you haven't visited yet.

1 While connected to the Internet, go to the AltaVista page by entering the URL

`http://www.altavista.digital.com`

AltaVista opens, as shown in Figure 5-10.

2 Click in the search term box and type dachshund **as shown in Figure 5-10.**

3 Click the Submit button to the right of the search term box.

heads up

The box shown in Figure 5-11 appears. When you just browse around the Web, you never *send* any information *to* the Web; you just *receive* information *from* it. When you submit a search term, however, your PC actually sends the search term to the search engine to be processed. Internet Explorer's built-in security system is preconfigured to caution you any time you send information to the Web, just to make sure that you don't inadvertently send your password or credit card number or other sensitive information. Sending a search term, however, is harmless, so you can safely move on.

4 Click Yes.

The search may take anywhere from a few seconds to a minute. When it's done, a list of hits appears, as shown in Figure 5-12. I scrolled down the list to a link to Links to Dachshund WWW Pages and clicked it to open the page shown in Figure 5-13.

5 Now jump to Yahoo! at

`http:/www.yahoo.com`

6 Click in the search term box and type dachshund.

7 Click the Search button.

Observe Yahoo!'s list of dachshund pages. Any different from AltaVista's?

heads up

When phrasing a search term, try to use the "typical" capitalization of the word. Some search engines do a better job of finding what you want if you capitalize it correctly (while others don't care). So capitalize the first letter of proper nouns, such as names (Lee Harvey Oswald), and observe any odd capitalization typically applied to the term (e. e. cummings, CompuAdd).

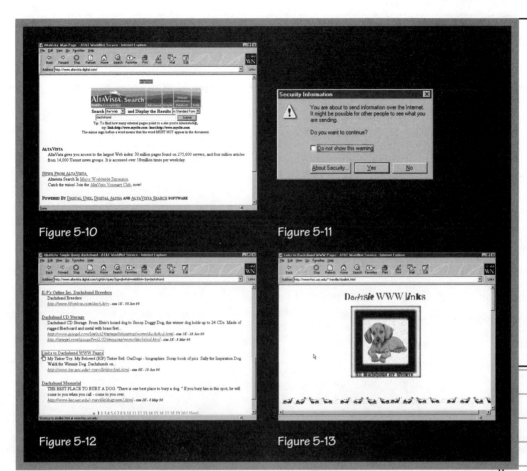

Figure 5-10: AltaVista is one of the newer and more powerful Web search tools.

Figure 5-11: Whenever you send information (such as a search term) to the Web, Internet Explorer cautions you about the possible dangers of sending sensitive information.

Figure 5-12: After the search engine finds all the matches to your search term, it shows a report that includes a link to each page it found.

Figure 5-13: Search successful — I found dachshunds.

Q&A session

Question: In some of the search tool pages I've visited, I've seen it said that the tool can search not only the Web but also "Usenet discussion groups." What are they?

Answer: The Web makes up part of the Internet, but not all of it. Usenet discussion groups, or *newsgroups,* are another part. A newsgroup is a public forum where visitors post questions or comments related to the newsgroup's topic. Other visitors read those messages and reply to them to answer the question or to expand upon (or, more often, argue with) the comments. Each of the roughly 13,000 newsgroups has a topic, from the serious (AIDS) to the important (asthma support) to the contentious (the many groups about politics) to the trivial (over two dozen newsgroups about *Star Trek*).

Newsgroups are not a part of the Web, but you can access them using some Web browsers. Other Web browsers can access newsgroups by opening a *helper application* — Internet Explorer, for example, can jump you to newsgroups by opening its companion, Internet News, which you discover in Unit 12.

☑ **Progress Check**

If you can do the following, you've mastered this lesson:

❑ Enter specific search terms, using a couple of search tools.

❑ Know when and how to broaden or narrow your search term.

Lesson 5-4

Power Searching

some techniques
work better with
some search engines
than others

With nothing but category browsing and basic searching in your arsenal, you're prepared to find material related to almost any topic. However, when time is short or your needs are very specific, applying a few advanced search techniques may get you exactly what you want, pronto.

To learn which of the following techniques are useful with a particular search engine, find a link on the search tool's page called Options, or a link that leads to instructions for using the search tool.

Phrasing the perfect search term

The Web is supposed to be easy, and in that spirit, I've left you free to phrase your search term however it rolls out of your brain. If you want to know about doughnuts, type **doughnuts**. And amazingly, phrasing your search terms so instinctively usually works just fine.

But you can adjust your phrasing to give the search engine a more accurate picture of what you want, which may result in a more useful list of hits.

Q&A session

Question: Can I enter a part of a word as a search term? For example, to find pages about my Scotch relatives, can I enter "Mc" as a search term, so that I'll see pages covering McGraw, McDuff, McDougle, McMendez, and so on.

Answer: Yes, and doing so can be a very clever way to produce some interesting results. Also, some search engines allow you to select a "search for whole words only" option. When you use that option, the search term *dog* matches only pages that have the precise word *dog* by itself — *dogs, doggy, doggerel,* and *moondoggy* would all be ignored by such a search.

Before trying a partial word with any particular search engine, however, check that search engine's instructions.

Tips for using multiple words

Remember high school algebra? (Me neither.) Remember when the teacher said it would come in handy someday in real life, even if you didn't become an engineer? Surprise! The time has come.

on the test

Actually, you need to remember only two basic ways of grouping things:

♦ **And:** When you use *and* between words in a search term, you tell the search engine to find only those pages that contain both of the words — pages that contain only one or the other are not included in the hit list.

♦ **Or:** When you use *or* between words in a search term, you tell the search engine to find all pages that contain either of the words — any page that contains either word, or both, is included in the hit list.

For example, the search term **doughnut or donut** finds all pages matching the word *doughnut* and all pages matching *donut* and includes *both* sets of pages in the list. The search term **doughnut and donut** finds only pages matching both the words *doughnut* and *donut* — pages containing only one term or the other are not considered matches.

extra credit

Search engines assume you mean *and*

When you use multiple words with most search engines, the engine does not usually search for the exact phrase you entered — it searches for each word with an *and* in between. For example, if I enter **Lee Harvey Oswald** as a search term, most search engines go looking for **Lee and Harvey and Oswald** — to hit any page containing all three parts of the name.

On the one hand, this approach may hit some pages you don't want; there may be pages containing all three words *Lee, Harvey,* and *Oswald,* separately, without saying a word about Lee Harvey Oswald. On the other hand, this approach prevents the order of the words from preventing possible matches. Because of the assumed *and,* this search finds pages with references to Oswald, Lee Harvey; Oswald (Lee Harvey); and other variants.

In some search engines, you can force the search to consider the exact order or your words by enclosing the term in quotes (**"Lee Harvey Oswald"**) or connecting the words with hyphens (**Lee-Harvey-Oswald**). In search engines that support this technique, the only pages hit will be those containing your exact words in the exact order you typed them.

To try out *and* and *or,* follow these steps:

1 **Go to the search tool of your choice.**

   You can revisit one of the tools you've seen in earlier lessons, choose one of the tools in Table 5-1 (see Lesson 5-2), or even try whatever comes up when you click your Search button (see Lesson 5-1).

2 **Enter the search term** star or trek **and click the Search button.**

3 **Examine the results. You should see many pages about *Star Trek* but also many about various kinds of "stars" and other "treks."**

4 **Press Back to return to the search engine.**

5 **Submit the search term** star and trek.

6 **Examine the results. Just about every hit should be *Star Trek*–related.**

Notes:

ballpark and browse
method = find
general area first
and then use links to
find specific topic

☑ **Progress Check**

If you can do the following, you've mastered this lesson:

❑ Use *and* and *or* in your search terms to control your search.

❑ Search for a general or related term if your original term doesn't work, and use links on the pages that come up to find what you're looking for.

Q&A session

Question: If I try the same search term with two different search engines, will I get the same results?

Answer: Nope. Certainly, you'll wind up with many of the same pages in the lists produced by the two search engines. But each search is likely to turn up pages that the other didn't find.

Each search engine searches through a different directory, either one made mostly by people (like Yahoo!) or one compiled by a crawler. Every directory's contents differ from all the other directories' contents. So naturally, the results of the search will differ, too. Also, the technical search methods used by each search engine differ. Even if you could apply two different search engines to the same directory, you'd probably get different results, or at least a similar list of pages presented in a different order.

That's why trying your search in a couple of different tools is always a smart move. The more tools you apply to the task, the greater your chances of locating the perfect page.

Searching without a search tool

Harry Truman is famous for saying, "If you can't stand the heat, stay out of the kitchen." Julius Caesar is famous for saying "*Et tu, Brute?*" (or at least Shakespeare thought Caesar said that). So it is with hopes of similar immortality that I offer a phrase I invented my own little self regarding a reliable search technique. Ned says, when searching the Web, apply the "ballpark and browse" method. (You may quote me freely.)

The ballpark and browse method is a compromise between browsing directories and using a search engine. First, you browse or search to reach the general ballpark of the topic you're interested in, and then you browse around that vicinity until you find what you're looking for.

Pages covering a subject often contain links to other pages covering the same subject, perhaps from a different angle. Often, the page holding the precise subject matter you want isn't a page turned up in a directory or a search, but rather, it's a page you found *in a link* on another page that you found in your search. The end of your journey may even be found on a page that you found through a link on a page… you found through a link on a page… you found through a link on a page you found through a search. (You get the idea.)

For example, if you want to find information about a particular movie, search for the studio that made the movie and then browse around. Or find a page that's generally about movies, on which you may find a link to the studio, on which you may find information about the film.

Other ballpark and browse ideas:

▶ Can't find info about a particular congressperson? Search for **U.S. Congress** and then browse around.

▶ Can't find info about a particular library? Search for **library** and browse the pages you find for links that may lead to the library you want.

▶ Can't find info about Ringo Starr? Search for **Beatles** and then browse around.

▶ Can't find info about knitting? Search for **needlecraft**, or **needle**, or even **wool**, and then browse. You'll find it.

Recess

Well, after five units, you pretty much know all there is to know about finding stuff on the Web. But don't put the book on the shelf yet — there's plenty more to learn before you can graduate to the level of master Web browser. If you want, shut down Internet Explorer and your Internet connection and take a break before tackling the quiz and exercise and moving on to the next unit.

Unit 5 Quiz

For each question, circle the letter of the correct answer. Some of the questions may have more than one right answer.

1. **Which of the following search tools can search the current contents of absolutely every single page on the Web?**

    A. Yahoo!

    B. AltaVista

    C. Either of the above

    D. None of the above

2. **To use a popular search tool, you can . . .**

    A. Click the Search button on the toolbar and then choose a tool offered on the page your Search button leads to.

    B. Click the Search button on the toolbar and then click a link that leads to the page of a search tool.

    C. Enter the URL of a search tool.

    D. Any of the above, depending purely on personal whim

3. **The Web grows and mutates like . . .**

    A. A fungus.

    B. Two fungi.

    C. Walt Disney Productions, Inc.

    D. Vancouver.

4. **When you're looking for information on a broad subject area, which technique is generally most rewarding?**

    A. Clicking through directory categories to locate a subdirectory covering the topic.

    B. Performing an automated search using the broad topic name as a search term.

    C. Calling a drive-time talk radio program.

    D. Inventing a likely Web address (`http://www.fungus.com`) and trying it out.

Notes:

5. **Which is probably the best search term for finding information about American bison, also known as "buffalo"?**

    A. Bisons

    B. Bison

    C. Bison or buffalo

    D. Bison and buffalo

6. **Which is the best search tool?**

    A. Yahoo!

    B. AltaVista

    C. Magellan

    D. Your brain, when applied creatively to any search tool

Unit 5 Exercise

Using the search page of your choice, find Web pages containing information about each of the following topics. (Never heard of some of 'em? That's the point. Go find out.) If the first directory or search engine you try comes up empty, try another. I guarantee that the Web has something to say about all of these subjects.

(If what you find doesn't tickle your neurons, go find something else. You're the boss, and besides, I'm doing this thing Pass/Fail.)

1. Marge Simpson.

2. Keeshond hounds.

3. NASDAQ.

4. Shemp (the fourth Stooge).

5. Taoism.

6. Sunny Delight enriched citrus beverage.

7. *The Celestine Prophecy.*

8. Harry Nilsson.

9. Fredo Corleone.

10. St. Augustine, Florida.

11. Land's End Direct Merchants (yuppie clothing by mail).

Downloading Files

Prerequisites

▶ Opening Internet Explorer and connecting to the Internet (Unit 1)

▶ Clicking links (Unit 2)

▶ Understanding and using URLs (Unit 3)

When you use the Web, you're really downloading files all the time. Every time you jump to a new page, Internet Explorer *downloads* (copies) the file containing the page from the Web server, through the Internet, to your PC.

on the test

The manner of downloading files that this unit offers is the more deliberate variety: You learn about a program or other file on the Web; you want the file; you go get it. *Downloading files* means deliberately selecting and copying them from servers to your PC's hard disk so you can use them for whatever purpose they fulfill (fun, work, global domination, and so on).

Downloading offers great rewards. On the Web, you can pick up free or inexpensive software programs, new drivers and utilities for Windows 95, games, photos, movie clips, books you can read right on your computer screen, tax instructions, music, and just about anything else that can be put in a computer file. Best of all, despite the many types of material you can get, the downloading steps are the same for all files, whether the file at hand is large or small, serious or trivial.

download = copy file from server to PC

Lesson 6-1   Understanding the Types of Files

Every type of computer file imaginable sits somewhere out on the Web, from tiny text files to huge applications (such as Internet Explorer). Although most of the files you come across on the Web are ready for you to use, some aren't. That's why you need to understand what's out there — and what you can actually use — before proceeding.

on the test

The many types of files that you find online can be divided up into three basic groups:

three types of files: program, document, and media

- ▶ **Program files:** Games, applications, utilities, and so on
- ▶ **Document files:** Books, manuals, presentations, spreadsheets, paranoid manifestos, and so on
- ▶ **Media files:** Pictures, photos, sound clips, music, video clips, animation

archive = ZIP file = compressed file or files of any type

Archives, also known as ZIP files, contain one or more files that have been compressed so that they take up less space. This compression allows the ZIP file to transfer to your PC in a fraction of the time that would be required to download the file or files uncompressed. An archive file can contain any of the other three file types — programs, documents, or media files. Most applications, which are made up of multiple files and can be very large, are stored on the Web as archive files. You usually need a decompression program to open a ZIP file (see Lesson 6-4).

heads up

Before downloading any file, ask yourself two very important questions:

before downloading file, check file's system/software requirements

- ▶ Will the file work on my computer? *Remember:* Windows users share the Web with users of other types of computers, including Macintosh, UNIX, and God only knows what else. Programs written for other types of computers don't work on PCs. (The type of system is really a consideration only with programs. Most document and media files can run on any system, as long as the system is equipped with the necessary software.)

♦ Do I have the software required to view or play the file? Document files require a program that can show them; for example, to look at a Word for Windows document, you need a program (Word, WordPad, or just about any other Windows-based word-processing program) that can display a Word file. To show or play a media file, you need the right viewer or player program.

Q&A session

Question: Can I use Windows 3.1– or DOS–based programs on my Windows 95 system?

Answer: Yes, you can, and that's a good thing because the Web offers many great programs that aren't available in Windows 95 versions. Keep in mind, though, that Windows 95 can run Windows 3.1– and DOS–based programs but does not run them as reliably as it does Windows 95–based programs. In particular, Windows 95 is much more likely to run into problems when running several programs at once if one of the programs is for Windows 3.1 or DOS.

When a page offers both a Windows 95 version of a program and a Windows 3.1 version, it may distinguish between them simply by calling the Windows 95 program a *32-bit version* and the Windows 3.1 version a *16-bit version*. In general, when given a choice, go for the 32-bit version, which will work better on your Windows 95 system.

Usually, the page on which you find a file tells you everything you need to know about whether you can use the file: the type of computer required, the type of file, and any special system or software requirements. If the page doesn't tell you what you need to know, you can deduce what you need to know from the file's *extension* — the last three letters (after the period) of the filename.

on the test

Table 6-1 describes the major types of Windows-compatible files that you may find on the Web and tells you what's required to use the files. For each type, the table shows the file extension; you can use the extension to determine whether you can use a certain file. For example, if the file is called FREDO.DOC, you can deduce that it's a Word file. If it's called FREDO.TXT, it's a text file, and if it's FREDO.AVI, it's probably a video clip of Fredo, whoever he is. For several types of files, you can view the file directly in Internet Explorer, as indicated in the table.

Note: Table 6-1 shows that you can view some types of files in WordPad, which is a word processor that comes with Windows 95. You can find WordPad by opening your Start menu and then choosing Programs⇨Accessories. But you don't really need to find WordPad; if you open a file that requires WordPad, WordPad opens automatically to show the file.

Internet Explorer can handle most PC-compatible file types

32-bit version = Windows 95 version

look at page containing file for requirements and file info

WordPad comes with Windows 95

can tell file type and software requirements from file's extension (last three letters of filename)

most file types can be viewed directly in Internet Explorer

self-extracting archive = compressed file or files, not requiring special decompression program

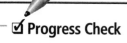

☑ Progress Check

If you can do the following, you've mastered this lesson:

❑ Recognize the types of files that you can use in a Windows 95 system with Internet Explorer.

❑ Identify a .ZIP file as an archive that you must decompress before you can use it.

Table 6-1	Common File Types You Can Use	
Filename Extension	*File Type*	*Required Software*
.EXE	Windows 95, Windows 3.1, or DOS program	None
.DOC	Word for Windows document	Internet Explorer, Word, or WordPad
.XLS	Excel spreadsheet document	Internet Explorer or Excel
.PPT	PowerPoint presentation	Internet Explorer or PowerPoint
.ZIP	Archive file containing one or more files compressed for faster downloading	WinZip (see Lesson 6-4), to uncompress and separate the files, which may themselves be any other type of file
.TXT	Ordinary text file	Internet Explorer, Windows Notepad, or WordPad
.WRI	Windows Write document	WordPad
.PDF	Adobe Acrobat document	Adobe Acrobat viewer
.AVI, .MOV, .QT, .MPG, .AU, .MID	Various types of media files	Internet Explorer (see Unit 7)

One special type of .EXE program file is called a *self-extracting archive,* which is a compressed file or files, just like a ZIP file. Unlike a ZIP file, however, a self-extracting archive file does not require a program (such as WinZip) to decompress it. Instead, it decompresses itself automatically when you double-click it. Internet Explorer is available through the Web as a self-extracting archive file.

Near a file link, look for a player link

You'll often find that near the link to a document or media file is a link to a page where you can download the required viewer or player for that file. For example, on many of the pages from which video clips can be downloaded, links for downloading video player software also appear.

As you can see in Table 6-1, you already have all the viewers and players you'll probably need, between what's built into Windows 95 and what's built into Internet Explorer. But you'll be happy to know that if some genius comes up with a cool new file format sometime in the future, the genius will probably also provide a link for downloading any special software required to enjoy that file type.

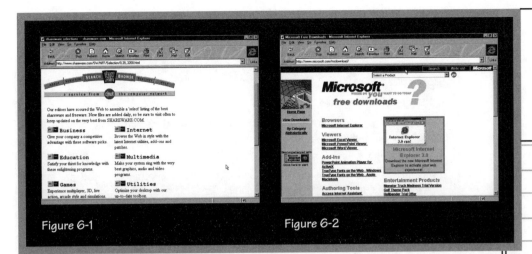

Figure 6-1: Shareware.com, a good source for program files.

Figure 6-2: Microsoft's Free Downloads page, another good source for files.

Figure 6-1   Figure 6-2

Finding Files   Lesson 6-2

Files are everywhere. They appear as links on all types of pages; clicking the link starts the download. More often than not, you won't go looking for files. You will be looking for information about a given subject and will come across a page containing links to files related to that subject.

Sometimes, a link to a file shows the name of the file that will be downloaded if you click it. Other times, the name of the application to be downloaded or some other description information appears in the link. In any case, either the link text or the descriptive text should inform you that the link downloads a file and what the file contains.

In the examples in this unit, you download files from the Dummies page, just for illustration purposes. But other great sources for files abound. Table 6-2 lists a few to get you started.

Table 6-2	Interesting Sources for Files to Download	
Place	*URL*	*Description*
Shareware.com (see Figure 6-1)	http://www.shareware.com	The major compendium of shareware and freeware on the Web
Microsoft's Free Downloads page (see Figure 6-2)	http://www.microsoft.com /msdownload	Links for downloading stuff Microsoft gives away, including Internet programs, games, and more
IDG Books Worldwide's Free & Downloadable	http://www.idgbooks.com /free/	Links to files and programs described in various books published by IDG Books
Digital Cinema	http://members.aol.com /flypba/index.html	Movie trailers (you learn how to watch them in Unit 7)
Internal Revenue Service	http://www.irs.ustreas. gov	Tax forms and instructions from you-know-who

time to download
file depends on how
fast modem is, how
busy server is, and
so on

☑ **Progress Check**

If you can do the following,
you've mastered this lesson:

❑ Identify a link that
downloads a file.

❑ Visit some good file-rich
sites.

Q&A session

Question: How long does downloading a file take?

Answer: Always at least too long. Actually, the exact length of a download depends on many factors, including the speed of your modem and Internet connection and the number of other surfers contacting the same server at the same time.

If you are especially good at math and have too much time on your hands, you may think that you can guess the length of a download by dividing the size of the file by the speed of your modem (converted from kilobits per second to kilobytes per second). But don't bother: A download from the Internet rarely takes place at your modem's full speed. The file leaves the server a little bit at a time, as fast as the server can send it — but the server is also busy sending files to other surfers and may take frequent, short pauses between its transmissions to you in order to serve its other guests. So predicting exactly how long a download will take is impossible. If you watch the progress report that Internet Explorer displays during downloads, you may notice that the download appears to stop from time to time, even for a minute or two, and then resume. Nothing's wrong — the server just put you on hold while it performed other tasks.

As a rule of thumb, across a 28,800 bps modem, expect each megabyte you download to take anywhere from about 10 to 20 minutes (for a 14,400 bps modem, figure 15 to 30 minutes). But always be prepared for downloads to take longer than you expect them to.

Lesson 6-3 | Downloading a File

Download time. In the upcoming example, you download a file from the IDG Books Worldwide page. I hope you enjoy it.

Retrieving the file

1 Start Internet Explorer and your Internet connection.

2 Go to IDG's Free and Downloadable files page at

`http://www.idgbooks.com/free/`

On the Free and Downloadable page, the column on the right lists Windows-compatible programs and files.

3 In the column on the right, click the link to HTML Assistant.

A page describing HTML Assistant, a handy tool for creating your own Web pages, appears.

4 In the bottom of the HTML Assistant page, click the link Download HTML Assistant.

Windows briefly displays a message reporting that it is Getting file information. After a moment, a dialog box like the one in Figure 6-3 appears.

5 Select Save it to disk and click OK.

A Save As dialog box appears, like the one in Figure 6-4. (Note that this dialog box does not appear if you choose Open it in Step 5.)

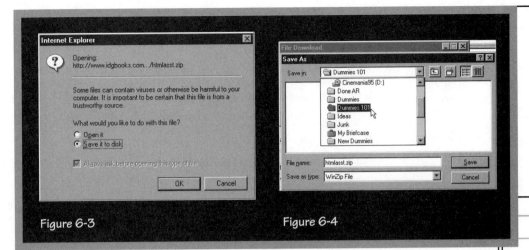

Figure 6-3: In this dialog box, you choose whether to open the file automatically after downloading or to save it to disk, to be opened later.

Figure 6-4: Choose a folder to store the downloaded file, or download it to your desktop.

Figure 6-3   Figure 6-4

extra credit

Open or save to disk?

In Step 5 of this example (refer to Figure 6-3), you have a choice to make about what Internet Explorer should do after downloading:

- **Open it:** Automatically opens the file (runs the program that the file contains or shows the document or multimedia that it contains)

- **Save it to disk:** Saves the file to your hard disk and allows you to go right back to browsing (you can open the file later simply by double-clicking its icon)

Choosing Open it saves you a step, but at a cost: The file is not permanently saved on your hard disk. Instead, Internet Explorer stores the file temporarily and runs the program or shows the document/media that the file contains. But when you close the file to return to browsing, the file is gone. Choosing the Save it to disk option allows you to open the file whenever you want (and as many times as you want) and to keep it on your hard disk for as long as you like.

Although using Open it offers some convenience in some situations, I recommend using Save it to disk for all downloads. First off, if you're concerned about viruses, saving the file allows you to scan the file for viruses before opening it. But I always use the Save option, not because I'm worried about viruses, but because I like to finish all of my downloading and surfing, go offline, and then use the files I've downloaded — why leave your Internet connection going when you're doing something else? This approach is especially important if you pay for your Internet connection by the hour.

heads up

In the Save As dialog box shown in Figure 6-4, you can change the filename in the File name box (although you have no reason to). However, do not change anything in the Save as type box. The information in that box ensures that the file is saved with its proper file extension (.EXE, .ZIP, and so on). When you use the file after downloading, Windows uses the filename extension to determine what to do with the file — run it as a program, show it in WordPad, and so on. If you change the file type, Windows won't know what to do with the file, so you may have problems using it.

don't change Save as type info

6 **In the Save As dialog box, click the folder in which you want the downloaded file saved.**

You may also choose to save the file on your desktop or in a desktop folder by opening the drop-down list next to the Save in box. Your Dummies 101 folder (created in Unit 1) is fine for this example.

Internet Explorer's time estimate for download can be highly inaccurate

click Cancel to stop download at any time

can multitask while file is downloading, but browsing Web slows down download

heads up

7 Click the Save button.

The download commences. During the download, Internet Explorer displays the File Download status message (as shown in Figure 6-5). When the file is large, the status message shows graphically how much of the file has been downloaded and also displays the estimated time left to complete the download (otherwise, the File Download status message reports "File Size Unknown" as in Figure 6-5).

Note that when the status message displays an estimate of the time remaining, the estimate can be extremely inaccurate, especially early in the download, fluctuating up and down while Internet Explorer tries to figure out how fast the file is coming off the server. The estimate offers a ballpark figure for how long the download will take — but don't plan dinner around it.

You can click Cancel at any time to stop the download. If you do, it's like you never started the download in the first place — you don't get a portion of the file saved to your hard disk so that you can pick up later where you left off. To download the file after canceling, you must start again at the beginning.

8 When the download is done, the File Download status message disappears, and you return to the current Web page.

You may continue browsing or go open the file that you just downloaded. The next lesson starts off at the Dummies Web page again.

Q&A session

Question: Can I do other stuff on my PC while my file is downloading?

Answer: Sure — that's what Windows 95 is all about, doing several things at once or, technically, *multitasking.* You can work in other applications, such as your word processor or Windows game software, during the download.

You can even browse the Web or start another download during a download — Internet Explorer can multitask Web activity. Keep in mind, though, that if you browse the Web while downloading a file, you will dramatically slow down your file download. Every time you jump to a new Web page, Internet Explorer must temporarily interrupt the file download, retrieve the page, and then resume the download. That interruption adds to the time required to download the file.

During downloads, I don't browse. I make coffee, play with my kids, eat an Italian ice, check the mail, or just happily procrastinate. Downloads are a terrific time to give yourself a break. After all, when you're downloading, you're always getting something done — even if you're doing nothing at all.

Opening a downloaded file

on the test

To use a file that you've just downloaded, go to the folder that you chose in Step 6 of retrieving the file and double-click the file's icon. What happens next depends on the file type:

 ♦ If the file is a program (.EXE), Windows runs it.

 ♦ If the file is any of the popular types of document or media files (refer to Table 6-1), Windows opens the necessary program to display or play the file. (Often, the program that Windows opens may be Internet Explorer, as Table 6-1 shows.)

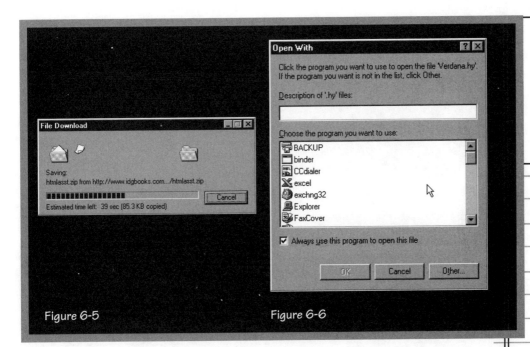

Figure 6-5: Internet Explorer displays a status message during the download.

Figure 6-6: When Windows doesn't know what to do with a file, it asks you what program to use to open the file.

Figure 6-5   Figure 6-6

▶ If Windows doesn't know what to do with the file, either the file is of a type incompatible with Windows or (more likely) you have not properly installed a program required to use the file. When Windows doesn't know what to do with a file, it opens the Open With dialog box shown in Figure 6-6. From the list, you can select the program that you want Windows to use to open the file.

If you see the dialog box shown in Figure 6-6, you need to find out what program is required to open the file type that you've selected, and then you need to acquire and install the program. You may find all the information you need (possibly including a link to the necessary program) on the Web page from which you downloaded the file.

extra credit

What's all this stuff about "FTP"?

Before advent of the Web, most files that you could download through the Internet were stored on computers called FTP servers. (FTP, in case you care, stands for *file transfer protocol,* but you don't need to know that; everybody on the Net just says "FTP.") Today, most of the good stuff you can download is on a Web server somewhere, but a great many files still live on FTP servers.

Just as you need a Web browser to get stuff off a Web server, you needed an FTP program on your PC to get stuff from an FTP server. Fortunately, Internet Explorer is a Web browser *and* an FTP program (and a few other things). You can download files from an FTP server right from within Internet Explorer. In fact, some Web links lead straight to a file that's actually on an FTP server. When you click the link to download the file, you're using FTP without even knowing it.

The only real difference between downloading via the Web and via FTP is that for FTP, sometimes, you have to click your way around a directory structure to get to a file. Files on FTP servers are organized into directories and subdirectories. Figure 6-7 shows an FTP directory, and Figure 6-8 shows a list of files in a subdirectory. Navigating an FTP directory may look trickier than browsing the Web, but it's not, really — everything you see is a link. Clicking a directory shows you the files or subdirectories that the directory contains; clicking a filename downloads the file.

(continued)

some files are on FTP servers; Internet Explorer can download FTP files

just click through directories and subdirectories on FTP server to get to file

Figure 6-7: Each of the FTP subdirectories is a link; clicking the link shows you the files (or more subdirectories) contained within.

Figure 6-8: To download a file from an FTP server, click the filename.

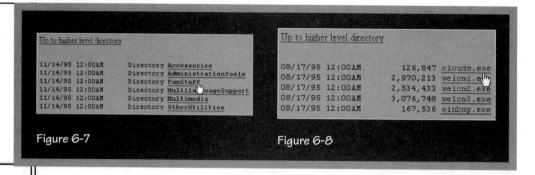

Figure 6-7   Figure 6-8

(continued)

If you feel that FTP is a little more than you want to deal with, then forget about it — nearly all the time (and more so every day), you can get what you want through an easy Web link. But just in case you feel adventurous, remember that FTP is out there and that using it is like using anything else through Internet Explorer: point, click . . . point, click . . . point, click . . . (repeat until confident).

☑ Progress Check

If you can do the following, you've mastered this lesson:

❑ Click a link to download a file.

❑ Choose whether to open the file automatically after downloading it or save it to your hard disk and open it later.

Lesson 6-4   Unzipping Compressed Files

zipped files
download more
quickly than
uncompressed files

Any file with the file extension .ZIP is an archive file, a special file made up of one or more files that have been packed together and compressed so that they take up less space. Archives are great because they allow you to collect a whole group of files — for example, all the files that make up an application program — merely by downloading a single archive file. The compression feature of archives allows you to download the archive in as little as one-fifth the time that would be required to download the file or files in their natural, uncompressed state.

unzip = decompress
zipped file

on the CD

Before you can use the contents of an archive, you must *unzip* that archive — decompress the file or files contained in the archive and restore them to their natural, ready-to-use state. WinZip, a program on the CD-ROM included with this book, decompresses ZIP files in a snap. Before performing the following steps, be sure that you have installed WinZip (see Appendix B for more details).

heads up

When you start to download a ZIP file, if you choose the Open it option (see the sidebar at the beginning of Lesson 6-3), the file is opened in WinZip automatically as soon as the download is complete. You must complete the decompression steps, however, beginning with Step 2.

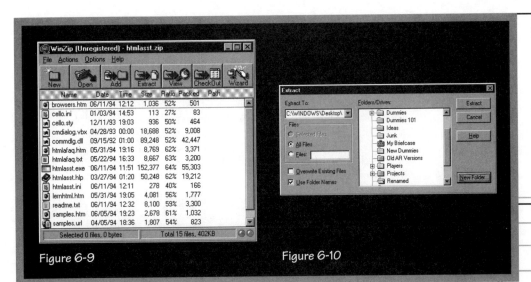

Figure 6-9

Figure 6-10

Figure 6-9: When you double-click a ZIP file, WinZip opens and shows you what the file contains.

Figure 6-10: When you click the Extract button shown in Figure 6-9, the Extract dialog box opens so you can decompress and separate the files.

1 **In your Dummies 101 folder (or wherever you saved it), locate the ZIP file icon for HTML Assistant (which you downloaded in Lesson 6-3).**

ZIP files use a file icon that looks like a little clamp (compression — get it?).

ZIP file icon

2 **Double-click the icon.**

WinZip opens and shows you the contents of the ZIP file, as shown in Figure 6-9.

3 **In WinZip, click the Extract button.**

The Extract dialog box opens, as shown in Figure 6-10. In the dialog box, choose a folder in which WinZip will store the files that it extracts from the ZIP archive, or click New Folder to create a new folder to store the files in. As a rule, try to extract files into an empty folder so that the extracted files don't get mixed up with other files.

Extract button decompresses file; put extracted files in empty folder

4 **Click OK.**

WinZip extracts the files and stores them in the folder you selected.

5 **Choose File⇨Exit to close WinZip.**

6 **Go to the folder where you told WinZip to store the files.**

The files are ready to use. Even though you now have the decompressed files, you still have the ZIP file as well. After unzipping, you can delete the ZIP file if you want to. See the "Zap ZIPs or keep 'em?" sidebar for more details.

ZIP file isn't deleted after decompression

may want to keep ZIP file

extra credit

Zap ZIPs or keep 'em?

After you unzip an archive, you have the files — so you no longer need the archive file whence they came. You can delete the ZIP file whenever you feel like it.

However, I usually hang on to the ZIP file for a while. First, it's nice to have the ZIP in case I accidentally do something stupid to the files — as long as I have the ZIP file, I can unzip again to get a clean batch o' files and try not to make the same mistake again. Second, if the archive contains files that I intend to use only occasionally, I delete the extracted version after each time I use it and save the ZIP instead. The ZIP takes up less disk space and reduces clutter on my hard disk. The next time I want to use the files inside it, I unzip, use 'em, and delete 'em when I'm done — keeping the ZIP on hand for next time.

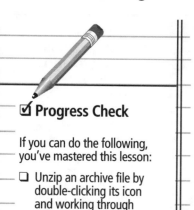

☑ Progress Check

If you can do the following, you've mastered this lesson:

❑ Unzip an archive file by double-clicking its icon and working through WinZip's dialog boxes.

❑ Look for SETUP and README files for programs.

heads up

If you've downloaded a media or document file, it's ready to use after it's unzipped. If you've downloaded a Windows program, further setup is usually required before you can use the program. Among the extracted files, look for a program file called SETUP; double-clicking that file usually runs a Wizard that leads you through setting up the program, step by step. Also look for a file called README, which usually contains installation instructions or other important information. README files are usually ordinary text files, so double-clicking a README file should open the file in Notepad or WordPad, where you can read it.

Unit 6 Quiz

For each question, circle the letter of the correct answer.

1. **When you download a file, you . . .**

    A. Compress it.

    B. Copy it from a server onto your PC.

    C. Move it from a server to your PC, deleting it from the server so that no one else can download it ever again.

    D. All of the above

2. **Which of the following types of files are opened automatically when you double-click them if you've installed Internet Explorer and the CD-ROM included with this book?**

    A. Word for Windows (.DOC) files.

    B. Adobe Acrobat (.PDF) files.

    C. Various types of media files (.AVI, .MOV, .AU, and so on).

    D. All of the above

3. **A ZIP file contains . . .**

    A. Zip codes.

    B. Zip guns.

    C. Zippy, the never-seen sister of popular greeting card personality Ziggy.

    D. One or more files, of any type, compressed together so that they download more quickly.

4. **To start a download, you . . .**

   A. Click a link.

   B. Type a filename in the Address box.

   C. Choose File⇨Download⇨File⇨Now⇨Please.

   D. Phone the server operator and ask him or her to send the file.

5. **The time required to download a 4MB file is . . .**

   A. Two hours (time = [MB/008]/[28,800] * X + your weight in kilograms).

   B. Anywhere from about an hour and a half to infinity (roughly).

   C. Directly proportional to the time it takes to sing *I Am the Walrus* (goo-goo-ga-choob!).

   D. It's a trick question — 4MB files cannot be downloaded without committee approval.

Unit 6 Exercise

1. Go to the Shareware page at

   `http://www.shareware.com`

2. Browse for a program that you'd like to try. See if you can find one that's ZIPped.

3. Download it.

4. Unzip it.

5. Enjoy it.

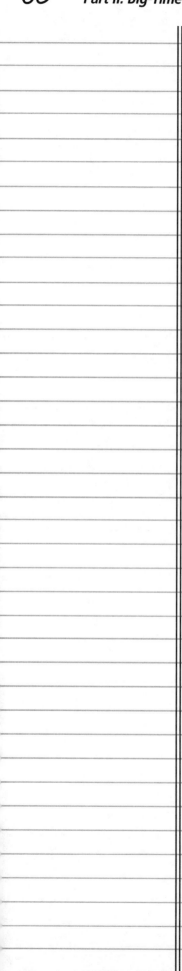

Playing Multimedia

Objectives for This Unit

✓ Understanding the ways in which multimedia appears on the Web

✓ Viewing (and hearing) multimedia built into Web pages

✓ Downloading and playing multimedia that's not built into a Web page

Prerequisites

▶ Opening Internet Explorer and connecting to the Internet (Unit 1)

▶ Browsing through links (Unit 2)

▶ Entering URLs (Unit 3)

M ultimedia happens.

That's about the size of it. There was a time when this unit would have been the longest and most difficult in the tutorial. Playing Web-based multimedia once involved acquiring and carefully installing a half-dozen "helper" applications, one to play each of the many different types of multimedia files. Now Internet Explorer comes pre-equipped to show or play virtually any type of *media file* (file containing multimedia).

The many different types and formats of media files — .GIF, .AVI, .MPG, .AU, and many more — all fall within one of three major categories:

▶ Pictures (of which you've already seen many in the Web pages you visited in preceding units)

▶ Sound clips (including speech, sound effects, and music — anything you hear)

▶ Video clips (including movie snippets, video, and animation)

on the test

In practical terms, all you need to think about when dealing with media files is whether the file is a picture, sound clip, or video clip. You really don't have to worry, for example, about whether a particular sound clip is a type .AU file or type .WAV. The steps for playing either file type are the same, and again, Internet Explorer automatically knows how to play all the popular media file formats — so you really don't need to even think about the file type. That's important to remember because some Web pages containing media files go to great pains to tell you the file type. But they're doing that to help out users of other browsers; Internet Explorer users don't care.

media file = file containing multimedia

media comes in three types: pictures, sounds, videos

Inline = media that appears or plays automatically and is integrated into page

External = media that doesn't play automatically but can be downloaded and played from hard disk

Active = integrated media that plays automatically and features control buttons

must have installed Internet Explorer with ActiveMovie option

need sound card and speakers/ headphones

display settings and PC speed affect quality of multimedia presentation

on the test

What you do need to consider is how the media file is presented on the Web. Pictures, sounds, and videos are presented on the Web in any of three ways:

- **Inline:** The media appears or plays automatically when you go to the page and is integrated into the page. For example, in your Web travels so far, all the pictures you saw in Web pages were inline pictures. While pictures are by far the most common inline media, a few pages also have inline sounds or video as well. Inline video clips appear as part of the layout of the page, and inline sounds play automatically in the background. You've probably come across the other types of inline media already, as well. (Did a page you visited suddenly play you a song?)

- **External:** External media files don't appear within the layout of a Web page and don't show up automatically when you access a page. They're just media files that you download and play by clicking a link. Most video clips and sound clips are presented as external media, although pictures can be external, too.

- **Active:** Active media content is a lot like inline multimedia because it is integrated into the layout of the Web page and appears more or less automatically when you go to the page. But unlike regular inline media, Active media often features buttons that allow you to control the presentation in some way. For example, when an Active video clip appears within a Web page, the clip may be accompanied by buttons that let you start, pause, or stop the playing of the clip.

In the three lessons of this unit, you take on each type of multimedia presentation — Inline, External, Active — one at a time. Before you go on, however, check out the "Is your PC media-ready?" sidebar for system requirements.

extra credit

Is your PC media-ready?

Before you embark on playing Web-based media, make sure that your PC is ready:

- To play most video and sound files, Internet Explorer must have been installed with its ActiveMovie option. See the note at the beginning of Lesson 7-2.

- To listen to sounds, you need to have a sound card installed in your PC, plus speakers or headphones. Any sound card supported by Windows will do.

- Any PC capable of running Internet Explorer can show any of the pictures and video on the Web, with no additional hardware. However, the quality of the image you see is affected by your display settings. For example, most pictures and video look best when the Windows Color palette is set to High-Color and the Desktop area (resolution) set to 800 x 600 resolution. Pictures and video still appear even if your display is set to 256 colors and 640 x 480 resolution (the minimum settings for Internet Explorer), but some may not look quite as nice. (To check or change your display settings, right-click any empty area of the Windows desktop, choose Properties from the context menu that appears, and then click the Settings tab.)

- Some types of video files play more smoothly on faster PCs. For example, a video clip that plays smoothly on a Pentium PC may appear a little jerky and jumbled on a 486 PC. (You can't really do anything about that, besides buying a new PC. But it's important to know.)

Playing Inline Multimedia

Wanna know how to play all the cool pages with inline pictures, videos, and sound? Okay, here it goes — pay attention. To see all the pictures and video and hear all the sound built into a page with inline multimedia:

1 **Go to the page.**

2 **Wait.**

That's it. Internet Explorer automatically knows what to do with inline multimedia, and just does it. (Remember: Multimedia happens.)

heads up

When you first go to a page containing inline media, not everything begins to play at once. As the page appears, keep an eye on the *e* logo. It may spin for several minutes while Internet Explorer gathers up all the media files. After the *e* logo quits spinning, all inline multimedia in the page should be apparent, to either your eyes or your ears. (If you're using the AT&T WorldNet℠ Service, your version of Internet Explorer has the AT&T logo rather than the *e* logo.)

Typically, the text, links, and inline pictures show up pretty quickly, and then the inline sound (if any) begins to play. Inline videos always show up last. In fact, several minutes may pass before a video begins to play. That's because video files are large and thus take a long time to travel from the server to your PC. While Internet Explorer retrieves a video clip, the spot on the page where the clip will appear may be filled with a placeholder or a temporary inline picture, or it may sit completely empty until the video shows up.

Tip: If you don't feel like waiting around for all the media in a page to show up, you can always click a link, choose a different URL from the Favorites menu (see Unit 4), or do anything else that jumps you to another page. Internet Explorer immediately quits retrieving media files and takes you wherever you want to go.

Q&A session

Question: How will I know when a page has inline sound?

Answer: When you hear something. Usually, when a page has inline sound, nothing that you see on the page tells you about it. Because you never know when a page you visit may have inline sound, keeping your speakers switched on while you browse is a good idea — otherwise, how would you know what you were missing?

Try it out:

1 **Make sure that your speakers are switched on.**

Most speakers have a little light on them that glows when they're switched on.

Notes:

Internet Explorer automatically plays all inline media on current page

media may take a while to appear and play, especially video files

always browse with speakers on to hear inline sounds

Figure 7-1: The Volcano Coffee page showcases inline pictures, sound, and video.

Figure 7-2: The Vero Beach page plays gentle music in the background.

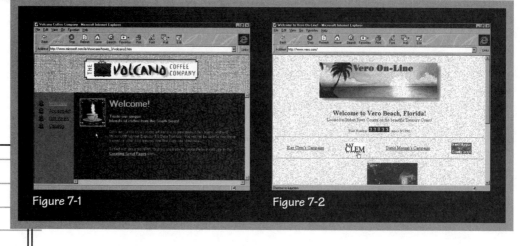

Figure 7-1   Figure 7-2

progressive =
Internet Explorer
shows rough version
of video while
waiting for rest of
file to download

☑ **Progress Check**

If you can do the following, you've mastered this lesson:

❑ Display a page containing inline media and experience what it has to offer.

❑ Distinguish among inline pictures, sounds, and videos.

2. **Go to the Volcano Coffee page at**

```
http://www.microsoft.com/ie/showcase/howto_3/
volcano3.htm
```

The Volcano Coffee page, shown in Figure 7-1, was set up as a demonstration for Internet Explorer's inline media capabilities (no, to my knowledge, there is no real Volcano Coffee Company). It includes

- Inline pictures — the logo at the top, the coffee beans in the background.

- Inline sound — thundering drums play when you go to the page.

- Inline video — the steaming coffee is a video clip of a spinning, steaming cup. (You have to wait a minute or two to see the cup spin; Internet Explorer displays a still picture of the cup while you wait.)

Head-start video

With some types of video files, the video begins to play fairly quickly but appears fuzzy and jerky at first; it sharpens up and smoothes out after a minute or two. What's happening is that Internet Explorer is trying to save your patience by showing you the video *progressively*.

Instead of waiting to download the whole video clip before beginning to play it, Internet Explorer starts playing the video as soon as it downloads enough of the clip to show a rough version, or a short version. As more of the video file arrives on your PC, Internet Explorer improves the image until at last the video clip appears in its complete glory.

---

3. **Now go to the Vero Beach page at**

```
http://www.vero.com/
```

This page (shown in Figure 7-2) promotes the lovely town of Vero Beach, Florida. (I've never been there, but it looks nice.) When you go to this page, the ever-popular *Pachelbel's Canon* plays gently in the background. Of course, it's unlikely that Pachelbel ever visited Vero Beach, but I guess the Vero Beach people simply wanted to play something soothing.

The next lesson takes you to another fun page that you may never have known about if not for this book: Jackie Chan's Web page. Stay tuned!

Playing External Multimedia

Lesson 7-2

Note: ActiveMovie, Internet Explorer's default player for most sound and video file types, is built into current versions of Internet Explorer supplied directly by Microsoft and some other sources. However, the AT&T WorldNet version of Internet Explorer supplied on the CD-ROM does not include ActiveMovie. If your copy of Internet Explorer was installed from the Dummies 101 CD-ROM (or if you are using any version but find that some video and sound file types don't play), download ActiveMovie and install it before proceeding with the rest of this unit.

To download ActiveMovie, go to `http://www.windows.com/ie/ download/ieadd.htm`. From the drop-down list on that page, choose ActiveMovie. Then click Next and follow the prompts. When the download is about to start, choose the Open it (not Save to disk) option. After the download finishes, follow the prompts to set up ActiveMovie; then restart your computer and proceed with Lesson 7-2.

Better media means bigger files. In other words, the sharper and more colorful a picture, the bigger its file. Sharper video clips and better-quality sound clips require larger files than fuzzy video and tinny sound. And, of course, longer clips mean bigger files, too. The best media files are fat, taking too much downloading time to be practical as inline media. That's just one of the reasons that the best media files are offered as external media.

But the real reason for external media is *choice.* Inline media forces itself upon you, whereas you can choose or ignore external media. Links to external media files appear in Web pages as either text links or picture links. If the page describes a file that you want to see or hear, you simply click the link to download the file (as you learned to do in Unit 6). If the link contains a file about which you care zip, leave it alone.

heads up

Keep in mind that external files can mean very long downloads. Most external pictures download within a minute or two. Short sound clips (lasting a few seconds) may be small, taking a few minutes to download, but longer clips may take up to an hour to download. And a video clip lasting as little as 30 seconds may take hours to download. Usually, the link to an external media file tells you the size of the file, so you can guesstimate the length of the download (see Unit 6) and decide whether the file is worth the time.

Finding an external media file

You don't usually go looking for external media. You go looking for information related to a topic that interests you, and on a page related to that topic, you find links to external files.

For example, a page about your favorite TV show may feature links to files containing pictures of the show's stars, the theme music, or a video clip from the show. A page about molecular biology may contain links to files containing

---

great media = huge files; best media files come as external media

external media does not appear as part of page

Figure 7-3: The *Rockford Files* Homepage offers links to Rockford-related external media.

Figure 7-4: Yahoo!'s multimedia archives directory is an external media trove of troves.

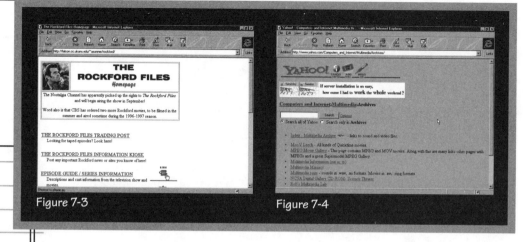

Figure 7-3   Figure 7-4

Notes:

views through the microscope. A page about Picasso may contain high-quality pictures of his drawings and paintings. A page about William Shatner may contain links to sound clips of him reading from Shakespeare's *Henry V.* You get the idea.

For example, Figure 7-3 shows the *Rockford Files* Homepage, where you can pick up assorted cast photos from the seminal 1970s private-eye show. The little telephone icon in the lower-right corner of the page is a link to a sound clip of the answering machine message that opens every episode: "Hello, this is Jim Rockford. Leave your name and message, and I'll get back to you. BEEP."

Tip: If you just want to dive in and see multimedia related to many different subjects, check out Yahoo!'s multimedia archives directory (see Figure 7-4). The pages listed in it are a great way to find and experiment with a wide variety of external media files. To reach the directory, open Yahoo!'s top directory (http://www.yahoo.com — see Unit 5) and then choose Computers and Internet⇨Multimedia⇨Archives.

Internet Explorer comes pre-equipped to play nearly all popular media file types

must unzip ZIP file before it can be played

Forget file types

When you come across external media, the text accompanying the link usually tells you the file type of the media file and may name a required "viewer" application. This information is principally for the benefit of people who don't use Internet Explorer. Internet Explorer plays all the common media file types, so you really needn't worry about file types.

Also, many pages divide video clips into versions designed to be played on a Macintosh (.QT or .MOV) and versions designed for Windows (.AVI). But even then, you needn't worry about file types — Internet Explorer plays .QT, .MOV, .AVI, and a few more video file types, such as .MPG.

Finally, to reduce downloading time, some external media files are presented on the Web as compressed archive (ZIP) files. Before you can play media files contained in a ZIP file, you must unzip the file (see Unit 6). After unzipping any media file, simply double-click the file's icon to play or display it.

Dealing with Internet Explorer's unpredictable behavior

Internet Explorer tries hard to make using external media easy. Unfortunately, it tries too hard, behaving unpredictably. Starting off is okay — to get any external media file, you simply click the link that leads to the file.

The problem is that what happens *after* you click the link varies from file to file. Internet Explorer always does either of two things when you click a link to a media file:

> ♦ It automatically downloads and plays the file with no further actions by you — you just click the file and wait.

> ♦ It starts the regular downloading procedure (see Unit 6). You must perform the regular downloading steps and then double-click the file's icon to see or play it.

heads up

As you can see, retrieving and experiencing external media is pretty simple either way. The problem is that I can't give you an easy way to predict exactly what will happen when you click that link. In general, you should expect the file to simply download and play all by itself. But you should always be ready to perform the downloading steps and then double-click the file icon to see or hear what you've downloaded.

When Internet Explorer can show a picture automatically, it does so right in the Internet Explorer window. In effect, it opens a new, blank page and shows the picture alone on that page. (Remember: External media is not contained within the layout of a Web page.)

Video clips and sound clips are played by Internet Explorer's built-in ActiveMovie program. ActiveMovie not only takes care of playing clips but also presents you with easy-to-understand buttons that allow you to start, stop, or pause the playing of a clip. The buttons look just like the controls on any tape player or VCR.

ActiveMovie has the ability to play some types of clips *progressively* — that is, it can begin to play the file while the file is still downloading. Whenever you click a link to an external media file that ActiveMovie knows how to play progressively, ActiveMovie opens immediately, manages the download, and begins playing the file as soon as it can. But again, sometimes the regular file-download procedure begins when you click a link to a sound or video clip. If that happens, just download the file and then double-click the file's icon to play the file in ActiveMovie.

Displaying a picture

Keeping Internet Explorer's quirks in mind, follow these steps to get some external media. First, view a picture:

1 **Go to the photo gallery of the Jackie Chan home page at**

`http://www.jackiechan.com/photo.htm`

The photo gallery page, shown in Figure 7-5, allows you to select and view publicity photos of the international action-movie superstar who does all his own stunts.

some media files play automatically; some don't

external media plays in its own new page

ActiveMovie plays some video and sound progressively; some not

Figure 7-5: When you see a gallery of small "thumbnail" pictures, each picture is a link to a larger version of the same picture.

Figure 7-6: When you click one of the little Jackie thumbnails, you download and display a big Jackie.

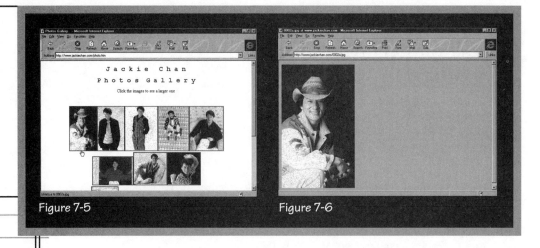

Figure 7-5   Figure 7-6

thumbnail = little picture that links to big picture

to print picture while viewing it, click Print button

Notes:

Each small picture on the page is actually a link to a larger version of the same photo. When little pictures serve as links to bigger versions of themselves, the little versions are called *thumbnails*. Thumbnails are a popular way to present links to pictures, although ordinary text links often lead to pictures as well.

2 **Click any thumbnail.**

I clicked the first one: Jackie relaxing in a cowboy hat. After a few moments, Internet Explorer displays the full picture (alone, on a blank page), as shown in Figure 7-6.

3 **Return to Jackie's photo gallery by clicking the Back button.**

Tip: While viewing a picture in Internet Explorer, you can print the picture by clicking the Print button on Internet Explorer's toolbar. To learn more about printing, see Unit 9.

Playing a clip

Now give ActiveMovie a spin by downloading a file that ActiveMovie plays progressively:

1 **Go to the MPEG Monster List at**

```
http://www.islandnet.com/~carleton/monster/
        monster2.html
```

The MPEG Monster List is a huge archive of video and sound clips in a file format called MPEG, one of the many types that ActiveMovie can play.

2 **Scroll down the page to the link for simpsons1.mpg.**

Figure 7-7 shows the simpsons1.mpg link on the MPEG Monster list.

3 **Click the link.**

ActiveMovie opens, as shown in Figure 7-8. ActiveMovie keeps track of how much of the clip has been downloaded; Figure 7-8 shows how ActiveMovie reports the progress. Observe in the figure that less than half the clip has been downloaded, but ActiveMovie already displays part of the clip.

Remember: Most video clips include sound, too. So when playing any video clip, make sure that your speakers are switched on.

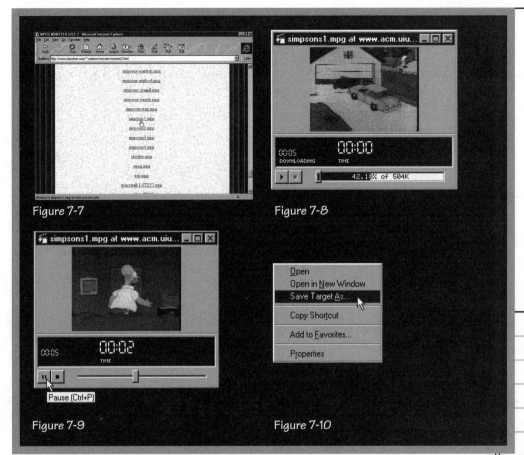

Figure 7-7

Figure 7-8

Figure 7-9

Figure 7-10

At some point near the end of the download, ActiveMovie plays the clip once (as shown in Figure 7-9) and then stops. You may then do any of the following:

- To play the clip again, click the Play button.
- To stop playing the clip, click the Stop button.
- To pause the clip during play, click the slider control that moves from left to right as the clip plays. To resume play from that point forward, click the Play button.
- To close ActiveMovie and return to your browsing, click the X button in ActiveMovie's upper-right corner.

Check out some of the other fun links on this Web page. The next lesson deals with something that's similar to external media: Active media. You'll go to one of Microsoft's pages to experience Active media.

plays a clip ▶
stops play ■
pauses play ❚❚

closes ActiveMovie ☒

ActiveMovie does not automatically save downloaded files to hard disk

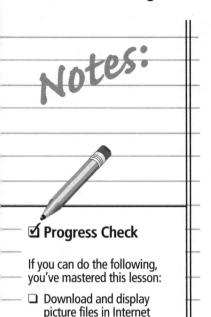

☑ **Progress Check**

If you can do the following, you've mastered this lesson:

❑ Download and display picture files in Internet Explorer.

❑ Download and play video and sound clips in ActiveMovie.

---

extra credit

Saving a file after ActiveMovie plays it

When ActiveMovie takes over a download, it does not save the file permanently to your hard disk. ActiveMovie assumes that you just want to see or hear the clip once or twice and then move on. So it stores the clip only temporarily. Eventually, Internet Explorer deletes the temporary file from your hard disk.

But right after you play the clip, the temporary file is still on your hard disk. That gives you an opportunity to copy the temporary file to create a permanent version that won't be erased. To keep a clip after ActiveMovie has interceded in the download:

1. **Close ActiveMovie.**

2. **Right-click the link from which you downloaded the file to open the link's context menu as shown in Figure 7-10.**

3. **Choose Save As from the context menu to open the Save Target As dialog box and save the file.**

Note that when saving a file that you've already downloaded and played, Internet Explorer does not have to download the file again when you save it this way. It simply copies the temporary file and saves the copy as a regular, permanent file.

Lesson 7-3   Controlling Active Multimedia

Active media is part of Microsoft's ActiveX strategy, which allows Web authors to automatically reprogram Internet Explorer, through the Web, to enable it to do stuff it doesn't yet know how to do. Using ActiveX, a programmer can put a new type of media file on the Web — one for which Internet Explorer has no built-in support. The programmer can attach to the media file some programming code that endows Internet Explorer with the ability to play the file.

Although Active media is cool, you won't find much of it outside Microsoft's Web pages. At this writing, Internet Explorer is the only browser that supports Active media. Most Web page authors want their pages accessible by users of more than one browser — Internet Explorer and Netscape Navigator at the very least. As support for ActiveX begins to appear in more browsers (as it inevitably will), more Active Web content will emerge.

You can't predict exactly what Active media may do on your PC — that's limited only by the programmer's imagination. But as a rule, Active media shows up in Web pages in either of two ways:

not much support for Active media yet

Active media appears within page and can do anything

▶ It looks and acts just like regular inline media and just does its thing. No action is required by you, other than experiencing whatever the media does.

▶ The media shows up within the layout of the page (like inline media) but is accompanied by control buttons such as Play and Stop (like external media). Any controls you see, like Play and Stop, are self-explanatory or are explained within the text of the Web page on which the media appears.

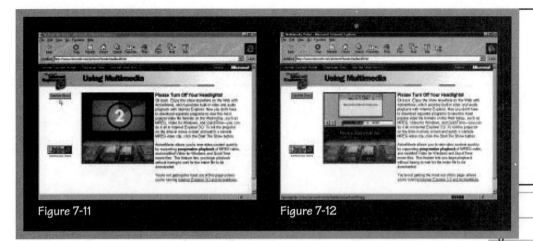

Figure 7-11

Figure 7-12

Figure 7-11: The big picture in this page is a special frame in which Active media will appear.

Figure 7-12: After you click Start the Show, ActiveMovie's controls appear within the layout of the Web page while the clip is retrieved.

Note: As with any page containing program code, many pages containing Active media display certificates when the program code runs. To learn more about certificates, see Unit 2.

The best place to try Active media, obviously, is Microsoft's Web page. Give it a spin:

1 **Go to the Internet Explorer Multimedia Video page at**

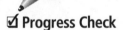
`http://www.microsoft.com/ie/most/howto/mediavid.htm`

The page appears, as shown in Figure 7-11.

2 **Click the Start the Show button on the left side of the page.**

While Internet Explorer retrieves the Active video, ActiveMovie's control buttons and download-status report appear (see Figure 7-12) — but not within a separate ActiveMovie window as they did in Lesson 7-2. The controls are now an integral part of the layout of the Web page, neatly tucked within the frame in which the video clip will play. That's what makes Active media unique.

Eventually, the clip (a TV commercial for you-know-who) plays once automatically and then stops. You may use the controls to play the clip again (or stop or pause it), or you can simply move on to another page.

Recess

That's probably enough browsing for one sitting. Shut down and take a nice, long break (after the upcoming quiz and exercise, of course).

Active media displays controls within frame for video clip

☑ Progress Check

If you can do the following, you've mastered this lesson:

❑ Display and enjoy a page containing Active media.

❑ Use on-screen buttons to control the play of Active media.

Unit 7 Quiz

Notes:

For each question, circle the letter of the correct answer.

1. **Which of the following may appear as integral parts of the layout of a Web page?**

   A. External media and inline media

   B. Inline media and Active media

   C. Active media and external media

   D. Entertainment media and media relations

2. **ActiveMovie jumps in to manage the download and start play automatically whenever you . . .**

   A. Click a link leading to any external media.

   B. Click a link leading to a video or sound clip that can be played before downloading is complete.

   C. Click the ActiveMovie button on the toolbar.

   D. Click a link leading to a picture.

3. **To play or show any of the media files on the Web, your PC needs only Internet Explorer and . . .**

   A. A sound card, game card, and MPEG playback card.

   B. A sound card and speakers.

   C. A VCR (for video), amplifier (for sound), and color printer (for pictures).

   D. None of the above

4. **If the regular download procedure begins when you click a link to a media file . . .**

   A. Press Esc to abort the download — the file is incompatible.

   B. Turn off your PC immediately and leave the room. Something's terribly wrong.

   C. Click the link again.

   D. Perform the download and then double-click the file's icon to display or play it, online or off.

5. **To play media contained in a ZIP file . . .**

   A. Play the ZIP file like any other media file.

   B. Unzip the ZIP file and then play the media.

   C. Play the file in Internet Explorer's ActiveZIP player.

   D. ZIP files cannot contain media files.

Unit 7 Exercise

1. List one or more of your favorites in the following categories:

   • Favorite recent films:

   _____

   _____

   • Favorite TV shows (recent or otherwise):

   _____

   _____

   • Favorite musicians/composers:

   _____

   _____

   • Favorite well-known painters:

   _____

   _____

2. Using the search techniques that you discovered in Unit 5, search for pages related to each item that you listed in Step 1.

3. Browse the pages you find and locate media related to your favorite films, TV shows, music, and painters. Watch for

   • Picture files containing movie or TV cast photos and stills and reproductions of paintings

   • Video clips containing movie trailers, commercials, and excerpts of movies and TV shows

   • Sound clips containing snippets of music from your favorite musician, TV/movie theme music, and dialog

Part II Review

Unit 5 Summary

- **Opening a search tool:** Click the Search button to reach a search page that offers a variety of popular search tools.

- **Clicking through categories:** Some search tools organize their directories of the Web into categories and subcategories; you can search for items that interest you by clicking down through the category tree.

- **Using a search term:** To search for something very specific, type a search term — a word or two that describes the item — in the text box of a search engine (the blank box next to the search tool name).

- **Phrasing advanced searches:** Use the word *and* between words in a search term to force the search engine to find only pages that contain both words, or use *or* between words to allow the search engine to find pages containing either word.

Unit 6 Summary

- **Downloading a file:** To download any file from the Web, click its link and then choose Save it to disk in the Open dialog box.

- **Opening a file:** Many types of multimedia files open automatically, in Internet Explorer or in ActiveMovie, as soon as you download them. If the file does not open automatically after downloading, locate its file icon and double-click the icon.

- **Unzipping a ZIP file:** After downloading a ZIP file, open it in WinZip by double-clicking the file's icon. In WinZip, click Extract to decompress the files so you can use them.

Unit 7 Summary

- **Playing inline multimedia:** To play inline sounds, pictures, and videos in a Web page, simply go to the page and wait for the multimedia to appear/play, which it does automatically.

- **Playing external media:** To play an external media file, click the link that leads to the file. During or immediately after downloading, the file opens and plays automatically in Internet Explorer or in ActiveMovie. If the file does not open automatically, locate its file icon and double-click the icon to play the file.

- **Playing Active media:** To play Active media in a Web page, go to the page and follow any instructions you see there. If controls — such as Play and Pause — appear, use them to control the media play.

Part II Test

The questions on this test cover all the material presented in Part II, Units 5 through 7.

True False

Each statement is either true or false.

T　F　1. Absolutely all media files open and play automatically when downloaded.

T　F　2. To use a search engine to find pages about mathematician Bucky Fuller, you can enter the search term **Buckminster Fuller**.

T　F　3. All files that you can download from Web pages are Windows-compatible.

T　F　4. Capitalization never matters when you type a search term.

T　F　5. ActiveMovie plays both sound and video clips.

T　F　6. Video clips are usually downloaded within a minute.

T　F　7. Files downloaded from the Web cannot contain viruses.

T　F　8. When you open an external picture file, it appears on a page alone in Internet Explorer.

T　F　9. Some search engines can locate not only Web pages but newsgroups as well.

T　F　10. Video clips may also contain sound.

Multiple Choice

For each of the following questions, circle the correct answer.

11. **To protect yourself from computer viruses . . .**

    A. Clean your computer often with a solution of vinegar and water.

    B. Always use the Save it to disk option (not the Open it option) when downloading; then scan the file with a virus-scanning program before opening it.

    C. Keep your computer warm at night.

    D. Do not allow your computer to play with other computers that have viruses.

12. **Which is a search tool?**

    A. Excite

    B. Yahoo!

    C. AltaVista

    D. All of the above

13. **To accurately estimate the time required to download a large file, calculate by using which of the following formulas?**

    A. Each KB = 1 second.

    B. Each MB = 15 minutes.

    C. Each kilobit = 1 nanosecond.

    D. Accurate download times cannot be calculated, because of unpredictable server pauses.

14. **Windows program files use the filename extension . . .**

    A. .WIN

    B. .PRO

    C. .EXE

    D. .NED

Part II Test

15. **To find only Web pages that contain information about boxer George Foreman, the best search term would be . . .**

    A. George and Foreman and box

    B. Foreman or George

    C. George Foreman or boxing

    D. Foreman

16. **When media files appear or play *progressively*, they . . .**

    A Materialize one scan line at a time.

    B Play faster and faster as they go.

    C Begin to appear or play before they've been completely downloaded.

    D Conceive new, innovative ways to appear or play.

17. **An archive, or ZIP, file is made up of . . .**

    A. A file, compressed so that it downloads more quickly.

    B. Multiple files, compressed so that they download more quickly.

    C. All the files that make up an application program.

    D. Any of the above

Matching

18. **Match up each button with what it does:**

    A. [▶]   1. Pauses the play of a sound or video clip.

    B. [❚❚]   2. Stops the play of a sound or video clip and returns to the beginning.

    C. [■]   3. Starts the play of a sound or video clip.

Part II Lab Assignment

This Lab Assignment tests your skills at using search terms and any media you may come across.

Step 1

Write down five things that interest you
Use the following space to record favorite movies, animals, occupations, musicians, actors, scientific breakthroughs, and so on.

_____   _____   _____

_____   _____   _____

_____   _____   _____

_____   _____   _____

_____   _____   _____

Step 2

Open Internet Explorer and connect to the Internet.

Step 3

Search for the first interest you wrote down in Step 1. Use one or more search tools to locate at least one page about your first interest. Explore and enjoy the page.

Step 4

Play media or download files shown on that page. If the page contains any media or other files related to your interest, play or download them.

Step 5

Repeat Steps 3 and 4 for each of the interests listed in Step 1.

Step 6

Quit Internet Explorer and the Internet.

Step 7

Enjoy a lovely beverage.

House-keeping

Part III

In this part...

You want to surf; I want you to surf, so up to this point, we been mostly surfin'. But not everything you can do in Internet Explorer involves jumping to a page or even going online. Some of what you do involves fiddling with your Internet Explorer setup so that your online experiences can be safer, more productive, or more personal.

In this part of the tutorial, you discover the ways you can customize your window on the Web and work with the information you discover there. For example, you can instruct Internet Explorer to avoid content you deem offensive. You can tap a range of features that can improve your productivity with the pages containing content that you want to see. And you can create shortcuts to take you straight to anywhere on the Web with nothing but a double-click.

Controlling Kids' Access to Web Content

Prerequisites

▶ Opening Internet Explorer and connecting to the Internet (Unit 1)

▶ Understanding URLs (Unit 3)

Internet Explorer has a built-in self-censorship system called Content Advisor that operates just like the V-chip that's being built into all new television sets.

Based on ratings that you control, Content Advisor prevents Internet Explorer from accessing Web pages containing levels of language, nudity, sex, or violence that you deem unacceptable for viewing by you or others who use your PC.

Once you enable it, Content Advisor can be disabled only with a password that you choose yourself. That prevents anyone else — smart kids, especially — from disabling Content Advisor, while it allows you to disable the censorship for your own browsing, if you want to.

heads up

The obvious and principal purpose of Content Advisor is to prevent kids from accessing (intentionally or otherwise) unsavory Web content, but it has other uses. In a company, the system administrator may enable Content Advisor to ensure that employees aren't checking out the *Penthouse* Web page when they're supposed to be working. Also, if you're especially sensitive, you may choose to use Content Advisor to protect yourself from stuff that may ruffle your own feathers.

> Content Advisor prevents access to Web pages that contain content you deem unacceptable

About the Web content controversy

A dose of tough love is coming. . . . Please wait while I steady my soap box.

Ahem.

uh-oh . . . soap box
stuff about seamy
side of Web

To anyone who reads the paper or watches TV news and hasn't spent much time on the Internet, the Web is a scary place. Pornographers, pedophiles, and other perverts lurk around every cyber-corner. It's Times Square online, a place of sin and danger that features a few friendly attractions only to lure innocent victims.

However, having done some surfing of your own by now, you know that the Web is a friendlier place than that. Is there stuff on the Web that you wouldn't want your kids to see? Absolutely. There's probably stuff out there that *you* wouldn't want to see, either. There's stuff out there that would make Hugh Hefner blush. But does that mean you really need to censor your Internet Explorer's Web access? Maybe not.

First, the unsavory stuff on the Web does not jump out at you. To see it, you've got to go looking for it. I suppose if you have clever, curious kids, then that's a problem — they might go looking for it. But if your kids are that clever and curious, they're probably going to find a way to see stuff you don't want them to see — offline, if not on. So Content Advisor is not a solution to your problem (if, in fact, clever and curious kids are really a problem).

Content Advisor isn't
foolproof

heads up

Second, Internet Explorer's Content Advisor cannot be an effective replacement for parental supervision. The existence of Content Advisor may lull some folks into a false sense of security — crank it up and leave the kids alone. But even with Content Advisor switched on full-blast, it does not protect your kids from

- **Unsavory content or people in chat sessions, e-mail exchanges, or newsgroups (see Units 11 and 12).** In fact, the infamous cases of children being stalked by online predators began not on the Web but in chat sessions and via e-mail. Content Advisor affects only Web content — e-mail, chat, and newsgroups are untouched by Content Advisor.

- **Racist or other hate-mongering content that does not also happen to include racist epithets or other material (nudity, for example) that Content Advisor would catch.** For example, many people are offended by broadcast commentator Rush Limbaugh, excerpts of whose diatribes may be found on the Web. While the ideas he espouses are offensive to many, he couches them in words that don't run afoul of the ratings.

- **Material of a political, religious, or other philosophical basis that may be personally offensive to you but doesn't violate the language/nudity/sex/violence boundaries of the ratings.**

The bottom line: If you feel that your kids aren't ready to exercise good online judgment, don't let them go online without your supervision — even with Content Advisor. If you feel that your kids have a strong-enough foundation to surf responsibly, they may not need your supervision — or Content Advisor.

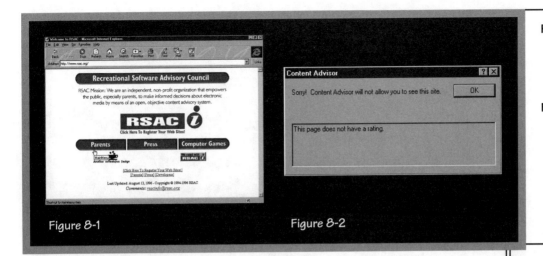

Figure 8-1

Figure 8-2

Figure 8-1: The home page of the RSAC (`http://www.rsac.org/`), the independent group in charge of ratings.

Figure 8-2: After you set up Content Advisor, Internet Explorer refuses to show you pages containing language, nudity, sex, or violence that you don't want to see — as well as pages that have not been rated.

Understanding the ratings

Content Advisor does not read Web pages to determine whether they meet your standards. Instead, pages are rated by their authors or by an independent board called the Recreational Software Advisory Council (RSAC). The RSAC's Web page (`http://www.rsac.org/`) appears in Figure 8-1. The RSAC is the acknowledged authority on rating not just Internet content but all kinds of recreational software, including video games.

In the RSAC's Internet rating system (RSACi — the *i* is for Internet), the raters review a page and assign it a number rating in each category. The categories are violence, language, sex, and nudity, and the ratings go from 0 (no instances of offensive content for that category) to 4 (highest level of offensive content for that category, or anything goes).

The final rating is built into the Web page so that Internet Explorer can read the rating before accessing the rest of the page. If the page's ratings exceed yours in any category, Internet Explorer refuses to show you the page (see Figure 8-2). For example, if a page has a violence rating of 3 and you configured Content Advisor with a violence rating of 2, the page will not appear.

heads up

Keep in mind the following about ratings:

▶ Ratings are subjective. Although the raters follow guidelines in making their determinations, their definition of "extreme violence," for example, may differ from yours and may not be applied consistently from page to page.

▶ Not all pages are rated — in fact, the majority of Web pages today are not rated. In addition to pages that exceed your ratings, Content Advisor blocks out all unrated pages (although you can configure it to permit unrated pages). Most of the unrated pages are harmless, so you'd be blocking out lots of great stuff for nothing. On the other hand, telling Content Advisor to permit unrated pages kind of defeats its purpose.

▶ In the future, new organizations will supply new ratings systems, maybe better ones. On the Advanced tab of the Content Advisor dialog box (you'll use that dialog box in this lesson), Internet Explorer allows you to add any new ratings system to Content Advisor. But for now, RSACi is all there is.

Web page ratings come from page's authors or RSAC

ratings are subjective

most Web pages are not rated, and Content Advisor blocks unrated pages by default

Figure 8-3: To enable ratings and choose the content levels you want blocked out, you begin at the Security tab of the Options dialog box.

Figure 8-4: Once you create your secret password, the Content Advisor settings cannot be disabled or changed without the password.

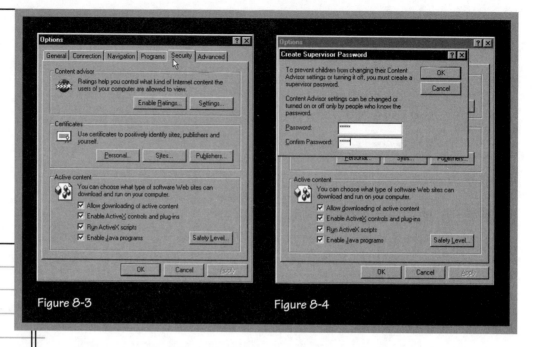

Figure 8-3   Figure 8-4

Lesson 8-1

Enabling Ratings and Choosing Types of Material to Block Out

When you first set up Content Advisor, you need to create a password so that no one else can fool with the settings later. After creating your password, you can customize the settings.

Security tab of
Options dialog box
controls ratings

1 **From the Internet Explorer toolbar, choose View⇨Options.**

The Options dialog box opens. Note that you don't have to be connected to the Internet to access the Options dialog box.

2 **Click the Security tab.**

The Security tab opens, as shown in Figure 8-3.

Enable Ratings
button sets
password

3 **In the Content Advisor section, click Enable Ratings.**

The Create Supervisor Password dialog box opens, as shown in Figure 8-4. You create your password in this dialog box — yes, at long last, *you're* the supervisor. After you set your password, anyone who wants to change the Content Advisor settings must type that password.

4 **Type a password in the Password box.**

As you type, asterisks appear in the box instead of the password. That way, no one can find out your password by peering over your shoulder.

The password can be anything you want it to be. But make sure that it's

make the password
easy to remember
but difficult for
someone else to
guess

- Easy for you to remember. The password **gjchusiix**, for example, is a bad choice unless it has a secret meaning for you or you secretly write it down someplace — and you don't want to write it down where someone else may find it.

- Difficult for someone else to guess. For example, **daddy** or **mommy** make bad passwords. **Remember:** Your kids are smarter than you are.

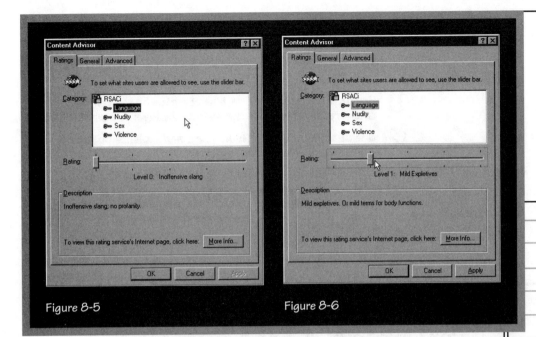

Figure 8-5

Figure 8-6

Figure 8-5: Choose rating levels here for each category of content: Language, Nudity, Sex, Violence.

Figure 8-6: When you click a marker on the scale, the rating level changes, and the Description box tells you what that rating will block out.

5 **Click the Confirm Password box and type your new password exactly as you typed it in Step 4.**

The Confirm Password box simply makes sure that when you first typed the password, you typed what you thought you were typing.

6 **Click OK.**

The Security tab reappears.

Once your Content Advisor is enabled, you need to tell it exactly how much nasty language, nudity, sex, or violence to permit. You set the level for each type of content individually. For example, if you're open-minded about language but skittish about sex, you can choose a high rating (permissive) for language but a low rating (restrictive) for sex.

7 **On the Security tab, click the Settings button.**

The Content Advisor dialog box opens, as shown in Figure 8-5.

8 **In the Category box, click Language.**

Observe that the Rating scale below the Category box is currently set at 0 (the first marker). The Description box below the Rating scale gives you details about what type of language will cause a Web page to be blocked out at this level: `Inoffensive slang; no profanity.`

9 **Click the Rating scale at some point to the right of the rectangular slider so that the slider jumps to the second marker (level 1).**

Each click to the right of the marker makes the slider jump to the next level. The Description box changes to `Mild expletives. Or mild terms for body functions.` (See Figure 8-6.) Now inoffensive slang is permitted, but mild expletives (or worse) are not.

10 **Repeat Step 9 to move the slider to level 2. Read the description and then move on to levels 3 and 4, following the same steps.**

The farther the slider moves to the right, the less restrictive the ratings are. So whereas the far-left setting for Language blocks out pages with even mildly rough language, the far-right setting blocks out only pages with the most extreme obscenities.

Settings button sets rating levels for categories

click Rating scale to right of slider to jump to next level

ratings get less restrictive as slider moves to right

More Info button brings up Web page with details about ratings

Tip: To find out precisely what a rating means and how it's determined, click the More Info button in the Description box to jump to a page at RSAC's Web server.

11 Having discovered what each level means (in the Language category, anyway), click the scale at the level you want to select.

12 One at a time, click the Nudity, Sex, and Violence options, reviewing the various levels for each and then selecting the Rating level you want.

13 After you have selected a Rating level for each of the four categories, click OK.

The next exercise picks up with the Content Advisor dialog box again — this time, the General tab.

Lesson 8-2

Setting General Options for Content Advisor

General tab of Content Advisor dialog box controls showing unrated pages, overriding blocked pages, and changing password

Content Advisor blocks unrated pages by default

can have option of overriding blocked pages on case-by-case basis

change password every so often

on the test

Using the General tab of the Content Advisor dialog box, you can modify Content Advisor's behavior in three useful ways:

- **Permit unrated pages:** Just to play it safe, Content Advisor automatically blocks access to all pages that have not been rated — which includes a majority of the pages on the Web. Obviously, that includes lots of perfectly harmless stuff; Content Advisor throws the baby out with the babes and bazookas. Using the General tab, you can instruct Content Advisor to permit unrated pages (some of which, inevitably, will contain the type of content you're trying to avoid).

- **Let the supervisor override a blocked page:** You can instruct Content Advisor to display a password box whenever accessing a page that it intends to block. If you type your supervisor password, Content Advisor allows the page to be shown, even if the page's content violates the ratings you've set or is unrated.

  Tip: This option is great because it permits you to browse the Web more freely while still leaving Content Advisor on. It also enables you to apply your own discretion. The kids can browse with Content Advisor on, and when Content Advisor won't let them see something they want to see, you can step in, evaluate the page, and then let the kids see it if you think that Content Advisor is being overprotective in that instance.

- **Change the supervisor's password:** Every so often, you should change your supervisor password — especially if you suspect that your kids may have figured it out. (Remember how easily Matthew Broderick figured out the password to the U.S. missile defense system in *Wargames*? He got away with it only because nobody had changed the password in a decade.)

To access the General tab and modify these settings:

1 If you're not already in the Security tab of the Options dialog box, choose View⇔Options from the Internet Explorer toolbar and click Security.

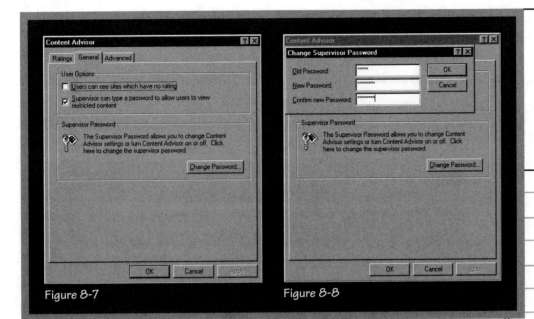

Figure 8-7

Figure 8-8

Figure 8-7: You can customize Content Advisor's behavior on the General tab.

Figure 8-8: To change your supervisor password, just type the old password and then type your new password twice.

2 **Click the Settings button to open the Content Advisor dialog box.**

3 **Click the General tab.**

The General tab opens, as shown in Figure 8-7.

4 **To prevent Content Advisor from blocking unrated pages, click the Users can see sites which have no rating check box.**

A check mark appears in the box. Now unrated pages will show up as if they were rated and passed your rating specifications. If you *want* Content Advisor to block unrated pages, click the check box again to remove the check mark.

5 **To allow a blocked page to be overridden by a password, click the Supervisor can type a password to allow user to view restricted content check box.**

Now Content Advisor will give the supervisor (or anyone who knows the supervisor password) the opportunity to override each page that it blocks. If you don't want blocked pages to be overridden by a password, click the check box again to remove the check mark.

6 **To change the password, click the Change Password button and fill out the Change Supervisor Password dialog box (shown in Figure 8-8) that appears.**

Type the current password in the Old Password box, just so Content Advisor can be sure that you are you. (Just as when you created the password, what you type does not appear on-screen — asterisks appear instead, so you know your keyboard works.) Type your new password in the New Password box and then again in the Confirm new Password box.

7 **Click OK.**

You're back in the Content Advisor dialog box.

8 **Click OK to save your changes.**

There's one more thing you can do with Content Advisor: Shut it off! Read on for more details.

when Users... check box is checked, all unrated pages show up

when Supervisor... check box is checked, password can override blocked page

Lesson 8-3

Disabling Content Advisor

Content Advisor
stays disabled until
it's manually
enabled again

heads up

If you're like a lot of people, you may want Content Advisor turned on while your kids browse the Web but switched off when you use it. If so, you can disable Content Advisor for your own browsings.

Once you disable Content Advisor, it stays disabled until you enable it again. Even after you quit the Internet, the next time someone connects to the Internet with your PC, Content Advisor remains disabled. So be sure to re-enable Content Advisor when you finish browsing.

To disable Content Advisor:

Disable Ratings
button turns off
Content Advisor

1 If you're not already in the Security tab of the Options dialog box, choose View⇨Options from the Internet Explorer toolbar and click Security.

2 Click Disable Ratings.

A dialog box pops up, prompting you for the password.

3 Type your supervisor password and click OK.

Recess

Shut off the computer and spend some (non-computer) time with the kids. Or the dog. Or whomever you've been neglecting with all this settings stuff. But be sure to take the quiz while the answers are all still fresh in your mind.

☑ **Progress Check**

If you can do the following, you've mastered this lesson:

❑ Understand the principles by which Content Advisor blocks content.

❑ Enable and disable Content Advisor.

❑ Set an individual rating level for each content category.

❑ Choose options for Content Advisor on the General tab.

Unit 8 Quiz

For each question, circle the letter of the correct answer.

1. **Content Advisor can shield a user of your PC from . . .**

    A. All offensive content on the Internet.

    B. All content that violates ratings you select, on the Web alone.

    C. All Web pages that have not been rated.

    D. B and C

2. **Your Content Advisor supervisor password should be . . .**

    A. Easy to remember.

    B. Hard to guess.

    C. One word (no spaces or punctuation).

    D. All of the above

3. **For what categories of content can the RSACi rating system block out pages?**

    A. Clarity, style, economy, and punctuation.

    B. Conservatism, Liberalism, Taoism, and Method Acting.

    C. Language, nudity, sex, and violence.

    D. Legislative, judicial, executive, and administrative.

4. **To override Content Advisor's blocking of any particular Web page, you can . . .**

    A. Configure Content Advisor to show blocked pages selectively when the supervisor password is typed.

    B. Press Ctrl+9 and then type the override command **STOP BEING SUCH A PRUDE**.

    C. The Content Advisor cannot be overridden without the signed approval of a Microsoft officer.

    D. E-mail the Webmaster a short essay describing a legitimate, scientific reason why you want to see a page containing unsavory content. Make it good.

5. **When you attempt to access a page that has not been rated, Content Advisor . . .**

    A. Shuts down your PC permanently.

    B. Refuses to show the page, unless you have configured Content Advisor to display unrated pages.

    C. Requests politely that you knock it off.

    D. Beeps loudly until help arrives.

Notes:

Unit 8 Exercise

1. Enable Content Advisor and set all four categories (Language, Nudity, Sex, Violence) to the far-left end of the scale (Level 0).

2. Browse, trying as hard as you can to find something potentially offensive that still manages to slip through Content Advisor. For example, you can conduct a Web search, using one of your favorite curse words as a search term. Then try to open the pages found by the search.

3. As you browse, write down the URLs (or save them as Favorites, temporarily) of pages that you were blocked from accessing.

4. Return to Content Advisor and reset all categories to Level 3.

5. Browse again and deliberately revisit pages you were blocked from in Step 2. Can you find pages that are blocked at Level 0 but acceptable at Level 3?

Printing Pages, Saving Pages, and Opening Pages on Disk

Objectives for This Unit

✓ Printing the current Web page

✓ Saving the current Web page to disk

✓ Opening and printing pages previously saved to disk

Prerequisites

▶ Opening Internet Explorer and connecting to the Internet (Unit 1)

▶ Browsing through links (Unit 1)

▶ Entering URLs (Unit 3)

So much information, so little time. . . .

On most subjects, you can find more information online than you could possibly read in a single sitting. One solution to that dilemma is to add to your Favorites menu (see Unit 4) any page that you don't have time to read. That way, you can easily return to and finish exploring that page the next time you go online.

There's a better way, though: You can capture any Web page to your hard disk and then read it later at your own sweet pace right through Internet Explorer. Or you can print pages and read the printouts later (even in bed, on the subway, in the bathroom . . .). Whichever way you choose, you have the ability to store pages and use them later, offline.

Tip: If you pay for your Internet connection by the minute, reading pages offline saves not just time but also money. When you come across a long page that you'd like to read, you needn't spend costly online minutes reading it — just print or save it, continue browsing, and read it later, offline, at your leisure, free of charge.

Although I don't pay for my Internet connection by the minute, I rarely read lengthy pages online. Instead, I browse around and *harvest* — print or save pages — as I go. Then I go offline, and *then* I read carefully. I don't save any money this way; I just find it an efficient way to work. You may, too.

save Web pages to hard disk, or print them, and read later to save time/money

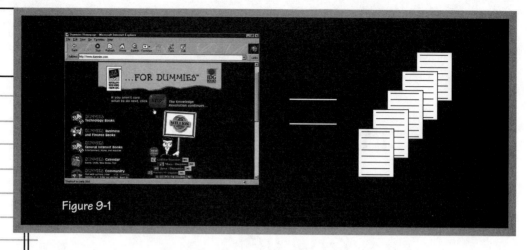

Figure 9-1: One Web page may print as one or many paper pages.

Figure 9-1

Lesson 9-1

Printing the Current Web Page

If you have any background with Windows-based applications, you've long since noticed the Print button on the toolbar and guessed what it does. But just in case you don't know, here's the scoop: The Print button on the toolbar prints the current Web page!

on the test

Before you try printing, you need to understand the difference between a "page" that you see online and a "page" that spits out of a printer. Because you can scroll around in it, a single Web page may be any length. It may take up a single screen or screen after screen after screen as you scroll through it. A paper page, on the other hand, has a fixed length. So when Internet Explorer prints a Web page, it must divide the contents of that page across as many sheets of paper as required. A single Web page may print out as several paper pages, as illustrated in Figure 9-1

To print a Web page:

single Web page may print out as multiple hard-copy pages

1 **Open Internet Explorer and your Internet connection, and visit any page you like (your choice!).**

If you don't feel like going anywhere, just print whatever page you're on — even the home page.

wait for all pictures to appear before printing

2 **Wait for all the pictures to appear completely (wait for the logo on the right side of the toolbar to stop animating).**

heads up

Waiting not only ensures that the pictures will be included in the printout but also helps Internet Explorer to format the pages properly for your printer. (In fact, Internet Explorer grays out the Print button until all the pictures have arrived.)

3 **Make sure that your printer is connected to your PC, plugged in, switched on, and loaded with paper.**

Print button brings up Print dialog box

4 **Click the Print button on the toolbar.**

The Print dialog box appears, as shown in Figure 9-2. At the top of the dialog box is a Printer section reflecting your current settings in Windows — your default printer. (If your printer isn't listed in the Name list box, you need to properly install your printer in Windows 95 and then return to Internet Explorer. See *Windows 95 For Dummies,* written by Andy Rathbone and published by IDG Books Worldwide, if you need help setting things up in Windows 95.)

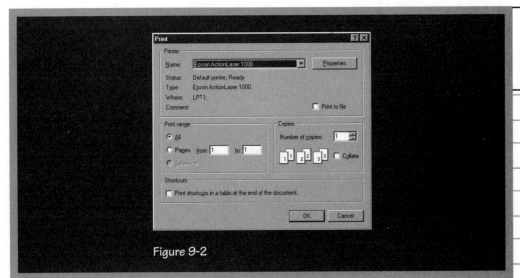

Figure 9-2

Notice that the default option in the Print Range section is All (the radio button next to All has a dot in it). That means that if you click OK, you print the entire Web page — however many printed pages that may be. If you want, you can click the radio button next to Pages and then enter just the page numbers you want to print, but this option is rarely useful because the pages aren't numbered on-screen — Internet Explorer doesn't figure out how the Web page is to be divided among paper pages until after you click OK.

A more useful option is Number of copies: Just click the arrow buttons beside the box to choose the number of copies you want to print.

5 **To print all of the current Web page, click OK.**

heads up

Internet Explorer splits the Web page up into as many individual pages as required and prints it. Depending on the Web page, Internet Explorer may change some things to make the printout legible; for example, if the Web page uses light-colored text against a dark background, Internet Explorer may print it as black text against a gray background to make it easier to read.

On the top of the printout, you can see the title of the Web page and the page number. On the bottom, the date and time you printed the page appear.

The date and time on the printout are more useful than you might think. Remember, Web pages change. If you keep printouts around for a while, you may want to know exactly when you printed the page you're reading. If the page was printed a while back, the time may have come to revisit the page online and see what's new.

Printing a page isn't the only way to have a page available for later reference, of course. The next lesson shows you how to save a page to your hard disk (stay online for that one).

extra credit

Printing shortcuts (a.k.a. links)

At the very bottom of the Print dialog box is an option unique to Internet Explorer: Print shortcuts in a table at the end of the document. If you enter a check mark there (by clicking the check box) and then click OK, the page prints as it normally would — except that a table is added to the end of the printout. The table lists all the links (Microsoft calls them *shortcuts* to confuse you; see Unit 10) in the page, along with the URLs that the links point to.

Printer section of dialog box shows current printer settings

default setting is to print entire Web page

can print more than one copy

Web page title and date/time of printout appear on printout

☑ **Progress Check**

If you can do the following, you've mastered this lesson:

❏ Understand how one Web page can equal many paper pages.

❏ Print a Web page on your printer.

Figure 9-3: To save a page to disk, choose File⇨Save As File and then give the page a name.

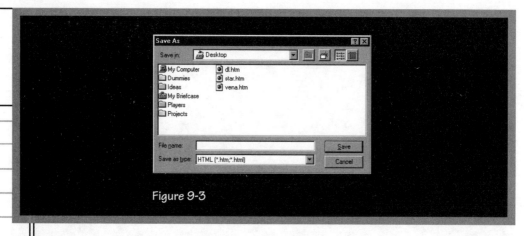

Figure 9-3

Lesson 9-2

Saving a Page to Disk

you often lose pictures/multimedia in saved pages — just text and links are saved

do not include extension in filename

on the test

You needn't kill trees to save pages for offline use. You can just save pages to your hard disk. Once they're there, you can view them later, as described in Lesson 9-3.

When you print a page, the pictures appear on the printout. But when you save a page, you save only its text and links — the pictures and other multimedia stuff, as a rule, are left behind. (Actually, in some cases, some of the pictures may appear on a saved page when you view or print it. But the reason for that is complicated, and if you wanted complicated stuff explained, you wouldn't have bought a book with the word *Dummies* in the title. All I'm sayin' is, don't be surprised if the pictures don't get saved along with the page.)

To save the current Web page to a file on your hard disk:

1 **With Internet Explorer and your Internet connection up and running, visit any page you like.**

If you don't feel like going anywhere, just save whatever page you're on — even the home page.

2 **From the Internet Explorer toolbar, choose File⇨Save As File.**

A standard Windows 95 Save As dialog box appears, as shown in Figure 9-3.

3 **Type a name for the file in the File name box:**

savetest

heads up

When typing a name for a page you're saving, do not type a filename extension (the period and three letters following the file name — like .DOC). Internet Explorer automatically assigns the extension .HTM to the file, which is the proper extension for a Web page file.

4 **Click in the Save in list box and choose your Dummies 101 folder from the drop-down list.**

Note that you can save files anywhere in Windows — even on your desktop.

5 **Click the Save button.**

You now have the page saved in your Dummies 101 folder. The next lesson shows you how to open that saved page. Close down Internet Explorer to prepare for the next lesson.

☑ Progress Check

If you can do the following, you've mastered this lesson:

❑ Save the current Web page as a file on your hard disk.

❑ Understand that media files are not always saved along with the text of the page.

Opening and Printing a Saved Page

Lesson 9-3

Once a Web page is saved as a file on your PC, you can view it in Internet Explorer — offline or on. While viewing it, you can print it if you want to.

You have two ways to open a saved page: from Windows (whether Internet Explorer is open or closed) or from within Internet Explorer.

When you open or print a saved page, whether you're connected to the Internet doesn't matter.

can be online or offline when opening or printing saved page

Opening a saved page from Windows

on the test

A saved page has the file extension .HTM. (Web pages have the extension .HTM *or* .HTML, but Internet Explorer saves 'em all as .HTM.) Windows knows that any .HTM file is a Web page and that the file is supposed to be viewed in Internet Explorer. So you don't even need to be in the Internet Explorer window to open the file. In fact, Internet Explorer can be closed — when you open an .HTM file, Internet Explorer opens automatically.

You open a file in Windows in a variety of ways. The easiest methods are to

- ▶ Double-click the file's icon anywhere in Windows (in its My Computer folder, in Windows 95 Explorer, and so on).
- ▶ Right-click the file's icon and choose Open from the context menu.

heads up

When you open a Web page file from its icon, Internet Explorer can be open or closed. If Internet Explorer is already open, Windows switches to it to display the page file. If Internet Explorer is closed, it opens automatically when you open the Web page file. When Internet Explorer opens in this automatic way, it does not connect to the Internet or access the home page; it just pops open and displays the page file.

if Internet Explorer is closed, opening a saved page opens Internet Explorer without connecting to Internet

To open a saved page:

1 **Close Internet Explorer, if you haven't already.**

Again, Internet Explorer can be open or closed when you open a file. But just for practice, start closed.

2 **Double-click the Dummies 101 folder on your desktop.**

The Dummies 101 folder opens. SAVETEST.HTM, the page you saved in Lesson 9-2, appears in the folder. Observe that saved Web pages all have the same icon — a little page with a globe on top of it.

Web page files use this icon 📄

3 **Double-click the file icon for SAVETEST.HTM.**

Internet Explorer opens (without connecting to the Internet), and the page appears on-screen (possibly minus pictures and other inline media).

4 **Choose File⇨Exit to close Internet Explorer.**

5 **Right-click the SAVETEST.HTM file icon.**

A context menu appears.

or right-click file icon and choose Open

Notes:

can open Internet
Explorer without
connecting to
Internet by clicking
Cancel in connection
dialog box

click OK to
disregard error
messages when not
connecting to
Internet

File→Open to get
Open dialog box

6 **Choose Open from the context menu.**

Internet Explorer opens (without connecting to the Internet), and the page appears on-screen. *Déjà vu.*

7 **Choose File⇨Exit to close Internet Explorer (in preparation for the next example).**

extra credit

Opening Internet Explorer without connecting

As you discovered in this lesson, opening a saved page from its icon opens Internet Explorer automatically (if it is not already open) but does not connect you to the Internet. This method allows you to read (or print) a page offline.

That's the easiest way to open Internet Explorer without going online. But you have another way:

1. Double-click the Internet icon.

Your connection dialog box opens.

2. In the connection dialog box, click Cancel.

The connection to the Internet is canceled, but Internet Explorer opens up anyway.

As Internet Explorer stirs to life, you may see an error message or two, explaining that a page can't be found. These messages are caused by Internet Explorer attempting — and failing — to access your home page through the Internet.

3. If an error message appears, click OK.

After any error messages, your home page appears anyway. Internet Explorer automatically *caches* (stores on disk) a number of pages you've visited, pictures and all. In fact, if you choose an item from your Favorites menu, it will probably appear, just as your home page did. You may feel like you're online, but you're not — you're just looking at echoes on your hard disk.

Opening a saved page from within Internet Explorer

Of course, if you're already working in Internet Explorer (offline or on), you needn't leave just to open a Web page file.

To open a page file from within Internet Explorer:

1 **Open Internet Explorer. Go ahead and connect to the Internet.**

When you open the page file, Internet Explorer can be connected to the Internet or not connected — doesn't make any difference.

2 **From the Internet Explorer toolbar, choose File⇨Open.**

The Open dialog box shown in Figure 9-4 appears. If you know the exact disk, folder, and filename of the page file (for example, C:\SILLY.HTM), you can type that in the Open dialog box and click OK. Usually, just clicking the Browse button is easier.

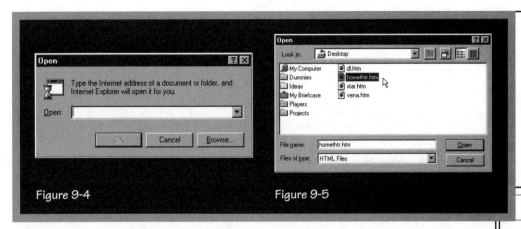

Figure 9-4: Choosing File⇨Open pops up the Open dialog box.

Figure 9-5: Clicking the Browse button from the Open dialog box opens a different Open dialog box in which you can choose a Web page file to open in Internet Explorer.

3 Click Browse.

You see a different dialog box, also called Open, as shown in Figure 9-5. From this dialog box, you navigate to the file that you want to open.

4 Click the Look in list box and choose the Dummies 101 folder from the drop down list.

All of the files in the Dummies 101 folder appear in the window beneath the Look in list.

5 Click SAVETEST.HTM. Then click OK.

The page file opens in Internet Explorer.

☑ Progress Check

If you can do the following, you've mastered this lesson:

- ❑ Open a saved Web page file from its icon on your desktop or in a folder.

- ❑ Open a saved Web page file from within Internet Explorer.

- ❑ Print a saved Web page.

Q&A session

Question: If I open a saved page and I *am* connected to the Internet, will the links in the page work even though the page is saved, not live?

Answer: Most of the time, all the links in a saved page still work when you view the page while you're online. In fact, if you open a page offline and then choose a link in it, Internet Explorer opens your connection dialog box. After you enter your password, Internet Explorer connects to the page that the link points to.

Occasionally, a link in a saved page doesn't work because the Web page author designed the link to find a page or other resource based on the page's location on the Web server. So the information stored in the link becomes meaningless when the page's location is changed to your hard disk. When you click such a link, Internet Explorer reports that it "can't find" the page the link leads to.

links in saved pages are usually functional

Printing a saved page

Whether you're online or off, and whether the page you're viewing is stored on your hard disk or on a Web server in Saskatchewan, printing is printing. Internet Explorer prints what you're looking at — it doesn't care where it came from.

So printing a saved page is identical to printing a page online — except, of course, that the saved version's printout may not include pictures. To review printing pages, see Lesson 9-1.

print saved page the same way as live pages

Recess

You don't even have to be online to enjoy the information that you find on the Web — one more way to exert control over that chaotic labyrinth. Take the following quiz and go through the unit exercise; you then have the instructor's permission to take a break from all this surfing and go hit some real waves.

Unit 9 Quiz

Notes:

For each question, circle the letter of the correct answer.

1. **How many paper pages are needed to print one Web page?**

    A. 1

    B. 7

    C. 3

    D. It depends on how long the Web page is.

2. **After you save a Web page to your hard disk, you can always . . .**

    A. Print it.

    B. View its text.

    C. View its pictures.

    D. A and B (and C only sometimes)

3. **If you view a saved page while online, will the saved page's links work?**

    A. Yes, always

    B. No, never

    C. Yes, usually

    D. Yes, obtusely

4. **When printing a Web page, you can select an option to add which of the following to the printout?**

    A. A table of the links in the page and the URLs the links point to.

    B. Your signature

    C. Mint flavor

    D. Consciousness

5. **The file type of a Web page is . . .**

    A. .WEB or .WEBB

    B. .PGE or .PAGE

    C. .NED or .EDDY

    D. .HTM or .HTML

Unit 9 Exercise

1. Using your favorite search engine, perform a search using a term that interests you (cross-stitch, *Star Wars,* African history, or whatever). Refer to Unit 5 if you get stuck.

2. When the search results — the list of pages found by the search — appear, save that search-results page to your desktop.

3. Close Internet Explorer and disconnect from the Internet.

4. On the desktop, double-click the icon of the page you just saved.

5. When the page opens in Internet Explorer, click one of the links in it.

6. When your connection dialog box opens, enter your password to connect to the Internet.

Making and Taking Internet Shortcuts

Objectives for This Unit

✓ Understanding Internet shortcuts

✓ Creating shortcuts

✓ Using shortcuts

Prerequisites

▶ Opening Internet Explorer and connecting to the Internet (Unit 1)

▶ Browsing through links (Unit 2)

▶ Entering URLs (Unit 3)

▶ Creating Favorites (Unit 4)

In Unit 4, you created a menu of Favorites. Each of your Favorites represents a Web page — choosing the Favorite instructs Internet Explorer to go to that page.

Although you didn't know it in Unit 4, each time that you create a Favorite, you create a small file called an *Internet shortcut,* which contains the URL of that Web page. Opening an Internet shortcut file tells Internet Explorer to go to that Web page. In fact, when you open an Internet shortcut, Internet Explorer opens automatically.

Internet shortcut = file containing URL

You can easily create your own Internet shortcuts in several different ways. After you create a shortcut, it works anywhere in Windows. You can put it anywhere you would put any file — on your desktop or in any folder. You can copy it (each copy works just like the original) or move it from folder to folder. And when you're done with it, you can delete it — it's just a file.

Why bother with shortcuts? You can do the following with 'em:

double-click shortcut on desktop to open Internet Explorer and jump to that page

▶ Put 'em on your desktop. By simply double-clicking an icon on your desktop, you open Internet Explorer and jump to a desired page — KAPOW! You don't even cruise by the home page on the way!

▶ Put 'em in folders, organized by subject or whatever, as a way of building a library of pages that you like to visit.

attach shortcut to
e-mail for recipient's
easy access to
that page

• Send 'em in e-mail messages to friends. You can attach an Internet shortcut to an e-mail message. When the shortcut arrives on the recipient's computer with your message, your recipient can use the shortcut to go where it leads (as long as your recipient uses Windows 95). This attachment idea is a great way to share your favorite pages with friends, or to invite guests to a chat session.

Interested? Read on. . . .

Is a link a shortcut?

In various places in Internet Explorer, you see links described as "shortcuts." For example, when you point to a link, the Internet Explorer status bar (in the lower-left corner) reports `Shortcut to` wherever the link leads. You may also see links called shortcuts in Internet Explorer's Help file.

Microsoft has apparently chosen to call links shortcuts as a way of standardizing Web terminology. Anything that leads to a page becomes a "shortcut," whether it's a link or the type of shortcut that you learn about in this unit. However, Microsoft's efforts create more confusion than they solve. A *link* is text or a picture in a Web page that jumps to another place. A *shortcut* is a little Windows file that you can create yourself and use to conveniently jump to a Web resource. They're two different animals, despite the fact that they both lead to pages.

More important, as you travel the Web, you'll see that everybody in the universe calls a link a link (or *hotlink* or *hyperlink*), except Microsoft. So there's no reason to adopt Microsoft's terminology — nobody else has.

In this tutorial, a link is a link, and a shortcut is a shortcut, and a rose is a rose. So there.

Lesson 10-1

Creating a Shortcut

Internet shortcut
icon; all Internet
shortcuts have the
extension .URL

An Internet shortcut is a small file that contains the URL of an Internet resource. In fact, all Internet shortcuts use the file extension .URL. When you see them on your desktop or in folders, Internet shortcuts use a little Internet icon (a globe), which makes them easy to spot.

Making an Internet shortcut from a page

create shortcut
while on that page —
but not on saved
version of page!

The easiest way to create an Internet shortcut is to do so while visiting the page to which you want a shortcut.

heads up

When creating a shortcut to a page, visit the page online — don't open a saved version, as you learned to do in Unit 9. If you create a shortcut while viewing a saved page, the shortcut will open the saved page on your PC instead of going to the one online.

Figure 10-1

Figure 10-1: While viewing a page, choose File⇨Create Shortcut to place a shortcut to the page on your desktop.

To create a shortcut to a page:

1 Open Internet Explorer and your Internet connection.

2 Visit any page you like.

3 From the Internet Explorer toolbar, choose File⇨Create Shortcut.

A message like the one in Figure 10-1 appears.

4 Click OK.

The shortcut is on your Windows desktop. You may leave it there or move it into any folder on your PC. The shortcut works the same way no matter where it is. You may also copy it as many times as you want; each copy works just like the original.

You don't have to even be on the page that you want to create a shortcut for — the next exercise shows you how to create a shortcut from a link..

File→Create
Shortcut to put
shortcut of current
page on desktop

can move shortcut
anywhere — works
the same

extra credit

Don't call me "Shorty"

You may rename a shortcut that you've created if the default name that Internet Explorer gives it is not descriptive enough. To rename a shortcut:

1. Find the shortcut's file icon and click the shortcut's name once, wait a second, and then click the name again.

The idea here is to wait long enough between each click so that Windows doesn't think you're double-clicking.

2. Type the new name.

3. Press Enter.

can rename
shortcut by clicking
shortcut's name
twice

Making a shortcut from a link

As you may recall from Unit 4, you can add a page to your Favorites menu from the page itself or from a link that leads to the page. The same is true for shortcuts.

To create a shortcut from a link:

1 Open a page on which links appear, and locate a link that leads to a page you'd like to have a shortcut to.

Figure 10-2: To create a shortcut from a link, right-click the link and choose Copy Shortcut. Then paste the shortcut on your desktop or in a folder.

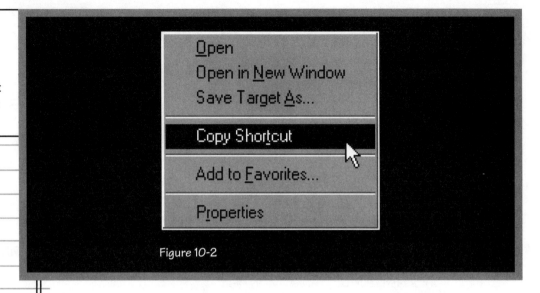

Figure 10-2

☑ Progress Check

If you can do the following, you've mastered this lesson:

❑ Create a shortcut to the current page.

❑ Create a shortcut from a link.

Your choice. If you need a starting place, try the Dummies home page at `http://www.dummies.com/`, and choose any link there.

2 **Right-click a link to open its context menu, as shown in Figure 10-2.**

3 **Choose Copy Shortcut.**

A message appears on the status bar (lower-left corner of the screen) to inform you that the shortcut has been copied to the Windows Clipboard. To finish the job, you must paste the shortcut where you want it to go.

4 **Paste the shortcut on the desktop by right-clicking an empty area of the desktop and choosing Paste Shortcut from the context menu.**

Or you can paste the shortcut in a folder by opening (or creating and opening) a folder and choosing Edit⇨Paste from the folder's menu bar.

When you use the shortcut (as described in the next lesson), it takes you to the page that the link pointed to, even with Internet Explorer closed. Go ahead and close your Internet connection to prepare for the next lesson.

Lesson 10-2

Using Shortcuts

on the test

Windows knows that any file with the extension .URL is an Internet shortcut and that Internet Explorer must be open to travel to the URL that the shortcut contains. So you can just open the shortcut file without bothering to open Internet Explorer first.

Opening a shortcut

To open a shortcut file so that Internet Explorer goes where the shortcut leads:

1 **If you haven't already, close Internet Explorer and disconnect from the Internet.**

Remember that shortcuts work just as well when Internet Explorer is open.

shortcuts work whether Internet Explorer is open or closed

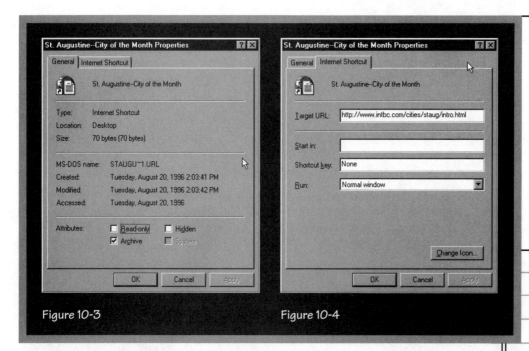

Figure 10-3

Figure 10-4

Figure 10-3: To see the Properties dialog box for an Internet shortcut, right-click the shortcut and choose Properties from the context menu.

Figure 10-4: In the Properties dialog box, click the Internet Shortcut tab to see the Target URL — the page to which Internet Explorer goes when you open the shortcut.

2 **On the desktop, double-click a shortcut icon that you created in Lesson 10-1.**

Of course, as with all Windows files, you have several different ways to open a shortcut file. The results are always the same. You can

- Double-click the file icon.
- Right-click the icon and choose Open from the context menu.
- In a folder, click the icon once to highlight it; then choose File⇨Open from the folder's menu bar.

3 **In the connection dialog box that appears, enter your password to connect to the Internet.**

Internet Explorer opens and displays the Web page to which the shortcut points.

Q&A session

Question: What if I create a shortcut and then forget where it leads? Can I find out where a shortcut leads without actually using it?

Answer: Like all files in Windows 95, every Internet shortcut has its own Properties dialog box. To see the Properties dialog box for a shortcut, right-click the shortcut and choose Properties from the context menu. The Properties dialog box appears, as shown in Figures 10-3 and 10-4.

The General tab of the Properties dialog box (see Figure 10-3) shows general information about the shortcut, such as the time and date it was created. Click the Internet Shortcut tab (see Figure 10-4) to see the Target URL — that's the URL to which the shortcut leads.

[margin notes]

double-clicking shortcut icon opens Internet Explorer and goes directly to that page

right-click shortcut and choose Properties to get details on shortcut

Target URL = URL to which shortcut leads

Figure 10-5: Your Favorites folder, packed with Internet shortcuts.

Figure 10-6: Right-click an empty area of the desktop to display the desktop's context menu. You can use it to paste a shortcut that you've copied to the Clipboard.

Figure 10-7: After copying a shortcut in your Favorites folder and pasting the copy on your desktop, you have the same shortcut in two places — and both work the same.

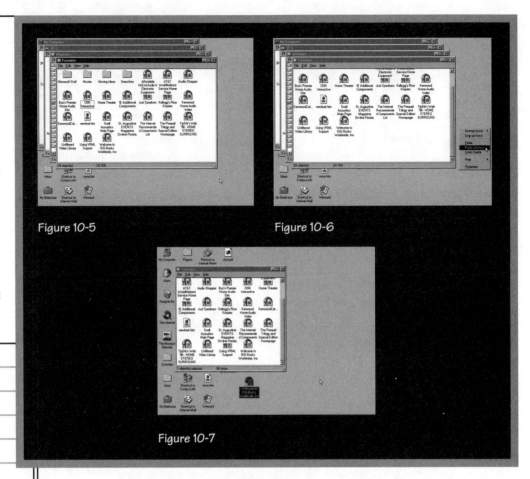

Figure 10-5   Figure 10-6

Figure 10-7

Favorites menu
items are Internet
shortcuts stored in
C:\Windows\Favorites
folder

can cut/copy and
paste shortcuts
from or to Favorites
folder

navigate to
Favorites folder in
My Computer and
drag and drop
shortcuts

Copying shortcuts from Favorites

Each item that you add to your Favorites menu is actually an Internet shortcut. The Favorites shortcuts (and folders containing Favorites shortcuts) are stored on your PC in a folder called Favorites (see Figure 10-5). Any Internet shortcut or folder stored in the Favorites folder appears automatically in your Favorites menu.

That means you can do any of the following:

▶ Cut a shortcut from your Favorites folder and paste it anywhere else to remove it from your Favorites menu and use it elsewhere as a shortcut.

▶ Copy a shortcut from your Favorites folder and paste it elsewhere so that you have two shortcuts to the same page — one in your Favorites menu and the other on your desktop or in another folder.

▶ Move or copy a shortcut that you've created into your Favorites folder to add it to your Favorites menu.

Try it out (you don't need to have Internet Explorer open for this exercise):

1 **Double-click the My Computer icon on the desktop.**

2 **In the My Computer window, double-click the icon representing your hard disk (usually C), double-click the Windows folder, and then double-click the Favorites folder.**

3 **Drag one of your Favorites shortcuts from the folder and drop it on your desktop.**

After you drop, the shortcut appears on your desktop, and it has been removed from your Favorites menu. (If you don't believe me, open Internet Explorer and click the Favorites button.)

4 **Return the shortcut to the Favorites folder by dragging it from the desktop to the Favorites folder and then dropping it.**

There — no harm done. The next steps show you an alternative way of doing the same thing you just did in Step 3.

5 **Right-click any shortcut in your Favorites menu.**

The shortcut's context menu appears.

6 **Choose Copy from the context menu.**

You've copied the shortcut to the Windows Clipboard.

7 **Right-click an empty area of the desktop.**

The desktop's context menu appears (see Figure 10-6).

8 **Choose Paste Shortcut.**

A copy of the shortcut appears on the desktop (see Figure 10-7). Now you have the same shortcut in two places: in your Favorites folder (and therefore in your Favorites menu) and on the desktop.

Recess

That was a quick and simple unit — go ahead and do some shortcutting before you take the quiz and do the unit exercise. Then you can move on to the Part Test and Lab Assignment.

☑ **Progress Check**

If you can do the following, you've mastered this lesson:

❑ Move a shortcut from folder to folder or to and from the desktop.

❑ Copy a shortcut.

Unit 10 Quiz

For each question, circle the letter of the correct answer.

1. **An Internet shortcut is . . .**

   A. The same thing as a link.

   B. Anything that speeds up your day.

   C. A toolbar button.

   D. A file containing an URL.

2. **You create shortcuts by . . .**

   A. Viewing a page and choosing File⇨Create Shortcut.

   B. Viewing a page and then clicking the Create Shortcut toolbar button.

   C. Right-clicking a link to copy a shortcut and then pasting the copy somewhere.

   D. A or C

3. **If you move a shortcut from the place where it was created to somewhere else . . .**

    A. It works just the same from its new location.

    B. It no longer works — the link has been broken.

    C. It no longer works, due to corporate downsizing.

    D. It works, but its work goes unrewarded.

4. **If you move a shortcut out of your Favorites folder . . .**

    A. You can still use the shortcut from its new location.

    B. You can rename the shortcut.

    C. The shortcut disappears from your Favorites menu.

    D. All of the above

5. **To learn the URL to which a shortcut points . . .**

    A. Point to the shortcut and wait a second.

    B. Right-click the shortcut, choose Properties, and click the Internet Shortcut tab.

    C. Drag the shortcut and drop it in your Recycle Bin.

    D. All of the above

Unit 10 Exercise

1. For your next several browsings, do not create any Favorites. Instead, create an Internet shortcut on your desktop for any pages that interest you.

2. After you have several shortcuts on your desktop, make a habit of using one to start each browsing session instead of simply opening Internet Explorer at the home page.

Part III Review

Unit 8 Summary

▶ **Understanding ratings:** Ratings are defined by an independent committee and applied to Web pages by the committee or by the page's authors. The ratings determine the levels of harsh language, violence, nudity, and sex on the page.

▶ **Enabling Content Advisor:** To enable Internet Explorer's Content Advisor, click the Enable Ratings button on the Security tab of the Options dialog box (View⇨Options).

▶ **Customizing Content Advisor:** To customize what Content Advisor blocks out, click Settings on the Security tab of the Options dialog box (View⇨Options) and customize the settings on the tabs of the Content Advisor dialog box.

Unit 9 Summary

▶ **Printing the current Web page:** To print the current Web page, click the Print button on Internet Explorer's toolbar, select any printing options you desire, and click OK.

▶ **Saving the current Web page as a file on your PC:** To save the current page, choose File⇨Save as File. Type a name for the page file (and select a folder, if you want) and then click Save.

▶ **Viewing a page saved on disk:** To open and view a Web page file that you saved to disk, double-click its file icon.

▶ **Printing a page saved on disk:** To print a Web page file that you saved to disk, double-click its file icon to open and view it in Internet Explorer; then print it as you would any other Web page.

Unit 10 Summary

▶ **Creating a shortcut to a Web page:** To create an Internet shortcut to the current Web page, choose File⇨Create shortcut.

▶ **Creating a shortcut from a link:** To create a shortcut from a link in a page, right-click the link, choose Copy Shortcut, right-click the folder (or the desktop) where you want to store the shortcut, and choose Paste Shortcut.

▶ **Using an Internet shortcut:** To use an Internet shortcut to go to a Web page, double-click the shortcut's file icon.

Part III Test

The questions on this test cover all the material presented in Part III, Units 8 through 10.

True False

Each statement is either true or false.

T   F   1. You can view saved pages while offline.

T   F   2. You use an Internet shortcut by double-clicking it.

T   F   3. When you print a Web page, you can choose to print multiple copies of it.

T   F   4. You can configure Content Advisor to either display or block unrated pages.

T   F   5. Content Advisor can block pages containing political or religious content that you don't approve of.

T   F   6. The links on a saved page don't work anymore.

T   F   7. You can create an Internet shortcut from the current page or from a link.

T   F   8. You can print only pages viewed online.

T   F   9. Saved pages often do not include pictures.

T   F   10. Most pages on the Web have been rated for content.

Multiple Choice

For each of the following questions, circle the correct answer.

11. Content Advisor can censor . . .

   A. The entire Internet.

   B. Web pages, but not any other Internet content (Chat, e-mail, and so on).

   C. All content stored on your PC.

   D. Web pages and newsgroups.

12. To open Internet Explorer without connecting to the Internet, you can . . .

   A. Open Internet Explorer and then click Cancel in the connection dialog box.

   B. Open Internet Explorer by opening a saved Web page on your PC.

   C. Right-click the Internet icon on your desktop and choose Open Si! — Connect No!

   D. A or B.

13. You open a saved Web page by . . .

   A. Double-clicking its file icon.

   B. Right-clicking the icon and choosing Open.

   C. Choosing File➪Open in Internet Explorer.

   D. All of the above.

14. An Internet shortcut can lead to . . .

   A. A migraine.

   B. Any URL.

   C. Harder, more dangerous shortcuts.

   D. Happiness.

Part III Test

15. **Your Favorites are really . . .**

    A. Somebody else's Favorites — you're a conformist.

    B. Ordinary saved pages, saved in the Favorites folder.

    C. Ordinary Internet shortcuts, saved in the Windows\Favorites folder.

    D. Boring.

16. **The RSAC, which defines the ratings system used by the Content Advisor, is . . .**

    A. The Royal Security Approval Committee.

    B. The Ratings System Advisory Committee.

    C. The Regional Strategic Air Command.

    D. The Recreational Software Advisory Council.

Matching

17. **Match up each icon with what it does:**

    A.   1. Opens a saved Web page (.HTM file)

    B.   2. Prints the current Web page

    C.   3. Opens a shortcut to an URL

Part III Lab Assignment

This Lab Assignment tests your ability to work with the Content Advisor.

Step 1: Reconfigure Internet Explorer

Enable the Content Advisor (View⇨Options⇨Security) and set all categories except Violence to rating level 5. Set Violence to level 0 (no violence whatsoever permitted).

Customize the Content Advisor to permit the display of blocked pages when the supervisor password is supplied.

Step 2: Browse the Web and notice effects

As you make your next few Web excursions, observe how the experience has changed.

Step 3: Override blocked pages

When Content Advisor blocks a page, override the block by entering your supervisor password; then save or print the page. Consider whether Content Advisor's ruling was appropriate.

Step 4: Reconfigure Content Advisor as desired

After evaluating your new configuration, go back and reconfigure or disable Content Advisor, according to your own needs.

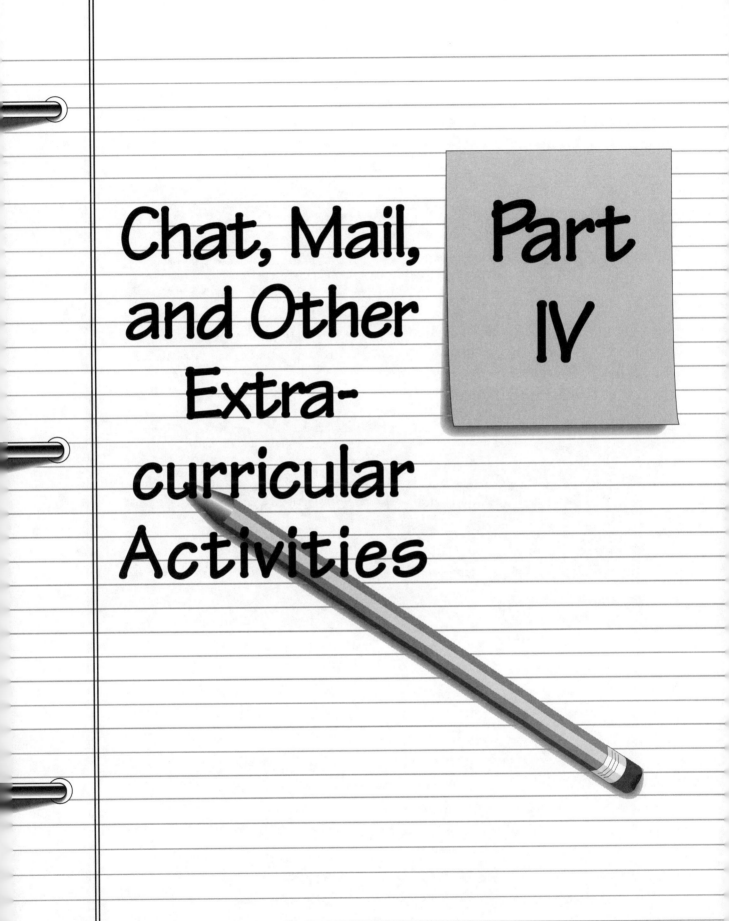

Chat, Mail, and Other Extra-curricular Activities

Part IV

In this part . . .

As you've seen in the preceding parts, all by itself, Internet Explorer takes you far and wide. But Internet Explorer is not alone; it's supplemented by a family of Microsoft companion products that take you even further. Of these companions (all of which are included on the CD-ROM with this book), the most important are

- **Comic Chat:** A program that allows you to participate in live, online disscusions.

- **Internet Mail:** A program for sending and receiving electronic mail (e-mail) through the Internet.

- **Internet News:** A program for reading and contributing to any of thousands of topical online discussion groups.

- **NetMeeting:** A program for conversing and collaborating in a variety of ways, including making voice telephone calls — right through your PC and the Internet.

Each of these companion products is integrated with Internet Explorer, and yet each also works on its own as an application unto itself. So in this part, you detour from Internet Explorer into the realms opened up by its companions: chat, mail, news and phone.

Chatting "Live" with Fellow Surfers

Objectives for This Unit

✓ Installing Microsoft Comic Chat

✓ Finding and choosing a chat room

✓ Chatting with others

Prerequisites

♦ Opening Internet Explorer and connecting to the Internet (Unit 1)

♦ Browsing the Web through links (Unit 2)

♦ Entering URLs (Unit 3)

♦ Comic Chat

on the CD

W hen you engage in a *chat* on the Internet, you join a live conversation with other Internet users, who may be anywhere in the world. The conversation is conducted through typed messages. Everything you type appears on the screen of everybody else participating in the chat. Everything the other chatters type appears on your screen. Each participant's statements are labeled with a nickname to identify who's talking, as shown in Figure 11-1. Note that the participants in a chat (known as *members*) choose their own nicknames and rarely share their real names — you can be whomever you want to be, and so can everyone else. When you chat, you often converse not with other people but with other people's alter egos.

Each of the many chats underway day and night on the Net takes place within a *chat room* (also called a *channel*), a window set aside exclusively for one conversation. In most rooms, the conversation is restricted to a given topic. In a *Star Trek* chat room, for example, folks chat about *Star Trek*; in a singles chat room, folks talk about stuff that singles like to talk about.

Chat can be a lot of fun, and it can be educational because it allows you to converse with and learn from folks who have widely differing backgrounds. But frankly, a large percentage of the folks who try chat tire of it quickly. The chat channels are often populated by too many lonely people with nothing to say, all hoping you will entertain them somehow. Common are exchanges like this one:

chats take place in chat rooms (also called channels)

most chats discuss given topic

chats are often boring but can be fun

Figure 11-1: A chat session, as it appears through a common chat program.

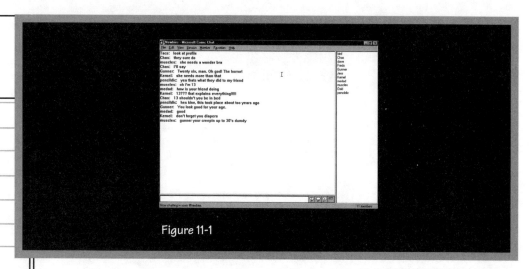

Figure 11-1

Notes:

FREDO: Hi.

VGER: Hi.

FREDO: What's up?

VGER: Not much. You?

FREDO: Not much.

VGER: Where is everybody?

FREDO: Dunno. I'm new.

VGER: Me, too.

FREDO: Expecting anybody?

VGER: Nope. You?

FREDO: Nope.

VGER: Well, bye.

FREDO: Wait . . . tell me what you're wearing. . . .

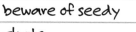

beware of seedy chats

heads up

Boring conversation isn't the only thing to be wary of with chats. Many chat rooms are devoted to so-called "adult" conversation, from the harmlessly erotic to the truly depraved. And frankly, some pretty seedy folks seem to visit even the most wholesome chat rooms when they can't find anybody else to talk to. Participating in a chat room is a little like striking up a conversation with strangers in New York's Times Square: You may enjoy a fascinating, enriching talk with people from any country or culture, or you may find yourself trapped with a militia member warning you to stock ammo for the coming revolt against the Commie liberals.

Fortunately, to escape an uncomfortable chat, you just exit the room — other chatters don't know your real name or e-mail address (unless you tell them), so nobody can follow you. Still, you should enter the world of chat with a measure of caution — unless, of course, "adult" talk is your thing and nutballs don't scare you.

Content Advisor offers no protection against X-rated chat rooms

on the test

Note: Internet Explorer's built-in censor, Content Advisor (see Unit 8), does nothing to protect you or your unsupervised kids from entering an X-rated chat room. If you allow your kids to use the Net without supervision and you're concerned about whom they may meet in a chat, you may want to consider leaving Comic Chat off your PC altogether.

But remember, you'll find at least as many decent chats as indecent ones on the Net. Many terrific chat rooms let you debate and discuss hobbies, politics, or other interests or just hang out and shoot the breeze. If you join the right chat room at the right time, chat offers wondrous rewards in fun, fascinating conversations, and the kick of communicating live with people who may be anywhere in the world.

So give chat a try. Just be prepared for anything.

Setting Up Comic Chat

Lesson 11-1

on the test

Real chats don't happen on Web servers — they happen on *chat servers,* more properly called *IRC servers* (IRC stands for Internet Relay Chat, the full formal name for Chat). Just as you need a Web browser to communicate with a Web server, you need a program called a *chat client* to communicate with a chat server.

on the CD

Internet Explorer has no built-in chat client. Fortunately, you'll find a fun chat client on the *Dummies 101: Internet Explorer 3 For Windows 95* CD-ROM. Microsoft Comic Chat not only gets you into sessions on chat servers but can also work in concert with Internet Explorer so you can jump easily from your Web browsing to chatting and back again.

Like any chat client, Comic Chat lets you communicate with chat servers. You can view the list of chat rooms, join a chat room, read what everyone says in the chat room, and make your own contributions to the discussion. What's different about Comic Chat is the way it shows the conversation.

A typical chat client, as shown earlier in Figure 11-1, just shows the text of the conversation, a line at a time, and labels each line with the speaker's nickname. Comic Chat displays the conversation like a comic strip (see Figure 11-2), using little cartoon characters to represent members and showing the member's words in cartoon word balloons. Folks at Microsoft think this approach makes chatting feel more human, more fun.

heads up

Not all chatters you'll encounter use Comic Chat. Most folks use ordinary text IRC clients; they see your statements labeled with your nickname but don't see your comic character. Conversely, on your display, Comic Chat converts all statements in a chat — even those made by users of text-only clients — into comics. On your display, other Comic Chat users appear in their chosen cartoon characters, while Comic Chat automatically chooses an unused character for each non–Comic Chat user.

Comic Chat is not installed automatically when you install Internet Explorer. You must install it yourself, which takes only a minute or two. You need to install this book's CD-ROM before going through the following steps (see Appendix B) and be sure the CD-ROM is in the drive.

To install Comic Chat:

1 **Click the Start menu and choose Programs⇨Dummies 101⇨ Dummies 101 - Internet Explorer 3 Installer.**

---

need chat client to communicate with chat (IRC) server

Comic Chat differs from other chat clients by displaying chats as comic strips

most chatters don't have Comic Chat

must have already installed book's CD-ROM

Figure 11-2: Microsoft Comic Chat makes chats look like comic strips.

Figure 11-2

Comic Chat icon

☑ **Progress Check**

If you can do the following, you've mastered this lesson:

❑ Understand that not all chatters use Comic Chat.

❑ Set up Comic Chat on your computer.

2 **Click the Comic Chat Add-On button.**

A dialog box opens, asking whether you want to install Comic Chat.

3 **Click Yes.**

The license agreement appears. Make sure that you read it before going to Step 4.

4 **Click Yes.**

Several status reports appear while Comic Chat sets up on your PC. After the installation is finished, a dialog box appears, thanking you for downloading Comic Chat (which you didn't do, but hey), and reporting, "Installation Complete!"

Q&A session

Question: If Microsoft updates Comic Chat, how do I get the new version?

Answer: Visit the Microsoft Comic Chat page, where new versions will be made available for downloading. The URL is

```
http://www.microsoft.com/ie/comichat/
```

Lesson 11-2

Entering a Chat Room

Ready to hit a chat? Here goes. In this lesson, I take you onto a chat server (where you can see a chat in progress) and also through a few final, niggling setup steps that must be performed after you open Comic Chat.

Programs→Microsoft
Comic Chat→
Microsoft Comic
Chat connects to
chat server

Opening Comic Chat and connecting to the server

You can be online or off when you begin this next procedure. If you're offline when you begin, Comic Chat connects to the Internet automatically.

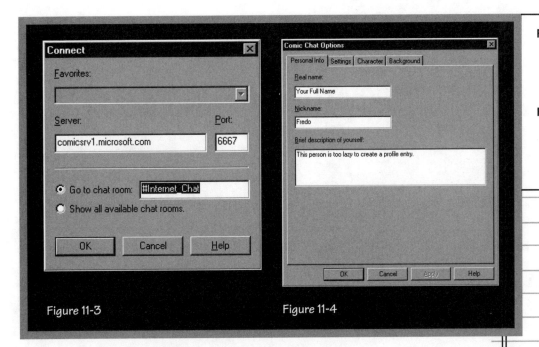

Figure 11-3

Figure 11-4

Figure 11-3: When you open Comic Chat, the connection dialog box opens to connect you to the chat server.

Figure 11-4: On the Personal Info tab, type a nickname for yourself — and leave the rest of the dialog box alone!

1 **Open Comic Chat by clicking the Start button and choosing Programs⇨Microsoft Comic Chat⇨Microsoft Comic Chat.**

A Connect dialog box like the one in Figure 11-3 opens.

2 **Click the radio button next to the Show all available chat rooms option and then click OK.**

If you're not already connected to the Internet, your connection dialog box opens so that you can connect.

Once you're online, a list of all chat rooms available on the server appears. You are now connected to a chat server and ready to chat — except that, as a new user, you have not yet selected a nickname and a comic character, as described next.

Choosing a nickname, character, and background

Before you can join in a chat, you must create a nickname for yourself — the name that all others in the chat room will know you by. Also, you must choose a comic character to play. On your display and on the display of all other Comic Chat users, the character you choose appears to "speak" the statements that you contribute to the chat. You can also select a background that appears behind the characters in each panel of the comic, as you see it on your screen (other Comic Chat users can pick their own backgrounds, too).

After you choose a nickname, character, and background, Comic Chat remembers them for future sessions. You do not need to choose them again, unless you want to. Note that you can change these selections whenever you feel like it.

To choose a nickname, character, and background:

1 **Choose View⇨Options.**

Comic Chat's Options dialog box appears, with the Personal Info tab selected (as shown in Figure 11-4).

Notes:

nickname/
character/back-
ground stay in place
for future sessions

Personal Info tab of
Comic Chat Options
dialog box controls
nickname,
character,
background

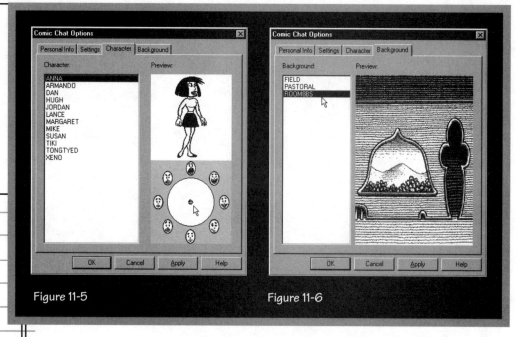

Figure 11-5: Click a name in the Character column, and you see the character in the Preview column.

Figure 11-6: On the Background tab, choose the background to go behind the characters in each panel of the Comic Chat.

Figure 11-5

Figure 11-6

Notes:

make nickname one
word and unusual

do not enter real
name or description
on Personal Info tab!

emotion wheel
(below Preview box)
changes
character's
expression

background
appears behind
characters in each
panel

heads up

2 **Click in the <u>N</u>ickname box and type a nickname for yourself.**

When choosing a nickname, keep the following in mind:

- Your nickname should be one word, using no spaces or punctuation.

- Your nickname should be unusual to reduce the chances that another chatter has chosen the same nickname. If you attempt to enter a room where someone is already using the same nickname as you, Comic Chat prompts you to change your nickname before entering.

On the Personal Info tab, you can also enter your real name and a description of yourself — but I *strongly* recommend against doing so. Users of some chat clients (including Comic Chat) have the ability to open profiles of the other chatters in the room. Any information that you supply as your real name and personal description goes into your profile and may be read by anyone you chat with. Most chat members are good folks, but maintaining your anonymity is your safest bet.

3 **Click the Character tab.**

The Character tab opens, as shown in Figure 11-5. When you select any name in the Character column, the Preview column shows what that character looks like — or rather, what you will look like to other Comic Chat users. Beneath the character preview, an emotion wheel appears. Click any of the faces in the emotion wheel to see what the character looks like in a given mood (see Lesson 11-3 for more about the emotion wheel).

4 **Select the character you want to play.**

Note that someone else in the chat may use the same character as you. That's OK. Chatters can share characters, but not nicknames.

5 **Click the Background tab.**

The Background tab (see Figure 11-6) allows you to select from several available cartoon backgrounds for the characters to appear with when chatting. When you select any entry in the Background column, the background appears in the Preview column.

6 **Choose a background and click OK.**

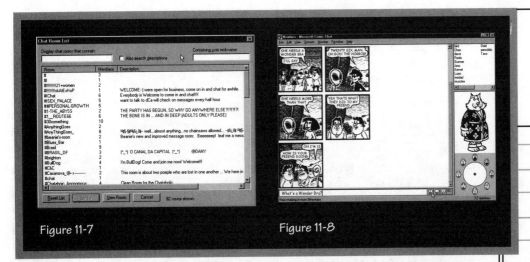

Figure 11-7

Figure 11-8

Figure 11-7: To enter any room in the list, double-click its name.

Figure 11-8: The Chat window is where chats happen.

Q&A session

Question: I see a Favorites choice on Comic Chat's menu bar, just like the Favorites item on Internet Explorer's menu bar. Does it do what I think it does?

Answer: A star sticker on your forehead! When visiting a chat room you like, choose Favorites⇨Add to Favorites. The next time you open Comic Chat, you can choose any of your Favorites from the pull-down list in the connection dialog box (refer to Figure 11-3).

Entering a room

To enter a chat, you select a room from the list that appears after you've chosen your nickname, character, and background. Figure 11-7 shows the list of all chats available on Microsoft's chat server when I visited it (the list changes from time to time). Observe that the name of each room begins with a hash mark (#). In the list, the name of the room is followed by the number of members currently in the room and a description of the conversation that takes place there.

Not every chat room has a description, but the subject of the chat is usually pretty easy to guess from the room's name. (Do you really need a description to guess what !!!!!!!!21+women is all about?)

For a safe and friendly first excursion, enter the room called #Newbies, designed as a practice room for new chat users.

1 **In the Chat Room List, scroll down the alphabetical Room column until you see the room #Newbies listed.**

2 **Double-click #Newbies.**

The Chat window opens, as shown in Figure 11-8. When you first enter a room, you won't see any comic panels immediately. The server shows you only what's been said since you entered the room. So after you enter, you may have to wait a few moments until statements begin appearing.

When you enter the room, everyone in the room is automatically notified that you've arrived. So don't be surprised if someone says hi.

heads up

The next lesson shows you how to contribute to the conversation, if you so choose.

Favorites→Add to Favorites puts current chat room on Favorites list for easy access later

every chat room name begins with #

#Newbies = practice room for new chatters

server shows only what's been said since entered room

everyone in room is notified when someone enters

Notes:

can try to connect
to chat servers not
listed, but Comic
Chat can't connect
to most

net-lag = variable
time between
sending message
and server
receiving message;
causes jumbled
messages

with practice, can
learn to follow
conversations

Q&A session

Question: Can I contact any IRC server with Comic Chat?

Answer: Yes and no. If you look back at Figure 11-3, you may notice that you can enter the address of any server in place of Microsoft's chat server. By entering a server address and selecting Show all available chat rooms, you should be able to connect to any IRC server and display the list of chat rooms there. You may double-click the name of any chat room in the list to join the chat.

Unfortunately, Comic Chat has a number of small, but debilitating, technical quirks that prevent it from successfully connecting to most common IRC servers. If you have the address of an IRC server, you're welcome to try entering it — it just may work. For now, though, there's more than enough chatting to be done on Microsoft's server. Hopefully, Microsoft will fix the incompatibilities in the next version of Comic Chat.

Understanding the chat display

on the test

When you first visit a chat room in which two or more members are already chatting, you may notice that the conversation appears a bit jumbled. Someone asks a question, someone else asks another question, someone answers the second question, and then someone answers the first question. The statements often seem not to follow the logical order of a conversation, making the chat a little hard to follow. The more people in the room, the more jumbled the conversation appears.

The jumbling is caused in part by *net-lag,* the time required for information to travel between the chatters and the server. Each chatter's words take a different amount of time to reach the server because of several factors, including the speaker's location in the world and modem speed. Also, some speakers take more time to compose and submit their statements than others. The result is a jumbled-looking conversation where you may see several statements appearing between any given statement and a direct response to that statement.

The solution? Practice. Hang around in chat rooms long enough, and by osmosis, you pick up the ability to follow conversations — seriously! Just watch the flow, and eventually your brain will develop the ability to sort it all out.

extra credit

Entering a Comic Chat from a Web page

Yes, you can jump from a Web page into a chat, although few Web pages are set up for that purpose. The best place to see how you can do this is on Microsoft's Comic Chat Rooms page.

1. **Open Internet Explorer and connect to the Internet.**

2. **Go to Microsoft's Comic Chat Rooms page at**

   ```
   http://www.microsoft.com/ie/comichat/rooms.htm
   ```

(continued)

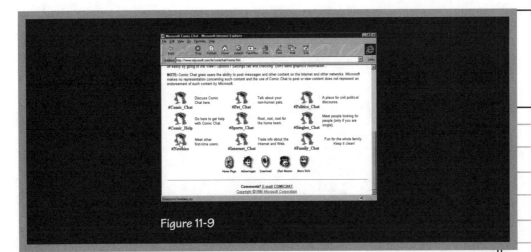

Figure 11-9

(continued)

Scroll down the page to the group of chat icons, shown in Figure 11-9. The nine chats shown on this page are only a small sampling of the chat rooms you may visit. However, these chat rooms are specially set up for users of Comic Chat. That means most, if not all, of the other members will be Comic Chat users.

3. **Click any of the chat icons.**

The Open dialog box appears, as if you were downloading a file. You see this dialog box whenever you open a chat room from a Web page.

4. **In the Open dialog box, click the radio button for Open it; then click OK.**

Comic Chat opens within the Internet Explorer window and takes you right into the chat room. You can now chat just as you would if you had opened Comic Chat the regular way. You can also change to any room on the server, as described in Lesson 11-3.

While in the chat room, you can click the Favorites button on Internet Explorer's toolbar to add the room to your Internet Explorer favorites — not your Comic Chat Favorites.

Open dialog box appears when opening chat room from Web page

☑ **Progress Check**

If you can do the following, you've mastered this lesson:

❑ Choose a nickname, character, and background for chatting.

❑ Enter a chat room from the Chat Room List.

Contributing to the Conversation

Lesson 11-3

on the test

The Comic Chat window has five parts, as shown in Figure 11-10:

▶ **Viewing pane:** Where the Comic Chat unfolds before your eyes

▶ **Member list pane:** List of all members in the room

▶ **Self-view pane:** A picture of what you look like to other Comic Chat users

viewing pane = where chat comic appears

can see all members in room in member list pane

Figure 11-10: The Comic Chat window has five parts.

Notes:

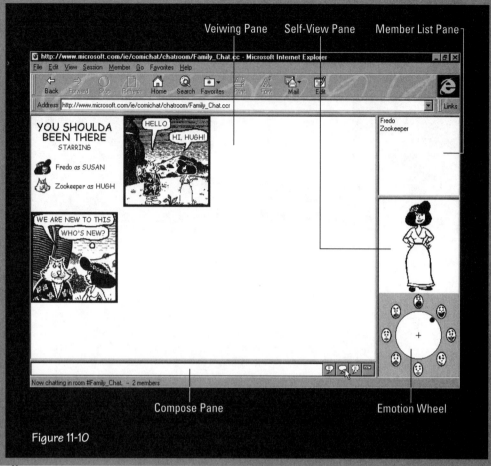

Figure 11-10

can see own character in self-view pane

pick character's expressions from emotion wheel

type messages and choose word balloon style in compose pane

can just lurk in chat room without saying anything

- **Emotion wheel:** A ring of different expressions that you can select for your character when making a statement

- **Compose pane:** The box where you type and send your messages, along with a set of buttons (on the right) that let you control the style of cartoon word balloon in which your statements appear

Unless somebody asks you a question that requires a response, you are not obligated to add anything to the conversation. In fact, just *lurking* in a chat room — watching the chat unfold while keeping your mouth, uh, fingers shut — is a great way to learn more about chats before diving in.

Adding your two cents' worth

To contribute to the chat:

1 **Click the Start button and choose Programs⇨Microsoft Comic Chat⇨Microsoft Comic Chat. Click the radio button next to the Show all available chat rooms option and then click OK. In the Chat Room List, choose #Newbies.**

As long as you're still just practicing, I suggest sticking to the #Newbies room.

2 **When you're ready to make your own earth-shattering (or not) contribution, just start typing.**

Anything you type appears automatically in the compose pane. You can type anything you want, but as a rule, be brief and to the point. Also, when choosing the wording of your statement, consider the gestures that Comic Chat automatically chooses based on your wording (see "Making gestures" later in this lesson).

While typing your statement, you can use the Backspace, Delete, Insert, and arrow keys to edit your statement and fix mistakes. Note that no one sees your statement while you're typing and editing it. Your statement does not appear to other members until you submit it as described in Step 3.

3 When your statement reads as you want it to, press Enter.

Your statement appears sometime soon in your viewing pane and in the displays of all others in the chat room. Comic Chat users see your character speaking the words in a *Say balloon,* the type that surrounds words that comic characters say aloud.

4 Type another statement; instead of pressing Enter, click the Think button (second from the left) in the compose pane.

Comic Chat users see your character thinking the words in a thought balloon, the type that surrounds comic characters' thoughts.

5 Type another statement, but instead of pressing Enter, click the Whisper button (third from the left) in the compose pane.

Now Comic Chat users see your character whispering the words in the type of balloon that surrounds comic characters' whispers.

6 When done chatting, quit by choosing File⇨Exit.

Changing expressions

on the test

The emotion wheel lets you enhance your character's performance by changing its expression for a given statement. Note, however, that you must always be sure that your words alone can carry your meaning — the expression will not be seen by chat members who aren't using Comic Chat. Expressions enhance your communication but should not be relied upon as communication in and of themselves.

To use expressions:

1 Go to Microsoft's Comic Chat Rooms page at `http://www.microsoft.com/ie/comichat/rooms.htm` **and choose the #Newbies group.**

2 Type your statement (don't press Enter) and then click an expression on the emotion wheel.

The character in the self-view pane changes to show you how your character will appear, using the selected expression, to other Comic Chat users. (To choose the character's neutral expression, click the + at the center of the emotion wheel.)

3 When the self-view pane appears the way you want it to, submit your statement by pressing Enter or clicking a button in the compose pane.

Stay in this chat room for the next exercise: making your character gesture.

---

can edit while typing before making statement public

press Enter to send statement to chat server

click Think button instead of Enter to make statement appear in thought balloon

Whisper button makes statement appear in whisper balloon

choose expression from emotion wheel before submitting statement

Making gestures

Your comic character changes its gesture depending on what you type. If a statement begins with certain words or contains certain words, Comic Chat automatically changes the gesture of your character to support the statement. Tables 11-1 and 11-2 describe the gestures that Comic Chat applies.

Table 11-1 Gestures Used Based on Words *Beginning* the Sentence

If Sentence Begins with This	Your Character Does This
I	Points to itself
You	Points to the other person
Hello or Hi	Waves
Bye	Waves
Welcome	Waves
Howdy	Waves

Table 11-2   Gestures Used Based on Words *in* the Sentence

If Sentence Contains This	Your Character Does This
are you	Points to the other person
will you	Points to the other person
did you	Points to the other person
aren't you	Points to the other person
don't you	Points to the other person
I'm	Points to itself
I will	Points to itself
I'll	Points to itself
I am	Points to itself

Try it out:

1 **If you're not still in a chat room, join one (see previous steps).**

2 **Look at the member list and find a name that interests you.**

For this example, I assume that the other member's name is Raoul.

3 **Submit the statement** Howdy, Raoul! **(substituting your chosen name for "Raoul").**

Your character appears in a panel, waving to Raoul while saying howdy to him.

4 **Submit the statement** I'm new here.

Your character points to itself.

Notes:

if sentence begins with certain word, character makes certain gesture

Figure 11-11

Figure 11-11: To switch to a new chat room, choose Session⇨New Room and enter the name of the room (including the # part).

When choosing gestures, Comic Chat favors words that start the sentence (Table 11-1) over words that lie within the statement (Table 11-2). In other words, if your statement begins with *I* but also contains the words *are you*, your character points to itself, not the other person.

heads up

Switching rooms

If you tire of a conversation and want to try a different one, you can switch rooms. Note that when you leave a room (whether you switch to another room or just quit), a message appears on other members' displays, reporting that you've split.

If you know the exact name of the room you want to go to:

1 **While in any room, choose <u>S</u>ession⇨<u>N</u>ew Room.**

The New Room dialog box opens, as shown in Figure 11-11.

2 **Type the name of the room.**

Be sure to include the hash mark (#) at the beginning of the room name.

3 **Click OK.**

If you don't know the exact name of the room you want to go to:

1 **While in any room, choose <u>V</u>iew⇨Chat Room <u>L</u>ist.**

The list of rooms on the server appears.

2 **Scroll to the name of the room you want to switch to.**

3 **Double-click the room name.**

extra credit

Seeing how the other half lives

Comic Chat doesn't have to show comics — it can show a display of plain-text statements, just like any regular chat client. In fact, take a look back at Figure 11-1, which shows how a typical text-only chat client shows a conversation. That's Comic Chat, switched to plain-text mode.

To switch Comic Chat to plain-text mode, choose <u>V</u>iew⇨Plain Te<u>x</u>t. The comic characters disappear, and the chat proceeds in text alone.

Comic Chat favors words that start sentence over words contained in sentence

Session→New Room to type name of desired room

View→Chat Room List to pick chat room from list

☑ **Progress Check**

If you can do the following, you've mastered this lesson:

❏ Contribute statements to the conversation.

❏ Choose the style of cartoon balloon in which your words appear.

❏ Choose your character's expression for a given statement.

❏ Understand how to word your statements so that Comic Chat assigns the desired gesture to your character.

Recess

Online chat is cool, but it's no substitute for the real thing. Keep your conversation skills sharp — go talk to somebody. When that somebody goes to bed, come back and take the quiz.

Unit 11 Quiz

Notes:

For each question, circle the letter of the best answer.

1. **To participate in a traditional online chat, you need . . .**
   A. An imagination.
   B. Major attitude.
   C. A cold Dr. Pepper.
   D. A chat client.

2. **In a chat with three or more members, the statements may appear jumbled because . . .**
   A. Each member's statements take different lengths of time to reach the chat server.
   B. Chat mavens are disorganized thinkers.
   C. The conversation is perfectly ordered — *you* are horribly confused. (Seek therapy.)
   D. Some chat clients are not fully compatible with all chat servers.

3. **When you use Microsoft Comic Chat . . .**
   A. All members see the conversation as a comic strip.
   B. All members see any statements made by you and other Comic Chat users as comics; other statements appear in plain text.
   C. You and other Comic Chat users see the conversation as a comic strip; members using other chat clients see plain text.
   D. You see the conversation as a Comic Strip when chatting on Microsoft's server but as plain text when chatting on other IRC servers.

4. **To prevent others with access to your PC from visiting unsavory chat rooms . . .**
   A. Supervise anyone who uses your PC.
   B. Don't install a chat client.
   C. Use Internet Explorer's Content Advisor (see Unit 8).
   D. A or B

5. **To reinforce (for other Comic Chat users) the intended tone of a statement . . .**

   A. Use **bold** and *italics* on important words.

   B. Choose an expression from the emotion wheel.

   C. TYPE ANGRY WORDS IN CAPITAL LETTERS!!!!!!!

   D. Add lengthy explanations of intent to all statements so everyone gets your drift.

Unit 11 Exercise

1. Open Comic Chat, connect to the server, and display the list of chat rooms.

2. Scroll through the list to find a chat room covering a topic about which you are absolutely, shamefully ignorant.

3. Enter the room and lurk awhile, soaking up the tone and vocabulary of the conversation.

4. When you feel ready, contribute to the conversation as if you were an expert. Don't be afraid to make bold, wholly insupportable assertions and to defend them adamantly.

5. See how long you can keep up the charade before somebody calls you a stooge.

6. When the jig is up, split. Never return to that room without first assuming a new identity (by choosing a new nickname).

Messaging through E-Mail and Newsgroups

Objectives for This Unit

✓ Sending e-mail to addresses that appear in Web pages

✓ Reading newsgroup messages in Web pages

✓ Sending and reading messages with Internet Mail and Internet News

Prerequisites
▶ Opening Internet Explorer and connecting to the Internet (Unit 1)
▶ Clicking links (Unit 2)
▶ Understanding and using URLs (Unit 3)

When you set up Internet Explorer in Unit 1, you simultaneously installed its two closest companions: Internet Mail, an e-mail program, and Internet News, a *newsreader* (the type of program required to use Internet newsgroups). Using these two helper programs, you can exchange e-mail with anyone else on the Net, and you can read — and respond to — the thousands of interesting messages publicly posted in Internet newsgroups (sometimes also called *discussion groups* or *Usenet news*).

newsgroups = discussion groups, or Usenet

Internet Mail and Internet News are, for all intents and purposes, individual programs, and either can be used from within Internet Explorer or all on its own. Their family relationship to the Web browser is important because links to e-mail and newsgroups appear ever more frequently in Web pages. Because Internet Mail and Internet News are tightly integrated with Internet Explorer, clicking an e-mail address in a Web page opens Internet Mail, and clicking a newsgroup link in a Web page opens Internet News.

Internet Mail and Internet News have one thing in common: They're both about sending and receiving messages. Before you can start dealing with messages, you need to familiarize yourself with the parts of a message, as illustrated in Figure 12-1.

header contains From, Date, To, Subject info

The top portion of the message is called the *header*. The header contains information that identifies the message:

▶ **From:** E-mail address of the person who sent the message

▶ **Date:** Date (and time) the message was sent

Figure 12-1: All Internet messages have a header (including To, From, and Subject information) and a body (the message itself).

Figure 12-1

always put description in Subject line

signature = standard text created by sender; appears below message content

▶ **To:** E-mail or newsgroup address to which the message was sent

▶ **Subject:** Brief description of the content or purpose of the message (e-mail programs consider the Subject line optional, but you should always fill it out anyway, as a courtesy to the recipient)

The header content shows up not just in the message but in the lists of messages that people see when they retrieve their e-mail or open a newsgroup. When you receive an e-mail message, its header information (or at least the From, Date, and Subject parts — the To part is obvious) appears in your list of messages. Clicking that header information opens the message.

Below the header, the *body* — the message content — appears. Sometimes, in the body but below the actual message content, a signature appears. A *signature* is a boilerplate block of text at the bottom of a message, included by the message's author as a way of personalizing his or her messages. Some folks put jokes in their signatures; others put business phone and fax numbers.

Lesson 12-1

On your Web travels, you've already seen e-mail addresses lurking on Web pages. For example, on the top page at many sites, a signature appears near the bottom of the page; the signature usually includes the e-mail address of the Webmaster (the person who maintains the Web page) or someone else responsible for handling e-mail inquiries.

e-mail addresses always contain @ symbol

E-mail addresses are easy to spot: They always have an *at sign* (@) in them.

To practice using an e-mail link in a Web page, send a message to the IDG Books Worldwide feedback staff:

e-mail link = e-mail address that appears as link on Web page

1 **Go to the IDG Books page at**

http://www.idgbooks.com/

2 **Click the link Contact Us.**

A page like the one in Figure 12-2 appears. Observe that many links on this page are also e-mail addresses. An e-mail address that appears as a link is called an *e-mail link.*

click e-mail link to open pre-addressed New Message window

3 **Click the e-mail link feedback@www.idgbooks.com.**

Internet Mail's New Message window opens, with the message pre-addressed to IDG Books (see Figure 12-3). Any time you click an e-mail link, this window opens a new message pre-addressed to the e-mail address that appeared in the link.

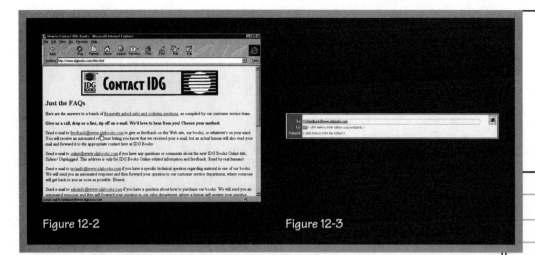

Figure 12-2   Figure 12-3

Figure 12-2: Four of the five links appearing on this Web page are e-mail links.

Figure 12-3: When you click an e-mail link, the New Message window opens, pre-addressed to the address in the link.

Notes:

 heads up

4 **Click in the Subject line of the header and type a subject:** E-mail test.

Although typing a subject may be optional, e-mail etiquette demands that you always supply a subject, and a few e-mail systems actually reject messages that don't have a subject. So get in the habit of always supplying a subject.

5 **Click in the body area of the message window and type your message:** Ned Snell told me to do this (Dummies 101: Internet Explorer 3 For Windows 95).

In general, you can simply type your message exactly as you would in any word processor. Words wrap automatically, and pressing Enter starts a new paragraph. But you can't use advanced formatting techniques, such as bold, italics, and different fonts. Most e-mail programs don't support such formatting reliably, so even if you could put fancy formatting in your message, the formatting probably wouldn't show up when your recipient read the message. That's okay — in e-mail, your content, not your style, is what matters.

6 **When finished typing your message, click the Send button on the toolbar.**

The Internet Mail window closes. Your message has been sent.

Send button sends message

☑ **Progress Check**

If you can do the following, you've mastered this lesson:

❑ Recognize e-mail links.

❑ Send a message to an e-mail link on a Web page.

Composing a New Message

Lesson 12-2

Ultimately, you'll want to send e-mail to someone whose address doesn't happen to pop up conveniently on a Web page. That task requires opening Internet Mail yourself and supplying the To line. When you send e-mail this way, a few other things work differently than they did in Lesson 12-1, as you'll soon see.

To practice sending e-mail, send yourself a message. You can be online or offline for Step 1.

1 **Open Internet Mail.**

You can open Internet Mail in these ways:

• From Internet Explorer, click the Mail button on the toolbar and then choose Read Mail.

• From Internet Explorer, choose Go⇨Read Mail.

• From the Windows 95 Start menu, choose Programs⇨Internet Mail.

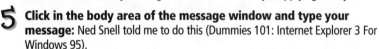

<u>Go</u>⇨Read <u>M</u>ail opens Internet Mail

so does <u>P</u>rograms⇨Internet Mail

Figure 12-4: This message reminds you that even though you've clicked Send, your message isn't *really* sent until you click Send and Receive.

Figure 12-4

New Message button opens window for addressing and composing message

separate multiple addresses on To line with semicolons

unlike when using e-mail links, Send button with regular mail sends message to Outbox, not to recipient, to await being sent

☑ **Progress Check**

If you can do the following, you've mastered this lesson:

❑ Open Internet mail and address and compose a message.

❑ Understand that with regular mail, clicking the Send button sends the message to your Outbox folder rather than directly to the recipient.

If you open Internet Mail offline, Internet Mail opens your connection dialog box automatically when you actually send the message that you compose here, as described in Lesson 12-3.

2 Click the New Message button.

The New Message window opens, just as it did in Lesson 12-1. However, the message is not pre-addressed because you didn't get here through an e-mail link. You must supply the e-mail address of your intended recipient in the To box. The edit cursor is already in the To box, ready to go.

3 Type your own e-mail address.

If you want to send the same message to multiple recipients, you can type as many e-mail addresses on the To line as you want. When using multiple addresses, separate the addresses by inserting a semicolon (;) after each e-mail address except the final one.

4 Click in the Subject line and type a subject: Hi, me!

5 Click in the body area of the message window and type Hello, Me!

6 Press Enter to start a new paragraph.

7 Type Just wanted to drop myself a note and say I'm swell! My self-esteem needs the boost.

8 Click the Send button.

heads up

A dialog box like the one shown in Figure 12-4 appears, to remind you that clicking Send does not actually send your message — it simply saves the message to your Outbox folder. The message is sent automatically the next time you send and receive messages, as described in the next lesson.

Q&A session

Question: Hey, what's the Cc part of the header for? You skipped it, Sparky.

Answer: You use the Cc (carbon copy) line to enter the address of someone who should receive a copy of the message. The addressee in the Cc line should not be the person to whom the message is written; rather, it's someone else who should see a copy. For example, when e-mailing your auto mechanic to complain that after an oil change your car was returned with no backseat, you may want to Cc your attorney.

To use Cc, simply click in the Cc line and type one or more e-mail addresses. If you want to send to multiple Cc recipients, separate addresses with semicolons, just as you do in the To line.

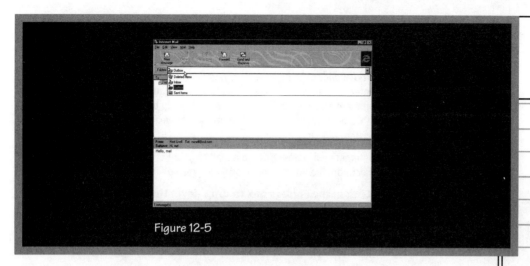

Figure 12-5

Figure 12-5: Drop down the Folders list to switch among your four Internet Mail folders.

Notes:

Sending and Receiving Messages

Lesson 12-3

After you click Send, your message is stored in the Internet Mail Outbox folder to await actual sending. To check your Outbox:

1 **Click in the Folders box to drop down the list of e-mail folders, as shown in Figure 12-5.**

2 **Click Outbox.**

The list of messages waiting to be sent appears. You can edit any message in your Outbox by double-clicking it in the list, making the changes you desire, and then clicking Send again.

on the test

To actually send the message to its recipient, you must click the Send and Receive button. Note that any time you use Send and Receive, Internet Mail does both of the following:

▶ Sends all messages waiting in your Outbox

▶ Retrieves any new messages sent to you by others

To send your message to yourself:

1 **Click Send and Receive.**

A message appears, informing you that your message is being sent. After all messages have been sent, Internet Mail reports that it is checking for new messages. For all I know, you may have some new messages waiting — if so, Internet Mail retrieves them now and stores them in your Inbox folder (you learn how to find and read them two steps from now). If you have no new messages waiting, No new messages appears in the status bar when the Checking for new messages box disappears.

2 **Wait a minute or two, just to give the mail server time to update itself with the message you just sent.**

While you're waiting, why not have a yummy donut?

---

click Folders box
and choose Outbox
to see messages
waiting to be sent

incoming messages
wait in Inbox folder

🖳

Send and Receive
button sends all
outgoing mail and
retrieves all
incoming mail

can edit messages
in Outbox by double-
clicking them

click Folders box and choose Inbox to see incoming messages

☑ **Progress Check**

If you can do the following, you've mastered this lesson:

❑ See and, if necessary, edit outgoing messages in the Outbox folder.

❑ Send messages to their recipients.

❑ Read incoming messages.

3 **Click Send and Receive.**

You already sent any mail from your Outbox in Step 1. Having nothing to send, Internet Mail immediately checks for new messages and retrieves them. If Internet Mail reports No New Messages in the status bar, your server may have been updated so quickly that you retrieved your message in Step 1, the instant after it was sent.

Internet mail stores retrieved e-mail on your PC. If you want, you can disconnect from the Internet and read your e-mail offline.

4 **Click in the Folders box to drop down the list of e-mail folders.**

5 **Click Inbox to display your Inbox folder.**

New, unread messages appear in bold at the top of the Inbox list (you may have to scroll up to see them if you have a long list in your Inbox).

6 **In your Inbox, click once on your message to yourself.**

The message appears in a pane below the Inbox folder. This "preview" mode is an efficient way to quickly read any new mail. To see the message in a large window by itself, double-click it.

Lesson 12-4

Replying to and Forwarding Messages

Notes:

So now you know how to send messages and receive messages — and in the great, mysterious scheme of things, what else can there be? *Variations* on sending messages, of course! Using a few simple options, you can conveniently

▸ **Reply** to a message you've received, without having to fill in the header (To and Subject)

▸ **Forward** to someone else a copy of a message you've received

For practice, reply to your "Hi, me!" message and forward the same message to IDG Books.

Replying to a message

1 **In Internet Mail, click Folders and choose Inbox.**

2 **Click the "Hi, me!" message and then click the Reply to Author button.**

A New Message window opens, as shown in Figure 12-6. Observe a few unusual things about this new message:

when replying, To line is already filled out

Subject line is filled out, with RE to indicate that message is reply

• The To line has already been filled in for you, with the e-mail address of the sender (in this case, you) of the message to which you are replying.

• The Subject line is the same as the subject of the message to which you are replying, except that the abbreviation RE (for *regarding*) has been added automatically.

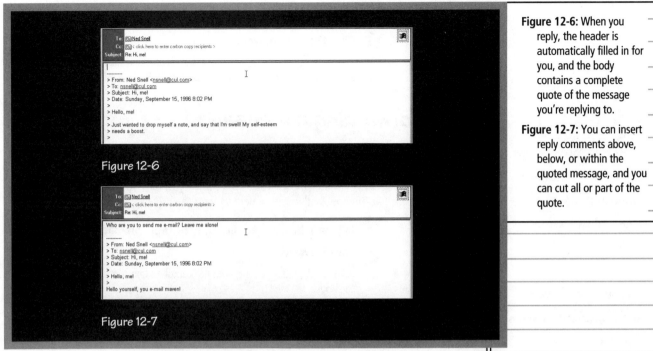

Figure 12-6

Figure 12-7

Figure 12-6: When you reply, the header is automatically filled in for you, and the body contains a complete quote of the message you're replying to.

Figure 12-7: You can insert reply comments above, below, or within the quoted message, and you can cut all or part of the quote.

- The entire text of the original message and a summary of the header appear in the message body. This quoting is done automatically to remind the original sender of the precise text of the message to which you're replying.

- Every line of the quote is preceded by a carat (>), which identifies it as a quote.

- Above the quote appears a dashed line, the *quote separator.*

The To and Subject lines are already filled in, so all you need to do now is type your reply, which appears automatically above the quote separator.

3 **Click in the body area (above the reply separator) and type** Who are you to send me e-mail? Leave me alone!

Optionally, you can insert your reply within the quote, which allows you to respond point by point to a message. Note that you may also delete any portions of the quote, including the quoted header, if you want.

4 **Within the quote, click in the spot between the two paragraphs of the quote.**

5 **Press Enter to start a new line.**

6 **Type** Hello yourself, you e-mail maven!

7 **Press Enter again.**

Your response now appears between the paragraphs of the quote. It's easy to spot within the quote because it's not tagged with carats (>).

8 **Point to the beginning of the second paragraph of the quote ("Just wanted to . . .").**

9 **Click and drag through the paragraph.**

Remember: To *click and drag* is to point the edit cursor at the beginning of the paragraph, hold down the mouse button, drag the mouse so that the whole paragraph is highlighted, and then release the mouse button.

10 **Press the Delete key.**

The second paragraph of the quote disappears, as shown in Figure 12-7.

original message is repeated in body of reply message

> = kind of quotation mark

can delete quoted original message or any portion of it

11 **Click the Send button.**

Your reply is saved in your Outbox and will be sent the next time you click Send and Receive (as described in Lesson 12-3).

Forwarding a message

Forward button for sending message to someone other than original message writer

usually shouldn't edit quoted original message when forwarding

☑ **Progress Check**

If you can do the following, you've mastered this lesson:

❑ Send a reply to someone who sent you a message.

❑ Forward a message you've received to someone other than the person who originally sent you the message.

Forwarding is a lot like replying. The only real difference is that you're not sending back to the author of the message — you're sending the author's message on to someone else. That means you have to supply the To line so that Internet Mail knows where to send the message copy.

1 **In your Inbox, single-click the "Hi, me!" message.**

2 **Click Forward.**

A Forward window opens, with the complete text of the message quoted in the body.

3 **Click in the To line and type**

feedback@www.idgbooks.com

As usual, you fill in the intended recipient's address in the To line.

4 **Click near the top of the body and type some explanatory comments — why you're forwarding this message and also what you think of *Dummies 101: Internet Explorer 3 For Windows 95* so far.**

Although you don't have to add comments or explanation — Internet Mail automatically adds a statement above the quoted header to tell the recipient that you forwarded the message — you should give the recipient some context for the forwarded message unless the reason that you're forwarding the message is absolutely obvious. And for this example, I'm sure that IDG Books Worldwide's feedback staff would appreciate getting some actual *feedback* from you (in return for the time spent reading your message).

heads up

When forwarding, you can edit the quoted message, just as you can when replying — but doing so may be a breach of etiquette. Recipients of forwarded messages generally assume that they're receiving the entire, unabridged original message.

5 **Click the Send button.**

Your forwarded message is saved in your Outbox and will be sent the next time you click Send and Receive (as described in Lesson 12-3).

Lesson 12-5

Getting Started with Internet News

newsgroup discussions not as immediate as Chat, but usually more thoughtful and informative

Think of newsgroups as if they were public e-mail mailboxes. Reading messages in newsgroups is a lot like reading e-mail messages, and sending messages to newsgroups is a lot like sending e-mail. The important difference is that newsgroups are public — anyone with access to a news server can read the messages stored there. Newsgroups are like bulletin boards, places where people with a common interest can post messages and can reply to messages posted by others.

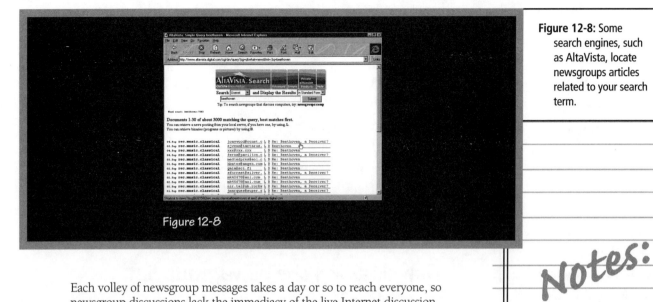

Figure 12-8

Figure 12-8: Some search engines, such as AltaVista, locate newsgroups articles related to your search term.

Each volley of newsgroup messages takes a day or so to reach everyone, so newsgroup discussions lack the immediacy of the live Internet discussion facility, Chat (see Unit 11). However, the discussion that takes place in newsgroups is generally more thoughtful and more informative than that in Chats. To put it another way, Chat supports largely social discussions; newsgroups are better for serious, analytical discussions.

heads up

Be warned, however, that so-called adult newsgroups exist on the Internet. Some access suppliers apply various methods to screen out the naughty newsgroups, with dubious success. The most common approach is to remove access to all groups beginning with the letters .alt (for *alternative*). That kills most of the really raunchy groups, but not all. Worse, the majority of the .alt groups are perfectly wholesome — so as usual, censorship efforts throw the baby out with the bath water.

Newsgroups are great, and I wouldn't hesitate to encourage anyone to explore them. In fact, you're often more likely to find truly insightful, authoritative information in a newsgroup than on a Web page. But if you're very sensitive to explicit or harsh language, tread newsgroups carefully.

heads up

And if you're concerned about your kids visiting unsavory newsgroups, note that Internet Explorer's Content Advisor (see Unit 8) does nothing to control newsgroup access. You'll need to supervise your kids' online forays (a good idea anyway), uninstall Internet News, or hope that your kids can't figure out how to use Internet News (a bad bet).

Opening a newsgroup from a Web page

On the Web, you come across links that lead to newsgroups and to individual newsgroup messages. In particular, search engines such as AltaVista (see Unit 5) may come up with newsgroups related to your search term, in addition to Web pages (see Figure 12-8).

Tip: To use these links, you don't need to have performed the remaining tasks in this lesson (downloading the newsgroup list and subscribing). Just click the link, and Internet News opens and goes to the newsgroup or message to which the link points. Once there, you can read or post messages, as described in Lessons 12-6 and 12-7.

Notes:

watch out for adult newsgroups

Content Advisor does not protect against unsavory newsgroups

don't have to subscribe to newsgroups to have access to them; search engine results can bring up newsgroups

if not accessing
newsgroup through
link, need to open
Internet News
manually

Opening Internet News

on the test

If you don't go to the newsgroup through a link, you need to open Internet News yourself. You can do that two ways:

♦ From Internet Explorer, click the Mail button and then choose Read News.

♦ From Internet Explorer, choose Go➪Read News.

♦ From the Start menu, choose Programs➪Internet News.

If you're offline when you open Internet News, your connection dialog opens so that you can connect to the Internet.

Downloading the newsgroup list

need to download
list of newsgroups
first (takes several
minutes)

The very first time you open Internet News, a message appears, asking whether you want to download the list of newsgroups. Before you can start using newsgroups, you need to download the latest list from the server.

To download the list, click Yes. The downloading takes several minutes — there are 11,000 to 14,000 newsgroups.

extra credit

Updating the newsgroup list

The list of newsgroups changes pretty often, although the changes are minor. Every week or so, a few unpopular newsgroups drop out of sight, and a few new ones pop up. So from time to time, you should download the list again. To do so:

1. **Open Internet News.**

2. **Click the Newsgroups button.**

3. **Click Reset list.**

Note that updating the list has no effect on your list of subscribed newsgroups.

---

update newsgroup
list every week or so

Subscribing to newsgroups

subscribing is
convenient way of
using newsgroups

To use newsgroups, you don't have to actually subscribe to any. But subscribing makes using newsgroups more convenient. Subscribing to newsgroups creates a sort of favorite newsgroups list, a list of groups that you plan to visit often.

Once you've subscribed to the groups you like, you can visit one by quickly choosing it from the list. Otherwise, you have to plow through the list of thousands of groups each time you want to visit one. Yeesh.

To subscribe to a newsgroup:

1 Open Internet News and click the Newsgroups button.

A dialog box like the one in Figure 12-9 appears. The All tab shows the entire newsgroup list, while the Subscribed tab shows just the groups to which you've subscribed.

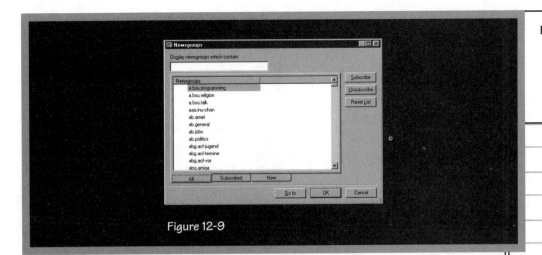

Figure 12-9

Figure 12-9: On the All tab of the Newsgroups dialog box, you find newsgroups that interest you, and subscribe to them.

Notes:

2. **Choose the All tab, if it is not already selected.**

3. **Click in the Display newsgroups which contain box.**

4. **Type a word related to a topic that interests you. Try** golf.

The list now shows only those newsgroups that contain the word *golf.*

5. **In the list, click** rec.sport.golf **to highlight it.**

6. **Click the Subscribe button.**

A news icon (like a little newspaper) appears next to rec.sport.golf. You're subscribed to it. (If you're not actually interested in golf — and who really is? — you can unsubscribe by highlighting rec.sport.golf and clicking the Unsubscribe button.)

7. **Repeat Steps 3 through 6 as many times as you want, subscribing to as many newsgroups as interest you.**

8. **When finished, click OK.**

Your subscribed newsgroups are all available from a handy list, as you'll discover in the next lesson.

extra credit

Choosing a default newsgroup

If you have a favorite newsgroup that you always visit first, set up that group as the default newsgroup. Internet News visits the default newsgroup automatically every time you open Internet News.

To make a newsgroup the default:

1. **Subscribe to the desired newsgroup, as described in Lesson 12-5.**

2. **Choose News▷Options; then click the Read tab.**

3. **Make sure that the last check box — Always start me in this newsgroup — is checked.**

4. **Drop down the list at the bottom of the dialog box and select the default newsgroup.**

5. **Click OK.**

Notes (right margin):

choose interesting newsgroups from All list by typing search term in Display newsgroups which contain box

for each desired newsgroup, click newsgroup and click Subscribe button

☑ **Progress Check**

If you can do the following, you've mastered this lesson:

❑ Click a link to open a newsgroup from a Web page.

❑ Open the Internet News program and download the current list of newsgroups.

❑ Subscribe to the newsgroups that you want to visit often.

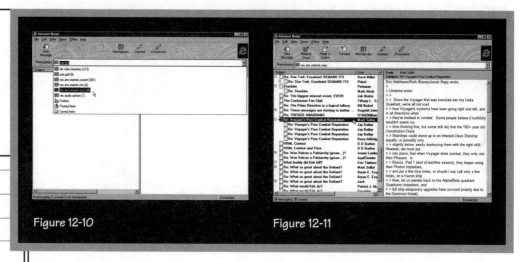

Figure 12-10: Drop down the Newsgroups list to select one of your subscribed newsgroups.

Figure 12-11: The messages making up a single conversation are grouped together as a thread.

Figure 12-10   Figure 12-11

Lesson 12-6

Reading a Message

After the setting up described in Lesson 12-5 is out of the way, you're all set to browse newsgroups and see what's there.

To read messages in a newsgroup:

1   **Open Internet News.**

2   **Drop down the Newsgroups list, which appears just below the toolbar.**

The list contains all your subscribed newsgroups, as shown in Figure 12-10.

3   **Select a group by clicking it.**

The list closes, the group name appears alone in the Newsgroups box, and Internet News retrieves the current header information — the list of messages — from the server. This process may take a minute or two if the list is long. Watch the left end of Internet Mail's status bar, which reports the progress of the retrieval.

When header retrieval is done, a list of current messages appears, like the one in Figure 12-11.

4   **Click any message to read it.**

If you single-click a message, it appears in the right-hand pane. If your double-click the message, it appears in a window by itself.

When scrolling through the message list, keep in mind the following:

- By default, messages are sorted by *threads*. A thread is a series of messages and replies that constitute a conversation of sorts. Typically, a thread is made up of a single message and all the replies directly related to that message, although you may see replies to replies to replies (and so on). At first, only the top message of each thread appears in the message list. That message is preceded by a plus sign (+). Click the plus sign to display the rest of the messages in the thread (see Figure 12-11).

Internet News first visits default newsgroup automatically

double-click message to make it appear in its own window

on the test

☑ **Progress Check**

If you can do the following, you've mastered this lesson:

❑ Go to one of the newsgroups you subscribed to.

❑ Follow along the various message threads in the newsgroup.

- You can change the way the messages are sorted: Choose <u>V</u>iew⇨<u>S</u>ort By. Then choose a sorting option. For example, to sort the message list by the time and date each message was sent, choose <u>V</u>iew⇨<u>S</u>ort By⇨<u>S</u>ent.

5 When done browsing a newsgroup, choose another group from the Newsgroup list or close Internet News by choosing <u>F</u>ile⇨E<u>x</u>it.

Posting Messages
Lesson 12-7

Eventually, you'll tire of simply reading other people's messages — you'll want to add your two cents' worth by *posting* a message of your own. Don't be in too big a hurry to do so, though.

heads up

Every newsgroup on the Internet has its own culture, its own little tribe. Typically, many of the regular visitors to a newsgroup are experts in the field that the newsgroup covers, or at least they believe themselves to be experts. They don't expect every visitor to be an expert, but they do expect visitors to appreciate the general expertise level of the group. For example, the group `alt.video.laserdisc` hosts mostly intermediate to advanced discussion of video laserdiscs and the technology behind them. Few in the group look kindly on a new visitor who posts a question such as "What's a laserdisc?" At the very least, such a question would probably be ignored. At the worst, irritated newsgroup regulars might *flame* the offender, sending angry messages to the group and/or e-mail to the offender.

Of course, in a better world, folks online would tolerate such innocent transgressions. But something about newsgroups brings out the worst in many people. To avoid stepping on any oversensitive toes, I suggest that you *lurk* — read without posting — in a group for a while before posting any comments or questions. Read the messages, follow the threads, and get a feel for the general level of the discussion and the vocabulary applied. If you feel you can join the conversation at the appropriate level, jump in.

Tip: If you know that the talk is over your head but you want to ask a question anyway, begin the Subject line of your message with something like **Newbie question**. That way, anybody who's annoyed by such questions knows better than to read it — and anyone who does read it has no right to complain.

Understanding netiquette

Internet etiquette — better known as *netiquette* — is a loosely followed code of conduct for behavior online. It's not especially relevant anywhere on the Internet except in newsgroups, and quite frankly, so many newbies are online today that few folks observe the tenets of netiquette anyhow.

Still, by observing the very basics of netiquette, you can avoid flames from sticklers. More important, netiquette isn't really a set of arbitrary rules — it's a common-sense code to keep the conversation focused and friendly. So why not follow it?

Notes:

flame = send angry message

don't post message or reply before studying the newsgroup's culture for a while

netiquette = unofficial code of online conduct

make sure that
message is relevant
to topic

keep it polite

keep it simple —
don't be coy or
sarcastic

delete all but
relevant parts of
quoted original
message when
replying

don't type in all caps

on the test

The most important rules of netiquette for posting to newsgroups are as follows:

- **Stay on topic.** When posting a new message, make sure that it falls within the range of topics discussed within the newsgroup — don't post a classical-music question in a grunge-rock newsgroup. When making a reply to a message, make sure that your reply follows the thread of the message to which you're replying.

- **Mind your manners.** Newsgroup discussions can get heated, and some folks can become patronizing, cruel, or just rude. Stay above it. Post polite messages. When a thread degenerates into an argument, stay out of it. And don't curse. Cursing, while a wonderful tool of expressive language and an essential part of my everyday vocabulary, not only is considered boorish by many but may also get your message automatically erased off the server before anyone even reads it.

- **Write what you mean.** A common mistake made by newbie posters is to try to use sarcasm to make a point. Readers of sarcastic messages often read them as sincere — and respond in kind. If you want your meaning to be clearly understood, don't be coy, don't be cute — just say it. (No, I'm not a hypocrite — we Dummies Press writers are *supposed* to write coy and cute, for your entertainment. But we're not so cute when we write newsgroup messages.)

- **Don't overquote.** When you reply to a newsgroup message, the whole message to which you're replying is quoted in your reply. If the quote is not essential to your reply, delete it — or at least delete any portions of the quote that aren't necessary. People shouldn't have to download a 100-line message just to read your 10-line reply.

- **Don't shout.** TYPING IN ALL CAPITAL LETTERS IS CONSIDERED SHOUTING AND IS GENERALLY THOUGHT OF AS AN ANNOYING BREACH OF NETIQUETTE. Exactly.

- **Don't get personal.** Again, newsgroup discussions can degenerate to petty arguments, even personal attacks. Don't participate. If attacked, don't take the bait.

Replying to a message

Most people find themselves wanting to reply to a message before they ever think up a new message. So try a reply as your first foray into posting newsgroup messages.

on the test

Note that you can reply in two ways, using either of two buttons on the Internet News toolbar:

Reply to Group sends
reply back to entire
newsgroup

Reply to Author
sends reply back to
just the author of
the message

- **Reply to Group:** Sends your reply to the newsgroup, to appear as an entry in the same thread as the message to which you're replying.

- **Reply to Author:** Sends nothing to the newsgroup but instead sends your reply as a private e-mail message directly to the author of the message to which you're replying. This option is valuable when you want to say something off-topic to the author (in which case the reply does not belong in the newsgroup) or when you want your reply to be private, just between you and the author.

In this example, you post your reply to the newsgroup. Just keep in mind, for those rare occasions, that you can click the Reply to Author button to make a private e-mail reply.

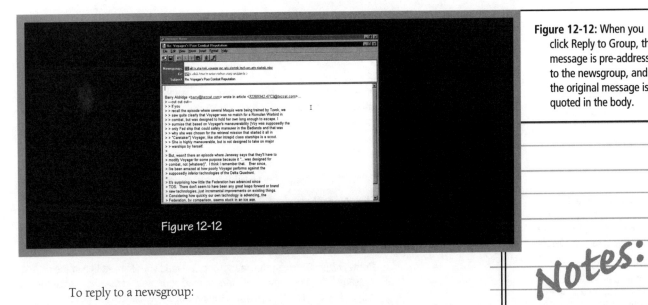

Figure 12-12

Notes:

To reply to a newsgroup:

1 Go to your favorite newsgroup and open a message to which you want to reply.

Make sure that you've carefully considered which newsgroup you're participating in and what message you're replying to, to avoid getting flamed by irritated members of the newsgroup.

2 Click the Reply to Group button.

A Reply window opens (see Figure 12-12), with

- The To line pre-addressed to the newsgroup

- The Subject line showing RE: *the message to which you're responding* (don't change the subject line, or your reply may not appear in the correct thread)

- The entire text of the original message quoted in the body

3 Click in the body and type your reply.

You can compose your reply just as you would an e-mail reply (see Lesson 12-4). You can type your whole reply above the reply separator (the dashed line above the quote), or you can insert your reply within the quote, at the relevant points. Be sure to delete any parts of the quote that aren't necessary to clarify your reply. Remember, anyone who wants to read the message you're replying to can do so on the newsgroup, so including the whole quote in your message is rarely necessary.

4 When finished with your reply, click the Post Message button.

After a moment, a message appears to inform you that your message has been posted but that it may not show up immediately on the server. In other words, if you re-open the newsgroup 15 minutes from now, you may not see your reply — servers take a while to update. But your reply will probably appear on your server within an hour.

heads up

When you post your message, it soon appears on your server. However, a day or more may pass before your reply shows up on all the other news servers in the world — so be patient in expecting replies to your messages. Also, note that not all newsgroups get copied to all servers. In particular, a few newsgroups on your server may be *local interest* groups covering your city or state. Such groups typically are not copied to other news servers or are copied only to other servers within the local region.

Reply window already has To and Subject lines filled in

not all newsgroups appear on all servers worldwide

Posting a new message

Posting a new message is really just like replying, except that you have no quoted message to fiddle with and your message starts a new thread instead of becoming part of an existing thread.

To post a new message:

1 **Open the newsgroup to which you want to post the new message.**

2 **Click New Message.**

A New Message window opens, pre-addressed to the open newsgroup.

3 **Click in the Subject line and type a brief, informative description.**

Remember: Others in the newsgroup will read your Subject line in their message lists to determine whether to read your message. A short, accurate subject line ensures that your message attracts the readers you desire.

4 **Click in the body area and type your message.**

5 **Click the Post Message button.**

Recess

E-mail and newsgroups are great ways to communicate, but paper still feels good. Write a nice note or card to a relative or long-lost friend (I *know* there's somebody you've been meaning to write to.) In the note, ask whether your friend has an e-mail address and include yours in the note. Soon, you may get an electronic response to your paper-based request. *Everybody* has an e-mail address these days. (Okay, my mother doesn't have one — but pretty much everyone else does. And Mom will probably cave in and get one soon. She did finally get a CD player.)

☑ Progress Check

If you can do the following, you've mastered this lesson:

❑ Know how to avoid getting flamed by following the rules of netiquette.

❑ Send a personal e-mail to the author of a newsgroup message.

❑ Add your message to a newsgroup thread by replying to a previous message.

❑ Create a new message that may spawn a whole thread of its own.

Unit 12 Quiz

For each question, circle the letter of the correct answer.

1. **The difference between e-mail messages and newsgroup messages is . . .**

   A. Newsgroup messages appear in Courier, e-mail in Times New Roman.

   B. E-mail sends slowly; newsgroup messages travel instantly.

   C. There is no difference.

   D. E-mail is private; newsgroup messages are public.

2. **In the To line of an e-mail message, you type . . .**

   A. Any infinitive verb form.

   B. The first name of your intended recipient.

   C. The e-mail address of your intended recipient.

   D. be, or not To: be

3. **Whether to an e-mail or newsgroup message, a reply automatically includes . . .**

    A. A presupplied To line entry.

    B. A presupplied Subject line entry.

    C. The text of the message to which you're replying (unless you delete it).

    D. All of the above

4. **To send a private e-mail reply to a newsgroup message . . .**

    A. Click Reply to Group.

    B. Click Return to Sender.

    C. Click Reply to Author.

    D. Click Return for Refund.

5. **When sending to an e-mail address that you did not get from a Web page link, the message actually goes out as soon as you . . .**

    A. Click Send.

    B. Quit Internet Mail.

    C. Turn your back.

    D. Click Send and Receive.

Unit 12 Exercise

1. Subscribe to the newsgroup `alt.newbies`

2. Post a message in which you ask newbies to reply to you via e-mail so you can test your ability to retrieve you mail.

3. Wait a few days.

4. Check your mail. Any answers?

Notes:

Making and Taking Internet Phone Calls

Prerequisites

▸ Opening Internet Explorer and connecting to the Internet (Unit 1)

Objectives for This Unit

✓ Setting up Microsoft NetMeeting to make Internet phone calls

✓ Calling and conversing with somebody else who uses NetMeeting

✓ Receiving a call

✓ Using the directory to find someone to talk to

▸ NetMeeting

on the CD

NetMeeting supports phone calls & other kinds of conferencing

NetMeeting, a free Microsoft program included on the *Dummies 101: Internet Explorer 3 For Windows 95* CD-ROM, is a sort of general-purpose conferencing and collaboration tool. Using NetMeeting, you can converse and collaborate with other NetMeeting users — who may be anywhere in the world — through the Internet.

The most exciting of the several forms of conversation enabled by NetMeeting is Internet phone calls. Using NetMeeting, you can enjoy a live voice conversation with another NetMeeting user. The effect is a lot like a telephone call, except that the Internet carries the call and your PC's sound card, speakers, and microphone do the job of the telephone handset. Depending on what you pay for your Internet service, a phone call through NetMeeting may be far less expensive than making the same call the regular way, especially if your caller lives in another state or country. Note, however, that the sound quality of an Internet phone call is not quite as good as that of a regular telephone call.

Besides Internet phone calls, NetMeeting enables

▸ **Whiteboard conferences:** All conference participants can see and sketch ideas on a collaborative online drawing board that's similar to an office whiteboard.

▸ **Chat:** Multiple users carry out a conference through typed messages, much like an Internet Relay Chat (refer to Unit 11).

Notes:

- **File transfer:** NetMeeting users can send each other files.
- **Application sharing:** Multiple NetMeeting users can see and, to some extent, control a program running on one participant's PC so that all may collaborate on a single project or document.

To introduce you to NetMeeting, this unit shows you how to install NetMeeting on your PC and how to make and accept Internet phone calls with other NetMeeting users. To learn more about NetMeeting's other capabilities, you can

- Consult NetMeeting's Help file (open the Help menu while in NetMeeting).
- Visit the NetMeeting home page at

  `http://www.microsoft.com/netmeeting/`

check out NetMeeting Help file or home page for more info

Q&A session

Question: If Microsoft updates NetMeeting, how do I get the new version?

Answer: Visit the Microsoft NetMeeting page, where new versions will be made available for downloading. The URL is

`http://www.microsoft.com/netmeeting/`

---

heads up

Before you begin, you need to know two important restrictions to making Internet phone calls through NetMeeting:

- The person with whom you plan to talk must also use NetMeeting.
- You and the other caller must have a sound card, a microphone, and speakers (or headphones) set up on your respective PCs and properly configured for use with Windows 95. (If you need help setting up your sound card or microphone, consult your PC's or sound card's manuals or see *Dummies 101: Windows 95*, written by Andy Rathbone and published by IDG Books Worldwide, Inc.)

Lesson 13-1

Setting Up NetMeeting for Phone Calls

Before you can begin making or taking calls, you must set up NetMeeting as described in the following sections.

heads up

NetMeeting can run within a minimum Internet Explorer system configuration (486 processor or faster, 8MB of RAM). However, Microsoft recommends a Pentium PC, at least 12MB of RAM, and a 28.8 Kbps or faster Internet connection for best performance. If you use NetMeeting on a PC/Internet connection that does not come up to these specifications, you may notice sluggish performance and possibly poor sound quality.

should have Pentium PC, 12MB RAM, 28.8 Kbps Internet connection

Installing NetMeeting

To install NetMeeting:

1 **Click the Start button and choose Programs⇨Dummies 101⇨ Dummies 101 - Internet Explorer 3 Installer.**

2 **Click the NetMeeting Add-On button.**

A dialog box opens, asking whether you want to install NetMeeting.

3 **Click Yes.**

The license agreement appears. Make sure that you read it before going to Step 4.

4 **Click Yes.**

Several status reports appear while NetMeeting sets up on your PC. After a few moments, a message appears, asking for the name of the folder into which NetMeeting will be installed and showing the default folder.

5 **Click OK to accept the default folder.**

If you know what you're doing, you can type a different folder name, but for most people, the default is the best choice.

Another status message appears while the installation finishes up. When the installation is finished, move on to the next setup procedure, "Opening and configuring NetMeeting."

heads up

You may (or may not) be prompted to restart your PC after installation. If you're prompted to restart, do so before continuing with the next section.

Opening and configuring NetMeeting

After NetMeeting has been installed, you must run the setup Wizard, which collects some final configuration information from you. The Wizard opens automatically the first time you open NetMeeting.

heads up

Before starting this part of the installation, close all programs (except, of course, Windows). Doing so will prevent conflicts that could arise in later steps.

1 **From the Start menu, choose Programs⇨Microsoft NetMeeting.**

The Wizard opens, and a Welcome screen appears.

2 **Click Next.**

The dialog box shown in Figure 13-1 opens.

3 **Type your First name, Last name, and E-mail address (all other blanks are optional) and click Next.**

on the test

Microsoft collects this information for the directory of NetMeeting users that it maintains on the *User Location Service* (ULS) server, the type of server required for all NetMeeting communications. You can choose not to be listed in this directory (see Step 4); if you do want to be listed, all information that you provide in this dialog box will be available to other NetMeeting users. Regardless of whether you choose to be listed, you must enter your name and e-mail address in this dialog box.

After you click Next, the dialog box shown in Figure 13-2 appears.

NetMeeting icon

restart computer if so prompted

close other programs before setting up NetMeeting

if listed in ULS directory, all info provided in Step 3 available to other NetMeeting users

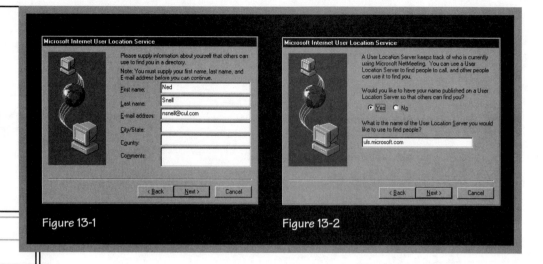

Figure 13-1

Figure 13-2

Figure 13-1: Enter your name and e-mail address to identify yourself to NetMeeting.

Figure 13-2: Click Yes to publish your name and other personal information in the ULS directory; click No to remain unlisted.

heads up

don't need to be listed on ULS to use NetMeeting

half duplex = only one person can speak at a time, like with CB radio

read passage in normal voice; Wizard uses voice to tune audio settings

☑ **Progress Check**

If you can do the following, you've mastered this lesson:

❑ Install NetMeeting.

❑ Run the Wizard to configure NetMeeting's audio settings.

4 Click Yes or No to tell Microsoft whether you want to be listed on the ULS server. Then click Next.

You don't need to be listed on the ULS in order to communicate with others through NetMeeting — the ULS is simply a directory that allows strangers to locate each other. Instead of letting Microsoft display the information that you provided in Step 3 on the ULS server, you may choose to privately inform your friends and associates that they can reach you directly through NetMeeting phone calls (as described later in this unit).

5 Click Next to begin tuning your audio settings.

You must tune your audio settings in order to make or accept phone calls with NetMeeting. After you click Next, a dialog box like the one in Figure 13-3 appears. The devices listed in Recording and Playback are the audio devices currently configured in Windows.

In Figure 13-3, notice the sentence under the Playback box, where the Wizard reports that my sound card is capable of half-duplex audio. *Half-duplex audio* means that when you have a phone conversation through NetMeeting, only one person can speak at a time, like a conversation over walkie-talkies or a CB radio. If your sound card supports full duplex, both callers can speak and hear one another at the same time, just like a regular phone call.

6 Click Next and click the radio button next to your modem speed.

7 In the next Audio Tuning Wizard dialog box that appears, click Start Recording and immediately begin reading aloud the paragraph directly beneath the Start Recording button.

In this dialog box, shown in Figure 13-4, the Wizard uses your voice to tune the microphone sensitivity, ensuring that others will hear you when you speak.

Read at a normal pace and volume, speaking just as you would if you were in a NetMeeting phone conversation. Watch the Time Remaining (at the bottom of the dialog box) to see when the Wizard is done recording. Whether you've finished reading the paragraph when time runs out doesn't matter.

8 When Time Remaining reads 0:00, click Next.

The Wizard reports that testing is complete. If your callers say that they have trouble hearing you, you can retune your audio settings at any time by opening NetMeeting and choosing Tools⇨Audio Tuning Wizard.

9 Click Next.

NetMeeting opens at last, as shown in Figure 13-5. The next time you open NetMeeting (from the Start menu, as described in Step 1), you go straight to this dialog box; the Wizard does not interfere.

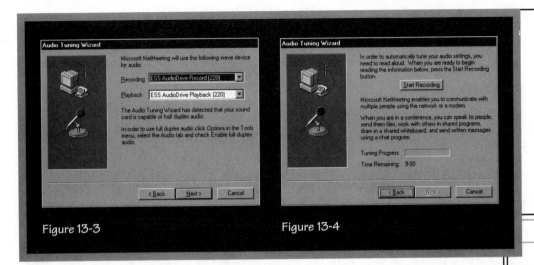

Figure 13-3

Figure 13-4

Figure 13-3: The Wizard checks the sound device to be used for phone calls.

Figure 13-4: Click Start Recording and then read aloud the paragraph beneath the button so that the Wizard can tune your audio settings according to your voice patterns.

Making a Call

Lesson 13-2

Before you can successfully call someone, the following must be true:

- You must know the e-mail address of the person you're calling.
- The person you're calling must have a sound card, a microphone, and speakers (just as you must).

Given these preconditions, prearranging your NetMeeting calls is the sensible thing to do. Using e-mail or a regular phone call, contact the person that you want to speak with and agree on a time and date for the call and the ULS server you will use. Then the person you're calling can be online, set up, and ready to take your call when the time comes.

Note: Any time you open NetMeeting, you can be online or off. If you're offline, NetMeeting opens your connection dialog box automatically so you can connect to the Internet.

To place a call, first make sure that your speakers and microphone are switched on. Connect to the Internet (if you haven't already done so) and then follow these steps:

1 **Open NetMeeting by clicking the Start button and choosing Programs⇨Microsoft NetMeeting.**

2 **Make sure that you're connected to the agreed-upon ULS.**

To check or change the ULS, choose Tools⇨Options⇨My Information and change the ULS listed there.

3 **In the Place a call box, type the e-mail address of the person you want to call.**

4 **Click the Call button.**

Completing the call may take a few moments. On the screen of the person you're calling, a message appears to indicate that a call is coming in. The person has the option of accepting or ignoring the call. When the person accepts, his or her name appears in the Name column of your NetMeeting screen.

---

set up calls in advance so that everybody's ready

can be online or offline when starting NetMeeting

Tools→Options→My Information to change ULS

Call button

Figure 13-5: Once set up, NetMeeting looks like this: simple.

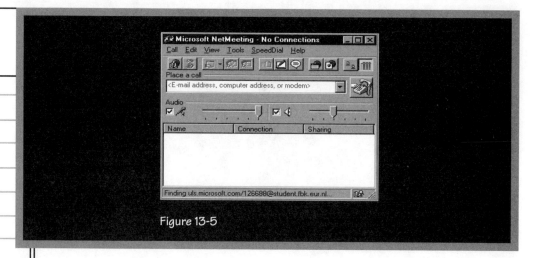

Figure 13-5

Hang button

5 **Talk and listen.**

You hear the other person's words through your speakers, and you talk into your microphone. *Tip:* When speaking, try to speak at roughly the same rate and volume level you used when you tuned your audio settings in Lesson 13-1.

6 **When you want to end the conversation, say good-bye and then click the Hang Up button.**

☑ Progress Check

If you can do the following, you've mastered this lesson:

❑ Open NetMeeting.

❑ Check and change the ULS.

❑ Place a call.

❑ Hang up.

extra credit

Using the ULS directory

ULS servers not only provide a medium for calls but also offer a directory of NetMeeting users who have permitted Microsoft to publish their listings (see Lesson 13-1). If you want to talk with someone in the directory, you can just click that person's listing to initiate a conversation. Doing so has the same effect as typing the person's e-mail address in the Place a call box, and the same preconditions apply — the person must be online and running NetMeeting in order to take your call.

You can open the directory in either of two ways (whichever you choose, NetMeeting must be open and connected to a ULS first):

- **Click the Directory button.** This method displays a list of users who are logged onto the server and who have allowed Microsoft to publish their listings (see Figure 13-6). To try to initiate a conversation, click the name of the person.

- **Click the Web Directory button.** This method opens Internet Explorer (if it's not already open) and displays a Web page listing of users who are logged onto the server and who have allowed Microsoft to publish their listings (see Figure 13-7). To try to initiate a conversation, click the name of the person.

When looking for someone in a directory, pay close attention to any information in the Comments section of the listing, where people indicate the topics they're interested in discussing. They may also indicate that they're not enabled for voice communication, or that they don't want to be contacted by strangers.

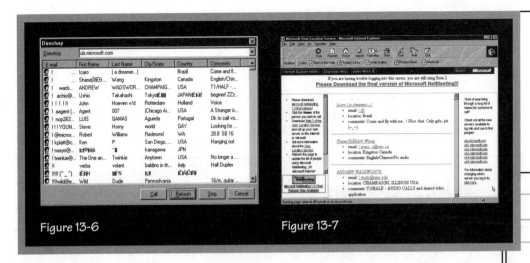

Figure 13-6

Figure 13-7

Figure 13-6: When you click NetMeeting's Directory button, the ULS directory appears in NetMeeting.

Figure 13-7: When you click NetMeeting's Web Directory button, the ULS directory appears in a Web page.

Taking a Call

Lesson 13-3

Some like to pitch; some like to catch. If you'd prefer taking the call to placing it, you'll need to set yourself up to receive the call when it's placed by the caller.

To accept a call:

1 **Prearrange the call, as described in the preceding lesson.**

Be sure to agree on the time for the call and the ULS server to use.

2 **Shortly before the time for the call, open NetMeeting (click Start and choose Programs⇨Microsoft NetMeeting) and connect to the Internet.**

If your default ULS is not the one the caller will use, choose Tools⇨Options⇨My Information and change the ULS listed there.

3 **Wait for the call.**

When the caller places the call, a dialog box appears, asking you to accept or ignore the call.

4 **Click Accept.**

You can now converse. When the call is over, hang up by choosing Call⇨Hang Up.

just need to open NetMeeting, connect to Internet, and check ULS to prepare for incoming call

dialog box appears when call comes in; click Accept

☑ Progress Check

If you can do the following, you've mastered this lesson:

❑ Prepare to accept a call.

❑ Accept a call.

Recess

This is a *big* recess — it's your last. Have a sandwich, take a shower, meditate. When you're refreshed and ready, snap through the easy quiz and exercise and then move on to the Part IV Test.

Unit 13 Quiz

Notes:

For each question, circle the letter of the correct answer.

1. **NetMeeting can be used for . . .**

   A. Software sharing.

   B. Voice calls over the Internet.

   C. Interactive conferences featuring both text and drawings.

   D. All of the above

2. **To use NetMeeting for voice calls, you must have . . .**

   A. A sound card, a microphone, and speakers (or headphones).

   B. The secret NetMeeting password.

   C. Something worthwhile to say.

   D. 16MB of RAM on your PC.

3. **If your sound card supports only half duplex audio . . .**

   A. The sound quality is only half as clear as with full duplex audio.

   B. You and the other caller each have your own front doors but share the house.

   C. When you finish a duplex call, you must unduplex.

   D. You and the other caller must take turns speaking.

4. **A User Location Service (ULS) server provides . . .**

   A. A medium for a call or conference between NetMeeting users.

   B. A search tool for finding any NetMeeting user in the world.

   C. A directory of NetMeeting users who have listed themselves with the server.

   D. A and C

5. **To accept a NetMeeting call from someone else . . .**

   A. You must be online.

   B. You must have NetMeeting open.

   C. You must click Accept when notified of the call.

   D. All of the above

Unit 13 Exercise

1. In your e-mail correspondence, ask people with whom you correspond frequently these questions:

   - Do you use Internet Explorer on Windows 95?
   - Do you have a sound card and a microphone?
   - Do you use NetMeeting?
   - Do you have voice capability?

2. If the answer to all three questions is yes, ask whether the person would like to have an Internet phone call. If the answer to the first two questions is yes but the answer to the last is no, inform your friend of the URL for downloading NetMeeting (`http://www.microsoft.com/ie`).

3. Plan a NetMeeting call, including date, time, and ULS server.

4. At the predetermined time, have a nice long Internet gabfest.

Part IV Review

Unit 11 Summary

▶ **Installing Comic Chat:** From the Start Menu, choose Programs⇨Dummies 101⇨Dummies 101 - Internet Explorer 3 Installer to open the CD-ROM Installer. Click the Comic Chat Add-On button and then follow the prompts.

▶ **Opening Comic Chat and connecting to the server:** Open your Start menu and then choose Programs⇨Microsoft Comic Chat⇨Microsoft Comic Chat. On the Connect dialog, click the radio button next to Show all available chat rooms; then click OK.

▶ **Choosing a nickname:** Choose View⇨Options, click in the Nickname box, and type a nickname for yourself.

▶ **Choosing a character:** Choose View⇨Options⇨Character and select a character from the list.

▶ **Choosing a background:** Choose View⇨Options⇨Background and select a background from the list.

▶ **Entering a chat room:** Double-click a chat room name in the Chat Room List.

▶ **Contributing a statement to the chat:** Type the statement and then press Enter or choose one of the buttons for different word balloon styles.

▶ **Changing your character's expression:** Before submitting your statement, click a face on the emotion wheel.

Unit 12 Summary

▶ **Sending e-mail straight from a Web page:** To send e-mail to an address that appears as a link in a Web page (an e-mail link), click the link, type a Subject, click in the body area, type your message, and click Send.

▶ **Opening Internet mail:** From the Start menu, choose Programs⇨Internet Mail.

▶ **Creating a new message:** Click New Message, enter an e-mail address in the To: line, enter a subject in the Subject line, type your message in the Body area, and click Send to save the message in your Outbox.

▶ **Replying to a message:** To compose a reply to a message you have received, open the message you received, click Reply to Author, compose the message, and click Send to save the message in your Outbox.

▶ **Sending messages and retrieving new mail:** To send all messages saved in your Outbox and retrieve any new mail waiting for you, click Send and Receive.

▶ **Opening Internet News:** To open Internet News from the Start menu, choose Programs⇨Internet News.

▶ **Subscribing to a newsgroup:** To subscribe to a newsgroup for easy access later, click Newsgroups, select the group from the list in the All tab, and click Subscribe.

▶ **Reading messages:** To see a newsgroup's current message list and read a message, choose one of your subscribed newsgroups from the Newsgroups drop-down list, wait for the headers to download, and then click any message in the list.

▶ **Replying to a message:** To post a reply to a message on the group, view the message, click Reply to Group, compose your reply over or within the quote, and then click Post Message.

▶ **Posting a new message:** To post a new message in a newsgroup, open that group, click New Message, enter a Subject, compose your message, and click Post Message.

Part IV Review

Unit 13 Summary

▶ **Installing NetMeeting:** From the Start Menu, choose Programs⇨Dummies 101⇨Dummies 101 - Internet Explorer 3 Installer to open the CD-ROM Installer. Click the NetMeeting Add-On button and then follow the prompts. When finished, click the Start menu and choose Programs⇨Microsoft NetMeeting and follow the prompts to complete setup.

▶ **Opening NetMeeting:** To open NetMeeting, click the Start menu and choose Programs⇨ Microsoft NetMeeting.

▶ **Placing an Internet phone call:** To make a voice call through NetMeeting, enter the e-mail address of the person you wish to call in the Place a call box and then click the Call button.

▶ **Receiving a call:** To receive a voice call placed by another NetMeeting user, click A̲ccept when prompted.

▶ **Hanging up:** To end a voice call, click the Hang Up button.

Part IV Test

The questions on this test cover all the material presented in Part IV, Unit 11 through Unit 13.

True False

Each statement is either true or false.

T   F   1. It's wise to strengthen important points in newsgroup messages by typing in ALL CAPITAL LETTERS.

T   F   2. Comic Chat makes you appear to be a comic character on the screens of all members in the chat, no matter what chat client they use.

T   F   3. When you compose a new e-mail message and click Send, the message doesn't go out right away (unless you clicked an e-mail link in a Web page), but is instead stored in your Outbox folder.

T   F   4. NetMeeting is used exclusively for voice telephone calls and no other purpose.

T   F   5. In order to visit a newsgroup, you absolutely must first subscribe to it.

T   F   6. When you Reply to a message (news or mail), you needn't type a Subject.

T   F   7. Using NetMeeting, you can converse only with other NetMeeting users.

T   F   8. Most newsgroups are open to discussion of any topic or question.

T   F   9. Always use your e-mail address or full name as your Comic Chat nickname.

T   F   10. You can find other NetMeeting users on the server by clicking the Directory button.

Multiple Choice

For each of the following questions, circle the correct answer.

11. **To send all e-mail messages waiting in your Outbox (and retrieve new incoming messages) . . .**

    A. Click Mail and News.

    B. Click Send and Receive.

    C. Click Forward.

    D. Click Send.

12. **The first time you run Internet News, you must . . .**

    A. Read the Help file to learn about Netiquette.

    B. Lurk in all subscribed groups.

    C. Send a greeting to each subscribed group.

    D. Download the full list of newsgroups.

13. **To call another NetMeeting user . . .**

    A. Enter the e-mail address and click Call.

    B. Enter the e-mail address and click Ring.

    C. Enter a server address and click Dial.

    D. Enter an ashram and click the lights.

14. **Which are the parts of a new message header (news or mail) that you should always enter?**

    A. To, From

    B. To, Subject

    C. To, Date

    D. To, RE

Part IV Test

15. **When you begin a statement in Comic Chat with the word "You", your character . . .**

    A. Slaps the other character.

    B. Points to the other character.

    C. Makes an open-handed gesture at the other character.

    D. Pokes the other character.

16. **Two participants in the same chat room cannot have the same . . .**

    A. Nickname.

    B. Character.

    C. Background.

    D. Attitude.

17. **To chat, you must have . . .**

    A. An Internet connection and a Web browser.

    B. A chat client, a connection to a chat server, and a nickname.

    C. An FCC chat license.

    D. Limitless free time.

Matching

18. **Match each button (from Comic Chat's Compose pane) with the type of word balloon it puts your statement in:**

    A.   1. Regular talking out loud

    B.   2. Thinking

    C.   3. Whispering

19. **Match each button with its action:**

    A.   1. Sends mail from Outbox and retrieves new mail

    B.   2. Sends a reply via e-mail

    C.   3. Posts a reply on a newsgroup

    D.   4. Sends to someone else a copy of a message you've received

Part IV Lab Assignment

This lab assignment enables you to hone your skills at communicating on the Internet.

Step 1

On Microsoft's chat server, find and join a chat covering a topic that interests you.

Step 2

In the chat, ask the other members if they know the names of good newsgroups covering the same subject. Jot down their suggestions.

Step 3

Visit the newsgroups your chat pals suggest.

Step 4

Return to the chat room another time and contribute your own suggestions.

Step 5

As friendships develop with your chat or newsgroup pals, ask for their e-mail addresses and begin a private correspondence.

Step 6

If a friendship deepens and your friend uses NetMeeting, arrange an Internet phone call.

Appendixes

Part V

In this part . . .

Appendix A is the section you'll probably flip to several times as you follow along in the book, as it contains the answers to all of the quizzes and tests. It's a cheater's paradise.

Appendix B is a guide to what's on the *Dummies 101: Internet Explorer 3 For Windows 95* CD-ROM. I use this appendix to describe the software, and I help you install the stuff that I didn't have you install in the lessons throughout the book.

Appendix C is a bonus lesson for the brave. It shows you how to create your own Web page.

Answers

Unit 1 Quiz Answers

Question	Answer	If You Missed It, Try This
1.	C	Review the introduction to Unit 1.
2.	B	Review Lesson 1-2.
3.	D	Review Lesson 1-2.
4.	A	Review Lesson 1-3.
5.	D	Review Lesson 1-4.

Unit 2 Quiz Answers

Question	Answer	If You Missed It, Try This
1.	D	Review Lesson 2-1.
2.	A	Review Lesson 2-1.
3.	D	Review Lessons 2-1 and 2-2.
4.	B	Review Lesson 2-3.
5.	D	Review Lesson 2-1.

Unit 3 Quiz Answers

Question	Answer	If You Missed It, Try This
1.	B	Review the introduction to Unit 3.
2.	D	Review Lesson 3-2.
3.	B	Review Lesson 3-1.
4.	B	Review Lesson 3-2.
5.	B	Review Lesson 3-2.

Unit 4 Quiz Answers

Question	Answer	If You Missed It, Try This
1.	D	Review Lesson 4-1.
2.	C	Review Lesson 4-2.
3.	D	Review Lesson 4-3.
4.	A	Review Lesson 4-3.
5.	B	Review Lesson 4-1.

Part I Test Answers

Question	Answer	If You Missed It, Try This
1.	True	Review Lesson 1-2.
2.	False	Review Lesson 2-1.
3.	False	Review Lesson 2-1.
4.	True	Review Lesson 3-1.
5.	True	Review Lesson 2-2.
6.	False	Review Lesson 2-3.
7.	False	Review Lesson 2-1.
8.	True	Review Lesson 2-2.
9.	False	Review Lesson 1-2.

10.	True	Review Lesson 1-3.
11.	C	Review Lesson 3-1.
12.	C	Review the introduction to Unit 1.
13.	A	Review Lesson 2-2.
14.	B	Review Lesson 2-2.
15.	D	Review Lesson 1-2.
16.	A	Review Lesson 1-2.
17.	A, 4	Review Lesson 4-1.
	B, 2	Review Lesson 2-2.
	C, 1	Review Lesson 2-2.
	D, 3	Peek ahead at Unit 5. (Trick! But you guessed it anyway, right?)

Unit 5 Quiz Answers

Question	Answer	If You Missed It, Try This
1.	D	Review the introduction to Unit 5.
2.	D	Review Lesson 5-1.
3.	A	Review the introduction to Unit 5 (A is the metaphor used in Unit 5 and is also funniest).
4.	A	Review Lesson 5-2.
5.	C	Review Lesson 5-4.
6.	D	Review the introduction to Unit 5.

Unit 6 Quiz Answers

Question	Answer	If You Missed It, Try This
1.	B	Review the introduction to Unit 6.
2.	D	Review Lesson 6-1.
3.	D	Review Lesson 6-4.
4.	A	Review Lesson 6-3.
5.	B	Review Lesson 6-2.

Unit 7 Quiz Answers

Question	Answer	If You Missed It, Try This
1.	B	Review the introduction to Unit 7.
2.	B	Review Lesson 7-2.
3.	B	Review the introduction to Unit 7.
4.	D	Review Lesson 7-2.
5.	B	Review Lesson 7-2.

Part II Test Answers

Question	Answer	If You Missed It, Try This
1.	False	Review Lesson 7-2.
2.	True	Review Lesson 5-3.
3.	False	Review Lesson 6-1.
4.	False	Review Lesson 5-3.
5.	True	Review Lesson 7-2.
6.	False	Review Lesson 7-2.
7.	False	Review the introduction to Unit 6.
8.	True	Review Lesson 7-2.
9.	True	Review Lesson 5-3.
10.	True	Review Lesson 7-2.
11.	B	Review the introduction to Unit 6.
12.	D	Review Lesson 5-1.
13.	D	Review Lesson 6-2.
14.	C	Review Lesson 6-1.
15.	A	Review Lesson 5-4.
16.	C	Review Lesson 7-2.
17.	D	Review Lesson 6-4.
18.	A, 3	Review Lesson 7-2.
	B, 1	Review Lesson 7-2.
	C, 2	Review Lesson 7-2.

Unit 8 Quiz Answers

Question	Answer	If You Missed It, Try This
1.	B	Review the introduction to Unit 8.
2.	D	Review Lesson 8-2.
3.	C	Review the introduction to Unit 8 and Lesson 8-1.
4.	A	Review Lesson 8-2.
5.	B	Review the introduction to Unit 8.

Unit 9 Quiz Answers

Question	Answer	If You Missed It, Try This
1.	D	Review Lesson 9-1.
2.	D	Review Lessons 9-2 and 9-3.
3.	C	Review Lesson 9-3.
4.	A	Review Lesson 9-1.
5.	D	Review Lesson 9-2.

Unit 10 Quiz Answers

Question	Answer	If You Missed It, Try This
1.	D	Review the introduction to Unit 10.
2.	D	Review Lesson 10-1.
3.	A	Review Lesson 10-2.
4.	D	Review Lesson 10-2.
5.	B	Review Lesson 10-2.

Part III Test Answers

Question	Answer	If You Missed It, Try This
1.	True	Review Lesson 9-3.
2.	True	Review Lesson 10-2.
3.	True	Review Lesson 9-1.
4.	True	Review Lesson 8-2.
5.	False	Review the introduction to Unit 8.
6.	False	Review Lesson 9-3.
7.	True	Review Lesson 10-1.
8.	False	Review Lesson 9-3.
9.	True	Review Lesson 9-2.
10.	False	Review the introduction to Unit 8.
11.	B	Review the introduction to Unit 8.
12.	D	Review Lesson 9-3.
13.	D	Review Lesson 9-3.
14.	B	Review the introduction to Unit 10.
15.	C	Review the introduction to Unit 10.
16.	D	Review the introduction to Unit 8.
17.	A, 2	Review Lesson 9-1.
	B, 1	Review Lesson 9-3.
	C, 3	Review Lesson 10-2.

Unit 11 Quiz Answers

Question	Answer	If You Missed It, Try This
1.	D	Review Lesson 11-1.
2.	A	Review Lesson 11-2.
3.	C	Review Lesson 11-1.
4.	D	Review the introduction to Unit 11.
5.	B	Review Lesson 11-3.

Unit 12 Quiz Answers

Question	Answer	If You Missed It, Try This
1.	D	Review Lesson 12-5.
2.	C	Review Lesson 12-2.
3.	D	Review Lessons 12-4 and 12-7.
4.	C	Review Lesson 12-7.
5.	D	Review Lesson 12-3.

Unit 13 Quiz Answers

Question	Answer	If You Missed It, Try This
1.	D	Review the introduction to Unit 13.
2.	A	Review the introduction to Unit 13.
3.	D	Review Lesson 13-1.
4.	D	Review Lesson 13-2.
5.	D	Review Lesson 13-3.

Part IV Test Answers

Question	Answer	If You Missed It, Try This
1.	False	Review Lesson 12-7.
2.	False	Review Lesson 11-1.
3.	True	Review Lesson 12-2.
4.	False	Review the introduction to Unit 13.
5.	False	Review Lesson 12-5.
6.	True	Review Lessons 12-4 and 12-7.
7.	True	Review the introduction to Unit 13.
8.	False	Review Lesson 12-7.

(continued)

Part IV Test Answers *(continued)*

Question	Answer	If You Missed It, Try This
9.	False	Review Lesson 11-2.
10.	True	Review Lesson 13-2.
11.	B	Review Lesson 12-3.
12.	D	Review Lesson 12-5.
13.	A	Review Lesson 13-2.
14.	B	Review Lessons 12-1, 12-2 and 12-7.
15.	B	Review Lesson 11-3.
16.	A	Review Lesson 11-2.
17.	B	Review Lesson 11-1.
18.	A, 1	Review Lesson 11-3.
	B, 2	Review Lesson 11-3.
	C, 3	Review Lesson 11-3.
19.	A, 3	Review Lesson 12-7.
	B, 1	Review Lesson 12-3.
	C, 4	Review Lesson 12-4.
	D, 2	Review Lessons 12-4 and 12-7.

Dummies 101 CD-ROM Installation Instructions

In this appendix, you learn how to install the CD-ROM packaged with this book. You also discover

- ♦ Which Unit of the tutorial covers the use of each program or file.
- ♦ How to set up programs that require further preparation to ready them for the steps in the tutorial.
- ♦ How to install the example file, COPYTST.DOC, which is required in one of the examples in Unit 3 and the Template folder, which you use in Appendix C.

Note: Because of the way the Installer program on the CD-ROM works, you must first install the AT&T WordNet software with Internet Explorer before the Installer will allow you to install NetMeeting, Comic Chat, Shockwave, or VRML ActiveX Control.

Installing the CD-ROM

To install the CD-ROM (Windows 95 must be running), follow these steps:

1 **Insert the Dummies 101 CD-ROM (label side up) into your computer's CD-ROM drive.**

2 **Wait a minute or so to give Windows a chance to activate the installation program automatically.**

Some Windows 95 configurations have a feature called AutoPlay installed. AutoPlay automatically plays/installs any CD-ROM shortly after you insert it. If AutoPlay is enabled for your PC, the Dummies 101 CD-ROM installation program starts up. Follow the instructions you see on screen to get icons installed in your Start menu; then proceed to the next section, "Installing Programs and Files."

If, after a minute or so, you see no messages regarding the CD, your PC does not have AutoPlay enabled, and you must perform Steps 3 and 4 to complete the CD installation.

3 **From your Windows 95 desktop, click the Start button and choose Run.**

4 **In the dialog box that appears, type** D:\ICONS **(substitute your CD-ROM's drive letter if different from D) and then click OK.**

After installation, proceed to the next section, "Installing Programs and Files."

Installing Programs and Files

After you've set up the CD-ROM Installer program as described in the previous section, the CD-ROM Install program appears on your screen. The Install program includes a button for installing each program on the CD-ROM, plus one more button — Install Exercise Files — that copies example files used in some units to your hard disk.

Do *not* click any of the buttons now. Clicking a button not only copies a program's files to your hard disk but also initiates the program's setup routine, which may require further input from you. Instead, click the Exit button at the bottom of the Installer and then proceed with the tutorials in the Units.

As you work through the book, you'll encounter complete instructions for installing each program as that program becomes necessary. (Two programs on the CD, Shockwave Add-On and VRML ActiveX Control, are not described in the tutorial but are instead described later in this appendix.)

Whenever a lesson prompts you to install a program from the CD-ROM:

1 Insert the CD-ROM in your drive (if it is not already there).

If your PC has AutoPlay enabled, the CD-ROM Installer program opens automatically. If the CD-ROM was already in the drive (and the Installer was closed previously) or if your PC does not have AutoPlay, you can open the Install program manually by opening your Windows 95 Start menu and choosing Programs⇨Dummies 101⇨Dummies 101 - Internet Explorer 3 Installer.

2 Click the button of a program to start the installation and then follow all setup steps described in the unit.

The remainder of this appendix briefly describes each program and file on the CD-ROM and tells you where you can find instructions for setting up and using the program or file.

Note: After a program or file has been completely installed and set up on your PC, you may remove the Dummies 101 CD-ROM; it is not required for the actual use of any program, other than to install that program.

Units 1 and 12: Using the AT&T WorldNet℠ Software

The AT&T WorldNet software file includes a special, AT&T-customized version of Internet Explorer, plus Internet News and Internet Mail.

Unit 1 describes how to set up the AT&T WorldNet software to establish your AT&T WorldNet account, and how to begin your Internet travels using Internet Explorer.

Unit 12 describes how to use Internet Mail and Internet News, which are both installed automatically when you set up the AT&T WorldNet software in Unit 1.

Unit 3: Using the COPYTST.DOC file

The file COPYTST.DOC, which is installed on your PC by the Install Exercise Files button, is used in an example in Unit 3. It requires no further setup.

Unit 6: Setting Up WinZip

Many files that you can copy from the Internet to your PC are compressed to copy more quickly and must be decompressed before you can use them. WinZip is a shareware program for decompressing compressed files. In Unit 6, you learn how to download files and how to decompress files with WinZip.

Before you can use WinZip, you must first set it up:

1 **Open the Installer program as described earlier in this appendix and then click the WinZip 6.1 button.**

A dialog box opens, asking you to choose a directory to store WinZip in. You may change the default directory shown or simply skip to Step 2 to accept the default directory.

2 **Click OK.**

Various status messages appear while WinZip files are copied to your PC. After a few moments, the WinZip setup Wizard appears.

3 **Click Next and follow the Wizard's prompts to complete the installation.**

You can set up WinZip using whatever options you like, but you'll get the best results if, when so prompted by the Wizard, you choose the Classic version (rather than the Wizard version) and Express (rather than custom) setup.

When the installation is complete, WinZip is ready to use as described in Unit 6.

Note: WinZip is shareware. Like all shareware, WinZip is licensed to you for a trial period, after which you are expected to pay a small fee to WinZip's publisher if you intend to continue using it. Every time you open WinZip, a screen appears briefly on which you can find details about registering and paying for continued use of WinZip. If you use AT&T WorldNet Service, please note that AT&T does not provide technical support for the WinZip software.

Unit 11: Using Comic Chat

Comic Chat enables you to join live, interactive discussion on the Internet and to view those chats in a fun, comic-strip-style presentation. Unit 11 describes how to set up and use Comic Chat.

Note: Comic Chat is a Microsoft product. If you use AT&T WorldNet Service, please be aware that AT&T does not provide technical support for the Comic Chat software.

Unit 13: Using NetMeeting

NetMeeting enables you to join live, interactive meetings (much like Comic Chat), and it also supports live phone conversations over the Internet (with no long-distance charges) if you have a sound card, speakers, and a microphone installed on your PC. Unit 13 describes how to set up and use NetMeeting.

Note: NetMeeting is a Microsoft product. If you use AT&T WorldNet Service, please be aware that AT&T does not provide technical support for the NetMeeting software.

Appendix C: Creating Your Own Web Page

In Appendix C, you learn how to create your own Web page using files included on the CD-ROM. Before proceeding to Appendix C, be sure to run the Installer and click the Install Exercise Files button to copy the Template folder to your hard disk. The Template folder contains files that together make up a template Web page called YOURHOME. HTM. You can edit this Web page to make your own. (The Install Exercise Files button also copies a file you need for Unit 3.)

Setting Up VRML ActiveX Control and Shockwave

Shockwave and VRML ActiveX Control add exciting new features to Internet Explorer. VRML (virtual reality modeling language) ActiveX Control, which comes from Microsoft, allows Internet Explorer to work with virtual, three-dimensional worlds, as you may have seen in some of the latest video games.

Shockwave, by Macromedia, allows Internet Explorer to play enhanced, interactive multimedia (sound, video, and animation) through the Web. Web pages that include interactive media designed for Shockwave are called *shocked sites*. You cannot see or use the interactive media on a shocked site unless you have the Shockwave add-on installed.

Note: Shockwave and VRML ActiveX Control are not AT&T WorldNet software products. Thus AT&T WorldNet does not offer support for these add-ons.

To install either Shockwave or VRML ActiveX Control, make sure that you already have Internet Explorer installed. Make sure that the Dummies 101 CD-ROM is in your drive and that all other programs, including Internet Explorer, are closed. Open the Installer as described earlier in this appendix and then click the button for the add-on that you wish to install. Follow the prompts during the setup procedure. When finished, restart your computer.

To explore how virtual worlds work, go to this Web site: `http://www.microsoft.com/ie/most/howto/vrml.htm`. Where can you find shocked sites? All over, actually, but the best place to start is at the Shockwave home page set up by Macromedia, Inc.: `http://www.macromedia.com/shockwave`.

Creating Your Own Web Page

The other day, an old friend and coworker of mine sent me the URL of a Web page he said I just had to visit. It turned out to be a brand new Web page for a company we both used to work for — a company that, at least officially, went out of business at least a year and a half ago.

At last, the world has come to this: Not only does everyone and everything have its own Web page these days, even *things that don't exist* have their own Web pages. Yeesh!

▶ Template folder

on the CD

Given that phenomenon, it's only reasonable for me to guess that you may want to create a Web page — for yourself or for your company — and publish it on the Internet so that anyone with an Internet account and a Web browser can visit it. In this appendix, you get a pain-free introduction to the wonderful world of Web authoring, including instructions for building a simple Web page with WebEdit, a handy Web-authoring tool.

Of course, Web authoring is a big topic, one to which whole books are devoted. So at the end of this appendix, I describe some great Web sites where you can expand your new Web authoring capabilities.

What's an HTML File, Anyway?

As you know from Unit 3 and Unit 9, a Web page is just a file in a format called HTML, which stands for *Hypertext Markup Language*. Although the file name extension of a Web page file is always .HTM or .HTML, the file itself is actually just an ordinary text file, one you can read in Windows Notepad or in any word processor. The text in that file, however, includes special codes — called HTML *tags* — that tell a browser how to display the file's contents.

a Web page is just a file in a format called HTML

In fact, if you look at any HTML file in Notepad or WordPad, you'll see the HTML tags — tags are enclosed within angle brackets (< >) — along with the text that actually appears in the Web page. You'll also see in the HTML file the filenames of pictures that appear in the Web page (the pictures themselves are stored separately as ordinary graphics files) and the URLs that any links in the page point to. Figure C-1 shows the actual text (in Notepad) of an HTML file. Figure C-2 shows how that very same file looks when viewed through Internet Explorer. As you can see if you compare the figures, the browser's job is to interpret the HTML codes in the text file, displaying the page's contents the way the author wants them to look.

Figure C-1: Viewed through Notepad or any word processor, the file YOURHOME.HTM appears to be nothing but the text of the Web page, the filenames of pictures, and the URLs of links, all surrounded by HTML tags enclosed in angle brackets (< >).

Figure C-1

Tip: While viewing any page in Internet Explorer (online or off), you can view the page's actual HTML text, sometimes known as *HTML source.* In Internet Explorer, choose View➪Source. The HTML text appears in a window (close the window when you're finished examining the HTML code). Viewing the HTML files of Web pages you visit is a great way to learn more about HTML and Web authoring.

Creating a Web page is a simple matter of composing the text to appear on the page, creating or acquiring any picture files to appear in the page, and then peppering the HTML text file with the desired HTML tags. In fact, it's possible to compose a Web page entirely in Notepad or any word processor that allows you to save a file in plain text format (with an extension of .HTM or .HTML, of course).

But creating Web pages in text editors requires expertise in HTML plus a lot of careful labor. Instead, most authors use special *HTML editors,* programs that automatically apply the proper HTML tags to the text you compose and the pictures you select.

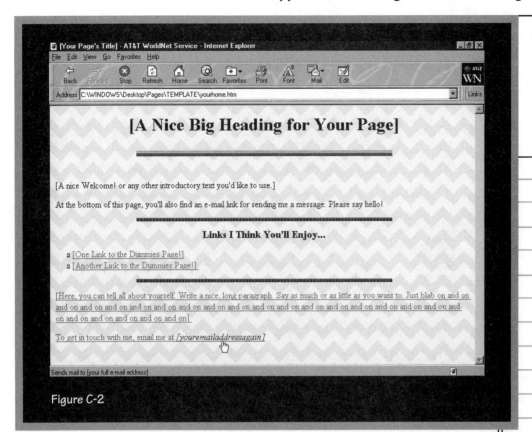

Figure C-2

Figure C-2: Viewed through Internet Explorer, the file YOURHOME.HTM appears as a Web page. The browser interprets the HTML codes to determine how to format the page for display.

The same page looks different in different browsers

Before you embark upon writing your own Web pages, it's important to understand that the same Web page looks different when viewed through different browsers. For example, if you put a heading in your page and center it at the top of the page, some browsers display the heading centered, but others will display the heading on the left side of the page because the browser does not support text centering. Remember as well that some browsers don't display pictures; be sure that any information contained in a picture — such as a company name in a logo picture — is repeated somewhere else on the page in text form.

Finally, as you expand your authoring capabilities beyond what you learn in this appendix, you'll begin to run into the term *extensions*. Extensions are new HTML tags created by a browser maker. Because the tags aren't part of the standard HTML language, not all browsers support them. For example, Microsoft created HTML extensions that allow Web authors to add inline video (see Unit 7) to Web pages. If an author uses inline video, only visitors using Internet Explorer can see the video.

Fortunately, nearly all of the extensions have been introduced by Microsoft and Netscape Communications (for its Netscape Navigator browser). To remain competitive, Microsoft and Netscape have been steadily enhancing their browsers to support most of each other's extensions. That means that even if you apply extensions in your page, visitors using Internet Explorer and visitors using Netscape will probably both see your page as you intended. However, a small percentage of your visitors — those using other browsers — will see all of the text on your page but may see it arranged and formatted somewhat differently than you intended, and they may not see all of your pictures or other multimedia.

Creating a Page in WebEdit

To illustrate how simple it is to compose a Web page using a typical HTML editor, the next several pages describe how you might create a Web page with a tool called WebEdit. I'm not necessarily recommending WebEdit; I'm just using it to illustrate the process.

Ultimately, you'll find your own favorite HTML editor. (See "Learning More about Authoring" at the end of this appendix to learn how to find other HTML editors and other authoring resources.)

heads up

If you want to learn more about getting the latest version of WebEdit, check out Luckman Software's Web page at `http://www.luckman.com`.

WebEdit allows you to create a page in three ways:

> ▶ **Home Page Wizard:** The Home Page Wizard shields you from having to deal with the HTML file and tags. Instead, it prompts you to type any text, URLs, and picture filenames you want in your page and then uses that information to automatically create a simple home page for you. (See "Using the Home Page Wizard" later in this appendix.)

> ▶ **New Blank Page:** A new, empty page is created on which you compose your page by typing text, picture filenames, and URLs and then applying the required HTML tags to them. (See "Composing a page" later in this appendix.)

> ▶ **Existing Page:** A pre-existing HTML file is opened so that you can change it. With an existing page, you can build a Web page from a *template*, a pre-fab Web page that you can edit to create a new page. (See "Using a template" later in this appendix.)

heads up

In the remainder of this section, you'll learn briefly about all three techniques. Be sure to read through the Home Page Wizard section first, even if you intend to apply one of the other techniques; the Home Page Wizard section contains important information about the elements of a Web page.

Opening WebEdit

If you chose to obtain a copy of WebEdit and installed it, you can open by selecting it from the Start menu.

When you use WebEdit for the first time, the program may prompt you to register. I suggest that you test it out for a few days before deciding whether or not to register. You may also be asked to read a license agreement. After you do so, WebEdit should open, ready for Web authoring.

Remember that WebEdit isn't free. If you like it and continue to use it, you must register it and pay the shareware fee.

Using the Home Page Wizard

Before starting the WebEdit Home Page Wizard, you must consider and prepare two items:

- **Picture files:** The Wizard enables you to optionally include a picture in your home page and to use a picture as a background for your page. Among browsers that can display pictures, all can display a picture in the GIF file format (extension .GIF), and most can display a picture in the JPEG format (extension .JPG). The preferred format is GIF because it's the most widely supported.

  You can create the pictures yourself; many drawing and paint programs allow you to save images you create in GIF or JPEG format. If you have a scanner, you can create pictures by scanning a photo or other image (be sure it's not copyrighted!) and saving the scan as a GIF or JPEG file. Finally, if you want to use pictures but don't want to create them yourself, you can download from the Web picture files called *clip art*. The final section of this appendix includes the addresses of several Web sites from which you may download free clip art.

  Important! When working with picture files, always store them in the same folder where you will store your HTML file when you finish it.

- **URLs for links:** You can include links in your home page. For example, you can feature a link that takes your visitors to your favorite place on the Web. Be sure you know the exact URL of the page you want to add a link for. The Home Page Wizard also enables you to include a link to another page you've created so that your home page can actually be made up of several pages linked together.

When you know your link URLs and have your picture files ready, open WebEdit. To start the Home Page Wizard, open WebEdit, choose File⇨New and then choose Home Page Wizard from the dialog that opens.

To work through the Home Page Wizard, supply the information the Wizard requests on each dialog and click <u>N</u>ext to proceed to the next dialog box. As you go, the Wizard displays a miniature version of your page on the left side of the dialog box, enabling you to see it as it develops. Each dialog box describes exactly what type of information is required.

Along the way, you'll be prompted to provide the following information:

- **Title** (required): Make sure that you supply a title that is brief but accurately descriptive of the contents or purpose of your page. The title identifies your page and is used by search engines (see Unit 5) to help decide whether your page matches a search term.

  Note: Technically, the title of an HTML file does not appear within the layout of the Web page itself. Instead, the title appears only in the title bar of the window in which the page is viewed through a browser. The Home Page Wizard cheats a little bit because whatever you supply for a title is used as the actual HTML title and then used again as the largest type of heading (heading 1), so that it appears big and bold at the top of the page layout. But when you create your own pages outside of the Home Page Wizard, the title does not appear within the layout of the page unless you also put the same text in a heading, as the Wizard does.

- **Subheading** (optional): The subheading is just a smaller heading to appear beneath the large heading in which the Wizard repeats the title text. Type anything you want.

- **Background** (optional): You can choose a "Plain" background (which is really no background at all), or you can choose a color for your background. Or you can enter the file name of a GIF picture file to use as an image background (you may have to click the Locate button to tell WebEdit where the image file is stored). The image background appears behind any text or other pictures in the page. If the image is not large enough to cover the whole background, it is automatically *tiled*, repeated over and over in a pattern, to cover the entire background of the page. Always use a GIF (not JPEG) file for an image background. Note that some browsers do not support color backgrounds or image backgrounds; visitors using those browsers simply won't see your background.

- **A picture** (optional): Click the checkbox next to <u>I</u>nclude a Picture and enter the full name of a GIF or JPEG file to include in your page (you may have to click the Locate button to tell WebEdit where the picture file is stored). You can optionally add a caption for your picture as well.

- **A paragraph** (optional): Type any general text you'd like to appear in your page.

- **Links** (optional): As the Site Location, type the complete URL of a page for which you want to supply a link. As the Site <u>D</u>escription, type the text that should appear on your page as the link itself. When a visitor clicks the Site Description in your page, the visitor jumps to the URL in Site Location.

- **Page links:** You enter Page Links just like the other Links, except that, because you're linking to other pages of you own, you needn't supply the entire URL. As long as the files for all of your pages will all be stored in the same server directory (see "Publishing Your Web Page" later in this appendix), the filename of the HTML file alone is sufficient.

- **Contact information** (optional): Enter your name and e-mail address to enable the Wizard to create a *signature* for the page, an e-mail link (see Unit 12) so that visitors can get in touch with you.

use a GIF file for an image background

When the Wizard closes, the HTML text file appears before you in WebEdit. You can then make changes to your new home page or simply save it. To save an HTML file in WebEdit:

1 Choose <u>F</u>ile⇨<u>S</u>ave.

2 Type a name for the file.

DO NOT add a filename extension; the extension .HTM is added automatically by WebEdit.

Be sure to save your HTML file in the same folder where any pictures it uses (including the file for any image background) are stored, or be sure to copy the picture files to the same folder as the HTML file.

Viewing a page you've created

In Unit 9, you learned how to use Internet Explorer to open and view an HTML file saved on your hard disk. The files you create yourself are no different. You can open a Web page you've created by locating its icon and double-clicking the icon or by choosing <u>F</u>ile⇨<u>O</u>pen⇨<u>B</u>rowse in Internet Explorer and browsing to the file.

Also, you can set up WebEdit's View Document with Browser button so that clicking it opens Internet Explorer and displays the file you're working on. The first time you click the View... button (the eyeglasses), you're led through a series of dialog boxes in which you tell WebEdit where your Internet Explorer program file (iexplore.exe) is stored. (You can probably find the file in C:\Program Files\Microsoft Internet\.) After that, any time you click View..., Internet Explorer opens and displays the file currently being edited in WebEdit. (Always save your file before clicking the View... button.)

always save your file before clicking the View... button

Composing a page

As I said at the beginning of this appendix, Web authoring is a big subject — so the best I can do here is get you started on creating and editing an HTML file without the Home Page Wizard's assistance. In a nutshell, you create a page by typing the page's text, picture filenames, and link URLs; you then apply the HTML tags to those elements.

You apply tags to text by highlighting the text and choosing formatting options from one of the buttons on WebEdit's toolbar. You add pictures and links by clicking the Inline Image or Anchor / Link button. The resulting dialog box opens up to collect the filename or URL and allows you to apply any special optional formatting.

A good way to get started is to use the Add Minimal HTML button (the + sign). With a completely empty document open, click the button. WebEdit adds the following HTML tags:

```
<HTML>
<HEAD>
<TITLE>Page Title</TITLE>
</HEAD>
<BODY>
```

(continued)

```
<H1>First Heading</H1>
Add body text here.
<HR>
</BODY>
</HTML>
```

You can then replace the words Page Title with a real title, First Heading with a real heading, and so on. After that, it's easy to add any new page elements you wish.

To learn more about composing a new Web page with WebEdit, consult WebEdit's Help file.

Using a template

Instead of creating your page from scratch, you can simply edit an existing file — a *template* — changing only what you want to and leaving alone what already works. In effect, WebEdit's Add Minimal HTML button starts you off with a template, but you can use a more elaborate template as well. For example, you can use the Home Page Wizard to throw together a basic page quickly and then expand and enhance that page by editing it in WebEdit.

To open an existing HTML file for editing, choose File➪Open.

The CD-ROM bundled with this book includes a template, YOURHOME.HTM, that includes some fancy formatting and a snazzy background. (The YOURHOME.HTM file appears earlier in this appendix, in Figures C-1 and C-2.)

1 Open YOURHOME.HTM in WebEdit.

You can find the file in c:\My Documents\Dummies 101 - Internet Explorer 3\ Template. It's installed when you click the Install Exercise Files button from the CD-ROM Install program, as described in Appendix B.

2 Locate any text enclosed in brackets ([ ]).

Change any of it you wish and delete the brackets, but *be very careful not to change* any of the coding outside the brackets. Don't forget to change the title (it appears near the top of the file).

3 Find and change the URLs in the page.

The current URLs point to the Dummies page, but you can replace the URL http://www.dummies.com with any URL you wish. Again, take care to change only the URL, not any of the surrounding code.

4 Near the bottom of the file, you need to enter your complete e-mail address in two different spots (both in brackets).

Enter your e-mail address and delete the brackets but do not disturb the surrounding code.

5 Save the file under a new name (so that you can use YOURHOME.HTM another time).

Note: If you edit YOURHOME.HTM and then save your edited HTML file in a folder that's different from the one where YOURHOME.HTM is stored (Template), be sure to copy the picture files from the Template folder to the folder where you've saved the new HTML file. The picture files used in YOURHOME are:

- alum.gif (the gray horizontal rule beneath the top heading)

- rule18.gif (the blue, animated horizontal rule used twice in the page)
- bullet4.gif (the star-shaped bullets on the links)
- pattern09.gif (the picture file that's tiled to create the image background)

6 **View your new page in Internet Explorer by clicking the View... button.**

7 **Return to WebEdit and make any further changes or edits you wish (it's your page, after all).**

Publishing Your Web Page

After you finish your Web page, you have to copy it onto a Web server so that others on the Internet can see it. Many companies have set up their own Web servers at a cost of many thousands of dollars. If you don't have permission to publish your Web page on your company's (or school's) server and don't plan to buy your own server, you'll need to acquire a little hard disk space on somebody else's Web server. You need enough space on a server to hold all of the files that make up your page (the HTML file plus any picture files). A typical Web page with a picture or two in it usually requires less than 100 kilobytes of space on a server. The larger and more picture-laden your page is, the more server space you'll need.

Finding Web server space is pretty easy. Odds are that your Internet Service Provider (whether a major online service or a local mom & pop service) has a Web server and will allow you to publish your page there. Rates for server space vary widely. Some providers offer a small amount of Web server space free to each of their Internet subscribers, and some don't. Most providers are willing to lease you space by the month; the monthly rate usually depends on how much hard disk space your files require. Also, some providers charge higher rates for business-related pages than for personal home pages because a business page is likely to receive more visits than a personal home page, thus having a greater impact on the provider's service capacity.

some Internet Service Providers offer Web server space free to each of their Internet subscribers

If your provider does not offer Web server space, contact other providers. Some may be willing to lease space to you even if you are not a subscriber to their Internet service. Usually, however, you get a better deal on server space from a provider when you also subscribe to that provider's Internet service. If your provider does not offer Web space, you may save money by switching your Internet subscription to a provider that does offer Web space.

When you know whose server will hold your Web page files, you must copy the files from your PC to the server — *upload* the files. The exact procedures for doing this task differ by provider; you must get complete uploading instructions directly from the company whose server you will use. Be careful that you also upload any picture files (including any used for an image background) and store them in the same server directory as the HTML file.

Finally, after your page is on the server, you'll probably want to put out the word that it's there. Depending on what you hoped to achieve by setting up a Web page in the first place, you may wish to do any or all of the following:

- E-mail friends and associates to give them your URL.

- Include your Web page URL in all of your correspondence and on your business cards, stationery, advertising, and so on.

- List your page in the appropriate categories of major search tool directories (see Unit 5). When you visit the page of most search tools, look for a link reading "Add URL" or something similar. Click the link and follow the instructions to add your Web page to the directory.

Learning More about Authoring

You've just had a taste of Web authoring, but there's so much more to learn. This final section describes a few Web pages where you can find resources to expand your Web authoring capabilities.

Keep in mind that WebEdit is just one of dozens of available HTML editors. Some are more difficult to use than WebEdit; others are easier. In Unit 6, you downloaded another such editor (HTML Assistant). You've got the file, so why not check out HTML Assistant and see if you like it? You'll find links to other editors in the following pages:

Microsoft's Site Builder Workshop, Authoring Page

```
http://www.microsoft.com/workshop/author/default.htm
```

Description: Links to guides and tutorials, authoring tools, media files, and more.

Microsoft Office Internet Tools Page

```
http://www.microsoft.com/office/MSOfc/it_ofc.htm
```

Description: Links to pages describing the Internet Assistants available for downloading from Microsoft. The Internet Assistants are free add-ins to Microsoft Office 95 programs (Word, Excel, PowerPoint, Access) that transform each program into a Web authoring tool. For example, the Internet Assistant for Word allows you to convert your Word documents to HTML or compose and view new HTML documents right in Word. (Office 97 programs have these capabilities built-in and require no Internet Assistant add-in.)

BevNet's Learning HTML

```
http://www.bev.net/computer/htmlhelp/
```

Description: A friendly tutorial in HTML plus links to editors and clip art pages.

Thomas Reed's Beginner's Guide to Web Page Creation

```
http://members.aol.com/thomasreed/instruct/web/
index.html
```

Description: A very friendly HTML tutorial.

Jeffrey Zeldman's Ask Dr. Web

```
http://www.zeldman.com/faq.html
```

Description: A great compendium of links to terrific sources for editors, clip art, and more.

Yahoo!'s Web Authoring Directory

```
http://www.yahoo.com/Computers_and_Internet/Internet/
World_Wide_Web/Authoring/
```

Description: Links to dozens of useful Web authoring sites.

Yahoo!'s Clip Art Directory

```
http://www.yahoo.com/Computers_and_Internet/Multimedia/
Pictures/Clip_Art/
```

Description: A great collection of links to clip art sites. Note that these sites have pictures in many file formats, but only the GIF and JPEG images are useful for Web pages.

Index

◆ A ◆

account security words, AT&T WorldNet, 19
account setups, AT&T WorldNet, 13–20
active multimedia, 100, 108–109
ActiveMovie videos
  playing video clips and sound clips, 105, 106–109
  saving after viewing, 108
Address box, entering URLs in, 44–47
addresses
  e-mail, 170–171
  URL (Uniform Resource Locator), 43–52
AltaVista search tool, phrasing search terms, 78–79
AND operator, multiple-word search terms, 80–81
answers to quizzes and tests, 205–212
archives
  See also compressed files
  file types, 86, 88
AT&T WorldNet accounts, 13–20
  account security words, 19
  credit card numbers, 18
  e-mail names, 18–19
  e-mail passwords, 19
  installing Internet Explorer, 20–21
  Member Directory listings, 19
  modem setups, 15–16
  passwords, 19
  phone numbers, 15–16
  registration, 16–20
  Search tools, 71–72
  Service Agreement and Operating Policies, 17
  setup Wizard, 14–15
AT&T WorldNet software, Dummies 101 CD-ROM, 214
audio settings
  multimedia, 101
  NetMeeting, 190, 191
authoring resources, 226–227

◆ B ◆

Back button, 36–37
backgrounds, Comic Chat, 157–158
ballpark-and-browse idea, 82

◆ browsers

browsers
  See also Internet Explorer
  defined, 2, 12
  HTML variations among, 219
browsing the Internet, 31–41
  aimless wandering, 74–75
  Back button, 36–37
  Forward button, 36–37
  Home button, 35–36
  links, 31, 32–35
  with purpose, 76
  search tools and, 74–76

◆ C ◆

categories, search tools and, 74–76
Cc lines, e-mail, 172
CD-ROM in back of book. See Dummies 101 CD-ROM
censorship. See Content Advisor
certificates, reprogramming Internet Explorer with,
    32–33
characters, Comic Chat, 157–158
chatting. See Comic Chat
children's supervision. See Content Advisor
clicking
  links, 32–33, 34–35
  right-clicking, 27
closing Internet Explorer, 24
collaboration. See NetMeeting
Comic Chat, 155–165
  chat servers, 155, 160
  contributing to conversations, 162–163
  Dummies 101 CD-ROM, 215
  entering from Web pages, 160–161
  entering rooms, 159
  expressions, 163
  Favorites, 159
  gestures, 164–165
  jumbled conversations, 160
  nicknames, characters, and backgrounds, 157–158
  opening and connecting to servers, 156–157
  plain-text mode, 165
  setting up, 155–156
  switching rooms, 165
  updating, 156
  window parts, 161, 162

compressed files, unzipping, 94–96
computers
  multimedia requirements, 100
  switching off to disconnect from Internet, 25
conferencing. *See* NetMeeting
Connect dialog boxes, 21
Content Advisor, 119–128
  controversy of Web content, 120
  disabling, 126
  enabling ratings and choosing types of material to
    block out, 122–124
  General tab, 124–125
  options, 124–125
  overriding, 124
  passwords, 122–123, 124, 125
  ratings, 121, 122
  unrated pages, 124, 125
context menus, right-clicking objects in Windows 95, 27
conventions in this book, 6
conversation. *See* chatting
copying Internet shortcuts from Favorites folder,
  144–145
copying and pasting URLs, 49–50
crawler search tools, 70
credit card numbers, registering AT&T WorldNet
  accounts with, 18

▸ D ▸

default newsgroups, 179
directories, search tool, 70
discussion groups. *See* newsgroups
displaying external multimedia, 105–106
downloading files, 85–97
  compressed files, 94–96
  defined, 85
  file types, 86–88, 92–93
  FTP (File Transfer Protocol), 93–94
  multitasking and, 92
  Open It option, 91
  opening after, 92–94
  retrieving files, 90–92
  Save As dialog box, 91
  Save It To Disk option, 91
  searching for files, 89–90
  sources for, 89
  time requirements, 90
  viewer links, 88
  viruses and, 86
downloading newsgroup lists, 178
Dummies 101 CD-ROM
  AT&T WorldNet software, 214

Comic Chat, 155–165, 215
  described, 4
  installing, 213
  installing programs and files, 214–216
  NetMeeting, 187–195, 215
  Web page creation, 216
  WinZip utility, 94–95, 215
Dummies 101 folder, 27

▸ E ▸

e-mail, 169–176
  addresses, 170–171
  AT&T WorldNet names, 18–19
  AT&T WorldNet passwords, 19
  Cc lines, 172
  composing messages, 171–173
  forwarding messages, 176
  message parts, 169–170
  quotes, 175
  replying to messages, 174–175
  sending and receiving messages, 173–174
  signatures, 170
editing URLs, 46
editors, HTML, 218
errors, URL, 45
exercises (end of unit)
  Unit 1, 29
  Unit 2, 41
  Unit 3, 52
  Unit 4, 62
  Unit 5, 84
  Unit 6, 96–97
  Unit 7, 111
  Unit 8, 128
  Unit 9, 137
  Unit 10, 146
  Unit 11, 167
  Unit 12, 185
  Unit 13, 195
Explorer. *See* Internet Explorer
expressions, Comic Chat, 163
extensions
  file type, 87, *88*
  HTML, 219
external multimedia, 100, 103–108
  ActiveMovie videos, 105, 106–109
  converting from inline multimedia, 103
  displaying graphics, 105–106
  file types, 104
  finding files, 103–104
  unpredictability of Internet Explorer, 105
Extract button, WinZip utility, 95

▸ F ▸

Favorites folder, copying Internet shortcuts from, 144–145
Favorites list, 53–62
  adding current page, 54–55
  adding page from links, 55–56
  Comic Chat, 159
  defined, 58
  folders within folders, 60
  jumping to, 56–57
  managing, 57–60
  organizing, 58–60
file types, 86–88
  archives, 86, 88
  extensions, 87, 88
  external multimedia, 104
  opening downloaded files, 92–93
  self-extracting archives, 88
  Windows versions, 87
  ZIP files, 86
filenames, slashes in URLs and, 48
files
  compressed, 94–96
  downloading, 85–97
finding files. *See* search terms; search tools; searching
Forward button, 36–37
forwarding e-mail messages, 176
friendly URLs, 47
FTP (File Transfer Protocol) servers, downloading files from, 93–94

▸ G ▸

General tab, Content Advisor, 124–125
gestures, Comic Chat, 164–165
graphics
  displaying external multimedia, 105–106
  Home Page Wizard picture files, 221
  links in, 33

▸ H ▸

highlighting URLs, 50
Home button, 35–36
Home Page Wizard, 220, 221–223
  information requirements, 222
  picture file graphics, 221
  URLs, 221
home pages
  customizing, 39
  defined, 22, 23

scrolling through, 26
  URLs and, 43–52
HTML (HyperText Markup Language), 217–219
  browser variations, 219
  editors, 218
  extensions, 219
  source viewing, 218
hyperlinks. *See* links

▸ I ▸

icons in this book, 7–8
inline multimedia, 100, 101–103
installing
  Dummies 101 CD-ROM, 213
  Internet Explorer, 20–21
  NetMeeting, 189
  programs and files on Dummies 101 CD-ROM, 214–216
Internet
  browsing, 31–41
  online exercise, 21–25
  overview, 1–2
  Service Providers. *See* ISPs
  signing off, 23–25
  World Wide Web and, 11
Internet Explorer
  See also browsers
  Back button, 36–37
  certificates, 32–33
  closing, 24
  Comic Chat, 153–167
  connecting to Internet, 21–23
  Content Advisor, 119–128
  disconnecting from Internet, 23–25
  downloading files, 85–97
  Dummies 101 folder, 27
  e-mail, 169–176
  Favorites list, 53–62
  Forward button, 36–37
  getting offline, 23–25
  getting online, 21–23
  Home button, 35–36
  installing, 20–21
  maximizing, 25
  moving-logo indicator, 26
  multimedia, 99–111
  opening saved Web pages from within, 134–135
  opening without connecting, 134
  printing Web pages, 130–131
  Quick Links, 38–39
  quitting, 24
  reprogramming with certificates, 32–33

Internet Explorer *(continued)*
  requirements for, 3–4
  scroll bars, 25–26
  search tools, 69–84
  Stop button, 35
  title bar, 25
  unpredictability of, 105
  updating, 20
  URLs, 43–52
  Web pages, 217–227
  Windows 95 and, 3
Internet Mail. *See* e-mail
Internet News. *See* newsgroups
Internet phone calls. *See* NetMeeting
Internet Service Providers (ISPs), account setups, 11–29
Internet shortcuts, 139–146
  See also links; URLs
  copying from Favorites folder, 144–145
  creating from links, 141–142
  creating from pages, 140–141
  defined, 139
  links comparison, 140
  opening, 142–143
  Properties dialog boxes, 143
  renaming, 141
  uses for, 139–140
IRC. *See* Comic Chat
ISPs (Internet Service Providers), account setups, 11–29

◆ L ◆

lab assignments
  Part I, 66
  Part II, 116
  Part III, 150
  Part IV, 201
links, 32–35
  See also Internet shortcuts; URLs
  certificates and, 32–33
  clicking, 32–33, 34–35
  creating Favorites pages from, 55–56
  defined, 32
  duplicating on same page, 34
  identifying, 33–34
  in pictures, 33
  printing, 131
  Quick Links, 38–39
  shortcuts comparison, 140
  underlining and, 33
logo indicator, 26

◆ M ◆

Magellan search tool, browsing categories, 76
mail. *See* e-mail
maximizing Internet Explorer, 25
media files. *See* multimedia
Member Directory listings, AT&T, 19
menus, context, 27
messaging. *See* e-mail; newsgroups
modem setups for AT&T WorldNet accounts, 15–16
moving around Web pages, 25–26
moving-logo indicator, 26
multimedia, 99–111
  active media, 100, 108–109
  ActiveMovie video, 105, 106–109
  categories of, 99
  external media, 100, 103–108
  inline media, 100, 101–103
  PC requirements for, 100
  sound, 101
  video, 102, 105, 106–109
  Volcano Coffee page, 102
multiple-word search terms, 77, 80–81

◆ N ◆

names, Comic Chat, 157–158
netiquette (Internet etiquette), 181–182
NetMeeting, 187–195
  audio settings, 190, 191
  Dummies 101 CD-ROM, 215
  hardware requirements, 188
  installing, 189
  making calls, 191–192
  opening and configuring, 189–191
  overview, 187–188
  setting up for phone calls, 188–191
  taking calls, 193
  ULS directory, 192, 193
  ULS servers, 189–190
  updating, 188
newsgroups, 176–184
  adult content, 177
  default, 179
  downloading lists, 178
  message parts, 169–170
  netiquette, 181–182
  opening from Web pages, 177
  opening Internet News, 178
  posting messages, 181–184
  reading messages, 180–181
  replying to messages, 182–183

search tools, 79
signatures, 170
subscribing to, 178–179
updating lists, 178
newsreaders, defined, 169
nicknames, Comic Chat, 157–158

◆ O ◆

offline, defined, 13
online
    See also Internet Explorer
    Connect dialog boxes, 21, 22
    defined, 13
    signing off Internet, 23–25
Open It option, downloading files, 91
opening
    Comic Chat, 156–157
    downloaded files, 92–94
    Internet Explorer without connecting, 134
    Internet News, 178
    Internet shortcuts, 142–143
    NetMeeting, 189–191
    newsgroups from Web pages, 177
    saved Web pages from Internet Explorer, 134–135
    saved Web pages from Windows, 133–134
    WebEdit utility, 221
OR operator, multiple-word search terms, 80–81
organizing Favorites list, 58–60

◆ P ◆

pages. *See* Favorites list; home pages; printing pages;
    Web pages
passwords
    AT&T WorldNet accounts, 19
    Content Advisor, 122–123, 124, 125
PCs
    multimedia requirements, 100
    switching off to disconnect from Internet, 25
phone calls. *See* NetMeeting
phone numbers, AT&T WorldNet accounts, 15–16
photos & pictures. *See* graphics
posting newsgroup messages, 181–184
printing
    pages, 130–131
    saved pages, 135
    shortcuts, 131
Properties dialog box for Internet shortcuts, 143
publishing Web pages, 225–226

◆ Q ◆

Quick Links, 38–39
quitting Internet Explorer, 24
quizzes
    See also tests
    answers, 205–212
    Unit 1, 28
    Unit 2, 40
    Unit 3, 51
    Unit 4, 61
    Unit 5, 83–84
    Unit 6, 96–97
    Unit 7, 110
    Unit 8, 127
    Unit 9, 136
    Unit 10, 145–146
    Unit 11, 166–167
    Unit 12, 184–185
    Unit 13, 194
quotes, e-mail, 175

◆ R ◆

ratings, Content Advisor, 121, 122
reading newsgroup messages, 180–181
receiving e-mail messages, 173–174
Recreational Software Advisory Council (RSAC), ratings
    for Content Advisor, 121
registration for AT&T WorldNet accounts, 16–20
replying to
    e-mail messages, 174–175
    newsgroup messages, 182–183
right-clicking, defined, 27
RSAC (Recreational Software Advisory Council), ratings
    for Content Advisor, 121
Run dialog box, entering URLs in, 47–48

◆ S ◆

saving
    ActiveMovie videos, 108
    Save As dialog box, 91
    Save It To Disk option, 91
    Web pages to disk, 132
scroll bars, 25–26
search terms, 77–79, 80–81
search tools, 69–84
    AT&T WorldNet, 71–72
    ballpark and browse, 82
    browsing, 74–76

search tools *(continued)*
  categories and, 74–76
  changing search pages, 73
  crawlers, 70
  directories, 70
  newsgroups, 79
  opening, 71–73
  overview, 69–71
  partial-word searches, 80
  phrasing search terms, 77–79, 80
  Search button, 71–72
  searching without, 82
  types of, 70
  URLs and, 73
searching
  for external multimedia files, 103–104
  for files to download, 89–90
self-extracting archives, 88
sending e-mail messages, 173–174
servers
  chat, 155, 160
  ULS for NetMeeting, 189–190
  Web, 11, 12
Service Agreement and Operating Policies, AT&T
    WorldNet accounts, 17
setting up
  AT&T WorldNet accounts, 13–20
  Comic Chat, 155–156
  NetMeeting for phone calls, 188–191
  WebEdit utility, 220
setup Wizard, AT&T WorldNet accounts, 14–15
shortcuts. *See* Internet shortcuts
signatures, e-mail and newsgroup, 170
signing off Internet, 23–25
sites, Web, 13
slashes in URLs and filenames, 48
sound
  multimedia, 101
  NetMeeting, 190, 191
source viewing, HTML, 218
spiders, 70
Stop button, 35
subscribing to newsgroups, 178–179
summaries
  Part I, 63
  Part II, 113
  Part III, 147
  Part IV, 197–198
switching rooms in Comic Chat, 165

tests
  See also quizzes
  answers, 205–212
  Part I, 64–65
  Part II, 114–115
  Part III, 148–149
  Part IV, 199–200
time requirements
  file downloads, 90
  Web page appearances, 23
title bar, Internet Explorer, 25
toolbar, Quick Links, 38–39

◢ U ◣

ULS directory, NetMeeting, 192, 193
ULS servers, NetMeeting, 189–190
underlined links, 33
updating
  Comic Chat, 156
  Internet Explorer, 20
  NetMeeting, 188
  newsgroup lists, 178
URLs (Uniform Resource Locators), 43–52
  See also Internet shortcuts; links
  copying and pasting, 49–50
  editing, 46
  entering in Address box, 44–47
  entering in Run dialog box, 47–48
  errors, 45
  friendly, 47
  highlighting, *50*
  Home Page Wizard, 221
  overview, 43
  search tools and, 73
  slashes and filenames, 48
Usenet. *See* newsgroups

◢ V ◣

video
  ActiveMovie, 105, 106–109
  multimedia, 102
viewers, downloading, 88
viewing Web pages with WebEdit utility, 223
viruses and downloading files, 86
Volcano Coffee page, multimedia demonstrations on,
    102

◢ T ◣

tags, HTML, 217–219
templates, WebEdit utility, 224–225

▸W▸

Web. *See* World Wide Web; Web pages
Web pages, 217–227
  See also World Wide Web
  authoring resources, 226–227
  defined, 13
  entering Comic Chat from, 160–161
  HTML (HyperText Markup Language), 217–219
  links and, 31, 32–35
  moving around, 25–26
  opening newsgroups from, 177
  opening saved, 133–135
  printing, 130–131
  printing saved, 135
  publishing, 225–226
  requirements for creating your own, 216
  saving to disk, 132
  time required to appear, 23
  URLs (Uniform Resource Locators),
    43–52
  WebEdit utility, 220–225
WebEdit utility, 220–225
  composing pages, 223–224
  Home Page Wizard, 220, 221–223
  opening, 221
  setting up, 220
  techniques, 220
  templates, 224–225
  viewing pages, 223
Windows 95
  context menus, 27
  entering URLs in Run dialog box, 47–48
  Internet Explorer and, 3
  multitasking and, 92
  opening saved Web pages from, 133–134
  switching off PCs and, 25
  versions and downloading files, 87
WinZip utility
  Dummies 101 CD-ROM, 215
  uncompressing files with, 94–95
World Wide Web, 1–2
  See also Web pages
  Internet and, 11
  servers, 11–12
  sites, 13
WorldNet. *See* AT&T WorldNet accounts
worms, 70

▸Y▸

Yahoo! search tool, 74–75

▸Z▸

ZIP files
  file types, 86
  unzipping, 94–96

Notes

Notes

The Internet For Macs® For Dummies® 2nd Edition	by Charles Seiter	ISBN: 1-56884-371-2	$19.99 USA/$26.99 Canada
The Internet For Macs® For Dummies® Starter Kit	by Charles Seiter	ISBN: 1-56884-244-9	$29.99 USA/$39.99 Canada
The Internet For Macs® For Dummies® Starter Kit Bestseller Edition	by Charles Seiter	ISBN: 1-56884-245-7	$39.99 USA/$54.99 Canada
The Internet For Windows® For Dummies® Starter Kit	by John R. Levine & Margaret Levine Young	ISBN: 1-56884-237-6	$34.99 USA/$44.99 Canada
The Internet For Windows® For Dummies® Starter Kit, Bestseller Edition	by John R. Levine & Margaret Levine Young	ISBN: 1-56884-246-5	$39.99 USA/$54.99 Canada

MACINTOSH

Mac® Programming For Dummies®	by Dan Parks Sydow	ISBN: 1-56884-173-6	$19.95 USA/$26.95 Canada
Macintosh® System 7.5 For Dummies®	by Bob LeVitus	ISBN: 1-56884-197-3	$19.95 USA/$26.95 Canada
MORE Macs® For Dummies®	by David Pogue	ISBN: 1-56884-087-X	$19.95 USA/$26.95 Canada
PageMaker 5 For Macs® For Dummies®	by Galen Gruman & Deke McClelland	ISBN: 1-56884-178-7	$19.95 USA/$26.95 Canada
QuarkXPress 3.3 For Dummies®	by Galen Gruman & Barbara Assadi	ISBN: 1-56884-217-1	$19.99 USA/$26.99 Canada
Upgrading and Fixing Macs® For Dummies®	by Kearney Rietmann & Frank Higgins	ISBN: 1-56884-189-2	$19.95 USA/$26.95 Canada

MULTIMEDIA

Multimedia & CD-ROMs For Dummies® 2nd Edition	by Andy Rathbone	ISBN: 1-56884-907-9	$19.99 USA/$26.99 Canada
Multimedia & CD-ROMs For Dummies® Interactive Multimedia Value Pack, 2nd Edition	by Andy Rathbone	ISBN: 1-56884-909-5	$29.99 USA/$39.99 Canada

OPERATING SYSTEMS:

DOS

MORE DOS For Dummies®	by Dan Gookin	ISBN: 1-56884-046-2	$19.95 USA/$26.95 Canada
OS/2® Warp For Dummies® 2nd Edition	by Andy Rathbone	ISBN: 1-56884-205-8	$19.99 USA/$26.99 Canada

UNIX

MORE UNIX® For Dummies®	by John R. Levine & Margaret Levine Young	ISBN: 1-56884-361-5	$19.99 USA/$26.99 Canada
UNIX® For Dummies®	by John R. Levine & Margaret Levine Young	ISBN: 1-878058-58-4	$19.95 USA/$26.95 Canada

WINDOWS

MORE Windows® For Dummies® 2nd Edition	by Andy Rathbone	ISBN: 1-56884-048-9	$19.95 USA/$26.95 Canada
Windows® 95 For Dummies®	by Andy Rathbone	ISBN: 1-56884-240-6	$19.99 USA/$26.99 Canada

PCS/HARDWARE

Illustrated Computer Dictionary For Dummies® 2nd Edition	by Dan Gookin & Wallace Wang	ISBN: 1-56884-218-X	$12.95 USA/$16.95 Canada
Upgrading and Fixing PCs For Dummies® 2nd Edition	by Andy Rathbone	ISBN: 1-56884-903-6	$19.99 USA/$26.99 Canada

PRESENTATION/AUTOCAD

AutoCAD For Dummies®	by Bud Smith	ISBN: 1-56884-191-4	$19.95 USA/$26.95 Canada
PowerPoint 4 For Windows® For Dummies®	by Doug Lowe	ISBN: 1-56884-161-2	$16.99 USA/$22.99 Canada

PROGRAMMING

Borland C++ For Dummies®	by Michael Hyman	ISBN: 1-56884-162-0	$19.95 USA/$26.95 Canada
C For Dummies® Volume 1	by Dan Gookin	ISBN: 1-878058-78-9	$19.95 USA/$26.95 Canada
C++ For Dummies®	by Stephen R. Davis	ISBN: 1-56884-163-9	$19.95 USA/$26.95 Canada
Delphi Programming For Dummies®	by Neil Rubenking	ISBN: 1-56884-200-7	$19.99 USA/$26.99 Canada
Mac® Programming For Dummies®	by Dan Parks Sydow	ISBN: 1-56884-173-6	$19.95 USA/$26.95 Canada
PowerBuilder 4 Programming For Dummies®	by Ted Coombs & Jason Coombs	ISBN: 1-56884-325-9	$19.99 USA/$26.99 Canada
QBasic Programming For Dummies®	by Douglas Hergert	ISBN: 1-56884-093-4	$19.95 USA/$26.95 Canada
Visual Basic 3 For Dummies®	by Wallace Wang	ISBN: 1-56884-076-4	$19.95 USA/$26.95 Canada
Visual Basic "X" For Dummies®	by Wallace Wang	ISBN: 1-56884-230-9	$19.99 USA/$26.99 Canada
Visual C++ 2 For Dummies®	by Michael Hyman & Bob Arnson	ISBN: 1-56884-328-3	$19.99 USA/$26.99 Canada
Windows® 95 Programming For Dummies®	by S. Randy Davis	ISBN: 1-56884-327-5	$19.99 USA/$26.99 Canada

SPREADSHEET

1-2-3 For Dummies®	by Greg Harvey	ISBN: 1-878058-60-6	$16.95 USA/$22.95 Canada
1-2-3 For Windows® 5 For Dummies® 2nd Edition	by John Walkenbach	ISBN: 1-56884-216-3	$16.95 USA/$22.95 Canada
Excel 5 For Macs® For Dummies®	by Greg Harvey	ISBN: 1-56884-186-8	$19.95 USA/$26.95 Canada
Excel For Dummies® 2nd Edition	by Greg Harvey	ISBN: 1-56884-050-0	$16.95 USA/$22.95 Canada
MORE 1-2-3 For DOS For Dummies®	by John Weingarten	ISBN: 1-56884-224-4	$19.99 USA/$26.99 Canada
MORE Excel 5 For Windows® For Dummies®	by Greg Harvey	ISBN: 1-56884-207-4	$19.95 USA/$26.95 Canada
Quattro Pro 6 For Windows® For Dummies®	by John Walkenbach	ISBN: 1-56884-174-4	$19.95 USA/$26.95 Canada
Quattro Pro For DOS For Dummies®	by John Walkenbach	ISBN: 1-56884-023-3	$16.95 USA/$22.95 Canada

UTILITIES

Norton Utilities 8 For Dummies®	by Beth Slick	ISBN: 1-56884-166-3	$19.95 USA/$26.95 Canada

VCRS/CAMCORDERS

VCRs & Camcorders For Dummies™	by Gordon McComb & Andy Rathbone	ISBN: 1-56884-229-5	$14.99 USA/$20.99 Canada

WORD PROCESSING

Ami Pro For Dummies®	by Jim Meade	ISBN: 1-56884-049-7	$19.95 USA/$26.95 Canada
MORE Word For Windows® 6 For Dummies®	by Doug Lowe	ISBN: 1-56884-165-5	$19.95 USA/$26.95 Canada
MORE WordPerfect® 6 For Windows® For Dummies®	by Margaret Levine Young & David C. Kay	ISBN: 1-56884-206-6	$19.95 USA/$26.95 Canada
MORE WordPerfect® 6 For DOS For Dummies®	by Wallace Wang, edited by Dan Gookin	ISBN: 1-56884-047-0	$19.95 USA/$26.95 Canada
Word 6 For Macs® For Dummies®	by Dan Gookin	ISBN: 1-56884-190-6	$19.95 USA/$26.95 Canada
Word For Windows® 6 For Dummies®	by Dan Gookin	ISBN: 1-56884-075-6	$16.95 USA/$22.95 Canada
Word For Windows® For Dummies®	by Dan Gookin & Ray Werner	ISBN: 1-878058-86-X	$16.95 USA/$22.95 Canada
WordPerfect® 6 For DOS For Dummies®	by Dan Gookin	ISBN: 1-878058-77-0	$16.95 USA/$22.95 Canada
WordPerfect® 6.1 For Windows® For Dummies® 2nd Edition	by Margaret Levine Young & David Kay	ISBN: 1-56884-243-0	$16.95 USA/$22.95 Canada
WordPerfect® For Dummies®	by Dan Gookin	ISBN: 1-878058-52-5	$16.95 USA/$22.95 Canada

DUMMIES PRESS™ QUICK REFERENCES

Fun, Fast, & Cheap!™

The Internet For Macs® For Dummies® Quick Reference
by Charles Seiter

ISBN:1-56884-967-2
$9.99 USA/$12.99 Canada

Windows® 95 For Dummies® Quick Reference
by Greg Harvey

ISBN: 1-56884-964-8
$9.99 USA/$12.99 Canada

Photoshop 3 For Macs® For Dummies® Quick Reference
by Deke McClelland

ISBN: 1-56884-968-0
$9.99 USA/$12.99 Canada

WordPerfect® For DOS For Dummies® Quick Reference
by Greg Harvey

ISBN: 1-56884-009-8
$8.95 USA/$12.95 Canada

Title	Author	ISBN	Price
DATABASE			
Access 2 For Dummies® Quick Reference	by Stuart J. Stuple	ISBN: 1-56884-167-1	$8.95 USA/$11.95 Canada
dBASE 5 For DOS For Dummies® Quick Reference	by Barrie Sosinsky	ISBN: 1-56884-954-0	$9.99 USA/$12.99 Canada
dBASE 5 For Windows® For Dummies® Quick Reference	by Stuart J. Stuple	ISBN: 1-56884-953-2	$9.99 USA/$12.99 Canada
Paradox 5 For Windows® For Dummies® Quick Reference	by Scott Palmer	ISBN: 1-56884-960-5	$9.99 USA/$12.99 Canada
DESKTOP PUBLISHING/ILLUSTRATION/GRAPHICS			
CorelDRAW! 5 For Dummies® Quick Reference	by Raymond E. Werner	ISBN: 1-56884-952-4	$9.99 USA/$12.99 Canada
Harvard Graphics For Windows® For Dummies® Quick Reference	by Raymond E. Werner	ISBN: 1-56884-962-1	$9.99 USA/$12.99 Canada
Photoshop 3 For Macs® For Dummies® Quick Reference	by Deke McClelland	ISBN: 1-56884-968-0	$9.99 USA/$12.99 Canada
FINANCE/PERSONAL FINANCE			
Quicken 4 For Windows® For Dummies® Quick Reference	by Stephen L. Nelson	ISBN: 1-56884-950-8	$9.95 USA/$12.95 Canada
GROUPWARE/INTEGRATED			
Microsoft® Office 4 For Windows® For Dummies® Quick Reference	by Doug Lowe	ISBN: 1-56884-958-3	$9.99 USA/$12.99 Canada
Microsoft® Works 3 For Windows® For Dummies® Quick Reference	by Michael Partington	ISBN: 1-56884-959-1	$9.99 USA/$12.99 Canada
INTERNET/COMMUNICATIONS/NETWORKING			
The Internet For Dummies® Quick Reference	by John R. Levine & Margaret Levine Young	ISBN: 1-56884-168-X	$8.95 USA/$11.95 Canada
MACINTOSH			
Macintosh® System 7.5 For Dummies® Quick Reference	by Stuart J. Stuple	ISBN: 1-56884-956-7	$9.99 USA/$12.99 Canada
OPERATING SYSTEMS:			
DOS			
DOS For Dummies® Quick Reference	by Greg Harvey	ISBN: 1-56884-007-1	$8.95 USA/$11.95 Canada
UNIX			
UNIX® For Dummies® Quick Reference	by John R. Levine & Margaret Levine Young	ISBN: 1-56884-094-2	$8.95 USA/$11.95 Canada
WINDOWS			
Windows® 3.1 For Dummies® Quick Reference, 2nd Edition	by Greg Harvey	ISBN: 1-56884-951-6	$8.95 USA/$11.95 Canada
PCs/HARDWARE			
Memory Management For Dummies® Quick Reference	by Doug Lowe	ISBN: 1-56884-362-3	$9.99 USA/$12.99 Canada
PRESENTATION/AUTOCAD			
AutoCAD For Dummies® Quick Reference	by Ellen Finkelstein	ISBN: 1-56884-198-1	$9.95 USA/$12.95 Canada
SPREADSHEET			
1-2-3 For Dummies® Quick Reference	by John Walkenbach	ISBN: 1-56884-027-6	$8.95 USA/$11.95 Canada
1-2-3 For Windows® 5 For Dummies® Quick Reference	by John Walkenbach	ISBN: 1-56884-957-5	$9.95 USA/$12.95 Canada
Excel For Windows® For Dummies® Quick Reference, 2nd Edition	by John Walkenbach	ISBN: 1-56884-096-9	$8.95 USA/$11.95 Canada
Quattro Pro 6 For Windows® For Dummies® Quick Reference	by Stuart J. Stuple	ISBN: 1-56884-172-8	$9.95 USA/$12.95 Canada
WORD PROCESSING			
Word For Windows® 6 For Dummies® Quick Reference	by George Lynch	ISBN: 1-56884-095-0	$8.95 USA/$11.95 Canada
Word For Windows® For Dummies® Quick Reference	by George Lynch	ISBN: 1-56884-029-2	$8.95 USA/$11.95 Canada
WordPerfect® 6.1 For Windows® For Dummies® Quick Reference, 2nd Edition	by Greg Harvey	ISBN: 1-56884-966-4	$9.99 USA/$12.99/Canada

For scholastic requests & educational orders please call Educational Sales at 1. 800. 434. 2086

FOR MORE INFO OR TO ORDER, PLEASE CALL ▶ 800. 762. 2974

For volume discounts & special orders pleas Corporate Sales, at 415. 655. 3000

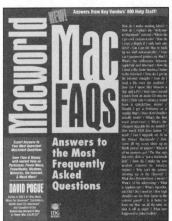

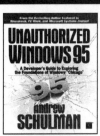

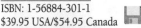

**COMPUTER
BOOK SERIES
FROM IDG**

For Dummies
who want
to program...

**Delphi Programming
For Dummies®**
by Neil Rubenking

ISBN: 1-56884-200-7
$19.99 USA/$26.99 Canada

**Access Programming
For Dummies®**
by Rob Krumm

ISBN: 1-56884-091-8
$19.95 USA/$26.95 Canada

TCP/IP For Dummies®
*by Marshall Wilensky &
Candace Leiden*

ISBN: 1-56884-241-4
$19.99 USA/$26.99 Canada

HTML For Dummies®
by Ed Tittel & Carl de Cordova

ISBN: 1-56884-330-5
$29.99 USA/$39.99 Canada

**Windows® 95 Programming
For Dummies®**
by S. Randy Davis

ISBN: 1-56884-327-5
$19.99 USA/$26.99 Canada

**Mac® Programming
For Dummies®**
by Dan Parks Sydow

ISBN: 1-56884-173-6
$19.95 USA/$26.95 Canada

**PowerBuilder 4 Programming
For Dummies®**
by Ted Coombs & Jason Coombs

ISBN: 1-56884-325-9
$19.99 USA/$26.99 Canada

Visual Basic 3 For Dummies®
by Wallace Wang

ISBN: 1-56884-076-4
$19.95 USA/$26.95 Canada

Covers version 3.

ISDN For Dummies®
by David Angell

ISBN: 1-56884-331-3
$19.99 USA/$26.99 Canada

Visual C++ "2" For Dummies®
*by Michael Hyman &
Bob Arnson*

ISBN: 1-56884-328-3
$19.99 USA/$26.99 Canada

Borland C++ For Dummies®
by Michael Hyman

ISBN: 1-56884-162-0
$19.95 USA/$26.95 Canada

C For Dummies,® Volume I
by Dan Gookin

ISBN: 1-878058-78-9
$19.95 USA/$26.95 Canada

C++ For Dummies®
by Stephen R. Davis

ISBN: 1-56884-163-9
$19.95 USA/$26.95 Canada

**QBasic Programming
For Dummies®**
by Douglas Hergert

ISBN: 1-56884-093-4
$19.95 USA/$26.95 Canada

**dBase 5 For Windows®
Programming For Dummies®**
by Ted Coombs & Jason Coombs

ISBN: 1-56884-215-5
$19.99 USA/$26.99 Canada

7/29/96

Official Hayes Modem Communications Companion
by Caroline M. Halliday

ISBN: 1-56884-072-1
$29.95 USA/$39.95 Canada

Includes software.

1,001 Komputer Answers from Kim Komando
by Kim Komando

ISBN: 1-56884-460-3
$29.99 USA/$39.99 Canada

Includes software.

PC World Excel 5 For Windows® Handbook, 2nd Edition
by John Walkenbach & Dave Maguiness

ISBN: 1-56884-056-X
$34.95 USA/$44.95 Canada

Includes software

PC World WordPerfect® 6 Handbook
by Greg Harvey

ISBN: 1-878058-80-0
$34.95 USA/$44.95 Canada

Includes software.

PC World DOS 6 Command Reference and Problem Solver
by John Socha & Devra Hall

NATIONAL BESTSELLER!

ISBN: 1-56884-055-1
$24.95 USA/$32.95 Canada

Client/Server Strategies™: A Survival Guide for Corporate Reengineers
by David Vaskevitch

SUPER STAR

ISBN: 1-56884-064-0
$29.95 USA/$39.95 Canada

Internet SECRETS™
by John Levine & Carol Baroudi

ISBN: 1-56884-452-2
$39.99 USA/$54.99 Canada

Includes software.

Network Security SECRETS™
by David Stang & Sylvia Moon

ISBN: 1-56884-021-7
Int'l. ISBN: 1-56884-151-5
$49.95 USA/$64.95 Canada

Includes software.

PC SECRETS™
by Caroline M. Halliday

ISBN: 1-878058-49-5
$39.95 USA/$52.95 Canada

Includes software.

IDG BOOKS WORLDWIDE

...SECRETS®

Here's a complete listing of PC Press Titles

Title	Author	ISBN	Price
BBS SECRETS™	by Ray Werner	ISBN: 1-56884-491-3	$39.99 USA/$54.99 Canada
Creating Cool Web Pages with HTML	by Dave Taylor	ISBN: 1-56884-454-9	$19.99 USA/$26.99 Canada
DOS 6 SECRETS™	by Robert D. Ainsbury	ISBN: 1-878058-70-3	$39.95 USA/$52.95 Canada
Excel 5 For Windows® Power Programming Techniques	by John Walkenbach	ISBN: 1-56884-303-8	$39.95 USA/$52.95 Canada
Hard Disk SECRETS™	by John M. Goodman, Ph.D.	ISBN: 1-878058-64-9	$39.95 USA/$52.95 Canada
Internet GIZMOS™ For Windows®	by Joel Diamond, Howard Sobel, & Valda Hilley	ISBN: 1-56884-451-4	$39.99 USA/$54.99 Canada
Making Multimedia Work	by Michael Goodwin	ISBN: 1-56884-468-9	$19.99 USA/$26.99 Canada
MORE Windows® 3.1 SECRETS™	by Brian Livingston	ISBN: 1-56884-019-5	$39.95 USA/$52.95 Canada
Official XTree Companion 3rd Edition	by Beth Slick	ISBN: 1-878058-57-6	$19.95 USA/$26.95 Canada
Paradox 4 Power Programming SECRETS™, 2nd Edition	by Gregory B. Salcedo & Martin W. Rudy	ISBN: 1-878058-54-1	$44.95 USA/$59.95 Canada
Paradox 5 For Windows® Power Programming SECRETS™	by Gregory B. Salcedo & Martin W. Rudy	ISBN: 1-56884-085-3	$44.95 USA/$59.95 Canada
PC World DOS 6 Handbook, 2nd Edition	by John Socha, Clint Hicks & Devra Hall	ISBN: 1-878058-79-7	$34.95 USA/$44.95 Canada
PC World Microsoft® Access 2 Bible, 2nd Edition	by Cary N. Prague & Michael R. Irwin	ISBN: 1-56884-086-1	$39.95 USA/$52.95 Canada
PC World Word For Windows® 6 Handbook	by Brent Heslop & David Angell	ISBN: 1-56884-054-3	$34.95 USA/$44.95 Canada
QuarkXPress For Windows® Designer Handbook	by Barbara Assadi & Galen Gruman	ISBN: 1-878058-45-2	$29.95 USA/$39.95 Canada
Windows® 3.1 Configuration SECRETS™	by Valda Hilley & James Blakely	ISBN: 1-56884-026-8	$49.95 USA/$64.95 Canada
Windows® 3.1 Connectivity SECRETS™	by Runnoe Connally, David Rorabaugh & Sheldon Hall	ISBN: 1-56884-030-6	$49.95 USA/$64.95 Canada
Windows® 3.1 SECRETS™	by Brian Livingston	ISBN: 1-878058-43-6	$39.95 USA/$52.95 Canada
Windows® 95 A.S.A.P.	by Dan Gookin	ISBN: 1-56884-483-2	$24.99 USA/$34.99 Canada
Windows® 95 Bible	by Alan Simpson	ISBN: 1-56884-074-8	$29.99 USA/$39.99 Canada
Windows® 95 SECRETS™	by Brian Livingston	ISBN: 1-56884-453-0	$39.99 USA/$54.99 Canada
Windows® GIZMOS™	by Brian Livingston & Margie Livingston	ISBN: 1-878058-66-5	$39.95 USA/$52.95 Canada
WordPerfect® 6 For Windows® Tips & Techniques Revealed	by David A. Holzgang & Roger C. Parker	ISBN: 1-56884-202-3	$39.95 USA/$52.95 Canada
WordPerfect® 6 SECRETS™	by Roger C. Parker & David A. Holzgang	ISBN: 1-56884-040-3	$39.95 USA/$52.95 Canada

IDG BOOKS WORLDWIDE

Order Center: **(800) 762-2974** *(8 a.m.–6 p.m., EST, weekdays)*

Quantity	ISBN	Title	Price	Total

Shipping & Handling Charges

	Description	First book	Each additional book	Total
Domestic	Normal	$4.50	$1.50	$
	Two Day Air	$8.50	$2.50	$
	Overnight	$18.00	$3.00	$
International	Surface	$8.00	$8.00	$
	Airmail	$16.00	$16.00	$
	DHL Air	$17.00	$17.00	$

*For large quantities call for shipping & handling charges.
**Prices are subject to change without notice.

Ship to:

Name _____

Company _____

Address _____

City/State/Zip _____

Daytime Phone _____

Payment: ☐ Check to IDG Books Worldwide (US Funds Only)

☐ VISA   ☐ MasterCard   ☐ American Express

Card # _____ Expires _____

Signature _____

Subtotal _____

CA residents add
applicable sales tax _____

IN, MA, and MD
residents add
5% sales tax _____

IL residents add
6.25% sales tax _____

RI residents add
7% sales tax _____

TX residents add
8.25% sales tax _____

Shipping _____

Total _____

Please send this order form to:

**IDG Books Worldwide, Inc.
Attn: Order Entry Dept.
7260 Shadeland Station, Suite 100
Indianapolis, IN 46256**

*Allow up to 3 weeks for delivery.
Thank you!*

Introducing
AT&T WorldNet^{SM} Service

A World of Possibilities...

With AT&T WorldNet^{SM} Service, a world of possibilities awaits you. Discover new ways to stay in touch with the people, ideas, and information that are important to you at home and at work.

Make travel reservations at any time of the day or night. Access the facts you need to make key decisions. Pursue business opportunities on the AT&T Business Network. Explore new investment options. Play games. Research academic subjects. Stay abreast of current events. Participate in online newsgroups. Purchase merchandise from leading retailers. Send e-Mail.

All you need is a computer with a mouse, a modem, a phone line, and the software enclosed with this mailing. We've taken care of the rest.

If You Can Point and Click, You're There.

Finding the information you want on the Internet with AT&T WorldNet Service is easier than you ever imagined it could be. That's because AT&T WorldNet Service integrates a specially customized version of a popular Web browser with advanced Internet directories and search engines. The result is an Internet service that sets a new standard for ease of use — virtually everywhere you want to go is a point and click away.

We're With You Every Step of the Way.
24 Hours a Day, 7 Days a Week.

Nothing is more important to us than making sure that your Internet experience is a truly enriching and satisfying one. That's why our highly trained customer service representatives are available to answer your questions and offer assistance whenever you need it — 24 hours a day, 7 days a week. To reach AT&T WorldNet Customer Care, call **1-800-400-1447**.

Safeguard Your Online Purchases

By registering and continuing to charge your AT&T WorldNet Service to your AT&T Universal Card, you'll enjoy peace of mind whenever you shop the Internet. Should your account number be compromised on the Net, you won't be liable for any online transactions charged to your AT&T Universal Card by a person who is not an authorized user.*

*Today cardmembers may be liable for the first $50 of charges made by a person who is not an authorized user, which will not be imposed under this program as long as the cardmember notifies AT&T Universal Card of the loss within 24 hours and otherwise complies with the Cardmember Agreement. Refer to Cardmember Agreement for definition of authorized user.

Minimum System Requirements

To run AT&T WorldNet Service, you need:

- An IBM-compatible personal computer with a 386 processor or better
- Microsoft Windows 3.1x or Windows 95
- 8MB RAM (16MB or more recommended)
- 11MB of free hard disk space
- 14.4 Kbps (or faster) modem (28.8 Kbps is recommended)
- A standard phone line

Installation Tips and Instructions

- If you have other Web browsers or online software, please consider uninstalling them according to vendor's instructions.

- At the end of installation, you may be asked to restart Windows. Don't attempt the registration process until you have done so.

- If you are experiencing modem problems trying to dial out, try different modem selections, such as Hayes Compatible. If you still have problems, please call Customer Care at **1-800-400-1447**.

- If you are installing AT&T WorldNet Service on a PC with Local Area Networking, please contact your LAN administrator for set-up instructions.

- Follow the initial start-up instructions given to you by the vendor product you purchased. (See Unit 1 of *Dummies 101: Internet Explorer 3 For Windows 95*.) These instructions will tell you how to start the installation of the AT&T WorldNet Service Software.

- Follow the on-screen instructions to install AT&T WorldNet Service Software on your computer.

When you have finished installing the software, you may be prompted to restart your computer. Do so when prompted.

Setting Up Your WorldNet Account

The AT&T WorldNet Service Program group/folder will appear on your Windows desktop.

● Double click on the WorldNet Registration icon.

● Follow the on-screen instructions and complete all the stages of registration.

After all the stages have been completed, you'll be prompted to dial into the network to complete the registration process. Make sure your modem and phone line are not in use.

Registering With AT&T WorldNet Service

Once you have connected with AT&T WorldNet online registration service, you will be presented with a series of screens that will confirm billing information and prompt you for additional account set-up data.

The following is a list of registration tips and comments that will help you during the registration process.

I. Use the following registration codes, which can also be found in Unit 1 of *Dummies 101: Internet Explorer 3 For Windows 95*. L5SQIM361 if you are an AT&T long-distance residential customer, and L5SQIM362 if you use another long-distance phone company.

II. We advise that you use all lowercase letters when assigning an e-Mail ID and security code, since they are easier to remember.

III. Choose a special "security code" that you will use to verify who you are when you call Customer Care.

IV. If you make a mistake and exit the registration process prematurely, all you need to do is click on "Create New Account." Do not click on "Edit Existing Account."

V. When choosing your local access telephone number, you will be given several options. Please choose the one nearest to you. Please note that calling a number within your area does not guarantee that the call is free.

Connecting to AT&T WorldNet Service

When you have finished registering with AT&T WorldNet Service, you are ready to make online connections.

● Make sure your modem and phone line are available.

● Double click on the AT&T WorldNet Service icon.

Follow these steps whenever you wish to connect to AT&T WorldNet Service.

Choose the Plan That's Right for You.

If you're an AT&T Long Distance residential customer signing up by March 31, 1997, you can experience this exciting new service for 5 free hours a month for one full year. Beyond your 5 free hours, you'll be charged only $2.50 for each additional hour. Just use the service for a minimum of one hour per month. If you intend to use AT&T WorldNet Service for more than 5 hours a month, consider choosing the plan with unlimited hours for $19.95 per month.*

If you're not an AT&T Long Distance residential customer, you can still benefit from AT&T quality and reliability by starting with the plan that offers 3 hours each month and a low monthly fee of $4.95. Under this plan you'll be charged $2.50 for each additional hour, or AT&T WorldNet Service can provide you with unlimited online access for $24.95 per month. It's entirely up to you.

AT&T

Explore our AT&T WorldNet Service Web site at:
http://www.att.com/worldnet

Over 200 local access telephone numbers throughout the U.S.

IDG BOOKS WORLDWIDE, INC.
<u>END-USER LICENSE AGREEMENT</u>

<u>Read This</u>. You should carefully read these terms and conditions before opening the software packet(s) included with this book ("Book"). This is a license agreement ("Agreement") between you and IDG Books Worldwide, Inc. ("IDGB"). By opening the accompanying software packet(s), you acknowledge that you have read and accept the following terms and conditions. If you do not agree and do not want to be bound by such terms and conditions, promptly return the Book and the unopened software packet(s) to the place you obtained them for a full refund.

1. **<u>License Grant</u>.** IDGB grants to you (either an individual or entity) a nonexclusive license to use one copy of the enclosed software program(s) (collectively, the "Software") solely for your own personal or business purposes on a single computer (whether a standard computer or a workstation component of a multiuser network). The Software is in use on a computer when it is loaded into temporary memory (i.e., RAM) or installed into permanent memory (e.g., hard disk, CD-ROM, or other storage device). IDGB reserves all rights not expressly granted herein.

2. **<u>Ownership</u>.** IDGB is the owner of all right, title, and interest, including copyright, in and to the compilation of the Software recorded on the disk(s)/CD-ROM. Copyright to the individual programs on the disk(s)/CD-ROM is owned by the author or other authorized copyright owner of each program. Ownership of the Software and all proprietary rights relating thereto remain with IDGB and its licensors.

3. **<u>Restrictions on Use and Transfer</u>.**

    (a) You may only (i) make one copy of the Software for backup or archival purposes, or (ii) transfer the Software to a single hard disk, provided that you keep the original for backup or archival purposes. You may not (i) rent or lease the Software, (ii) copy or reproduce the Software through a LAN or other network system or through any computer subscriber system or bulletin-board system, or (iii) modify, adapt, or create derivative works based on the Software.

    (b) You may not reverse engineer, decompile, or disassemble the Software. You may transfer the Software and user documentation on a permanent basis, provided that the transferee agrees to accept the terms and conditions of this Agreement and you retain no copies. If the Software is an update or has been updated, any transfer must include the most recent update and all prior versions.

4. **<u>Restrictions on Use of Individual Programs</u>.** You must follow the individual requirements and restrictions detailed for each individual program in Appendix B of this Book. These limitations are contained in the individual license agreements recorded on the CD-ROM. These restrictions may include a requirement that after using the program for the period of time specified in its text, the user must pay a registration fee or discontinue use. By opening the Software packet(s), you will be agreeing to abide by the licenses and restrictions for these individual programs. None of the material on this disk(s) or listed in this Book may ever be distributed, in original or modified form, for commercial purposes.

5. **<u>Limited Warranty</u>.**

    (a) IDGB warrants that the Software and CD-ROM are free from defects in materials and workmanship under normal use for a period of sixty (60) days from the date of purchase of this Book. If IDGB receives notification within the warranty period of defects in materials or workmanship, IDGB will replace the defective disk(s)/CD-ROM.

    (b) IDGB AND THE AUTHOR OF THE BOOK DISCLAIM ALL OTHER WARRANTIES, EXPRESS OR IMPLIED, INCLUDING WITHOUT LIMITATION IMPLIED WARRANTIES OF MERCHANTABILITY AND FITNESS FOR A PARTICULAR PURPOSE, WITH RESPECT TO THE SOFTWARE, THE PROGRAMS, THE SOURCE CODE CONTAINED THEREIN, AND/OR THE TECHNIQUES DESCRIBED IN THIS BOOK. IDGB DOES NOT WARRANT THAT THE FUNCTIONS CONTAINED IN THE SOFTWARE WILL MEET YOUR REQUIREMENTS OR THAT THE OPERATION OF THE SOFTWARE WILL BE ERROR FREE.

    (c) This limited warranty gives you specific legal rights, and you may have other rights which vary from jurisdiction to jurisdiction.

6. **<u>Remedies</u>.**

    (a) IDGB's entire liability and your exclusive remedy for defects in materials and workmanship shall be limited to replacement of the Software, which may be returned to IDGB with a copy of your receipt at the following address: Disk Fulfillment Department, Attn: Dummies 101: Internet Explorer 3 For Windows 95, IDG Books Worldwide, Inc., 7260 Shadeland Station, Ste. 100, Indianapolis, IN 46256, or call 1-800-762-2974. Please allow 3-4 weeks for delivery. This Limited Warranty is void if failure of the Software has resulted from accident, abuse, or misapplication. Any replacement Software will be warranted for the remainder of the original warranty period or thirty (30) days, whichever is longer.

    (b) In no event shall IDGB or the author be liable for any damages whatsoever (including without limitation damages for loss of business profits, business interruption, loss of business information, or any other pecuniary loss) arising from the use of or inability to use the Book or the Software, even if IDGB has been advised of the possibility of such damages.

    (c) Because some jurisdictions do not allow the exclusion or limitation of liability for consequential or incidental damages, the above limitation or exclusion may not apply to you.

7. **<u>U.S. Government Restricted Rights</u>.** Use, duplication, or disclosure of the Software by the U.S. Government is subject to restrictions stated in paragraph (c) (1) (ii) of the Rights in Technical Data and Computer Software clause of DFARS 252.227-7013, and in subparagraphs (a) through (d) of the Commercial Computer — Restricted Rights clause at FAR 52.227-19, and in similar clauses in the NASA FAR supplement, when applicable.

8. **<u>General</u>.** This Agreement constitutes the entire understanding of the parties and revokes and supersedes all prior agreements, oral or written, between them and may not be modified or amended except in a writing signed by both parties hereto which specifically refers to this Agreement. This Agreement shall take precedence over any other documents that may be in conflict herewith. If any one or more provisions contained in this Agreement are held by any court or tribunal to be invalid, illegal, or otherwise unenforceable, each and every other provision shall remain in full force and effect.

Dummies 101 CD-ROM Installation Instructions

The CD-ROM in the back of this book contains the AT&T WorldNet^{SM} software that you can use throughout the lessons in this book. It also contains other useful programs that are described in Appendix B and an exercise file that is covered in Unit 3. You can easily install these files by using the special *Dummies 101* Installer program that's also stored on the CD-ROM.

Note: The CD-ROM does *not* contain Windows 95. You must already have Windows 95 installed on your computer.

With Windows 95 running, follow these steps:

1. **Insert the *Dummies 101* CD-ROM (label side up) into your computer's CD-ROM drive.**

   Be careful to touch only the edges of the CD-ROM.

   Wait about a minute before you do anything else; the Installer program should begin automatically if your computer has the AutoPlay feature. If the program does not start after a minute, go to Step 2.

2. **Wait a minute or so to give Windows a chance to activate the installation program automatically.**

   Some Windows 95 configurations have a feature called AutoPlay installed. AutoPlay automatically plays/installs any CD-ROM shortly after you insert it. If AutoPlay is enabled for your PC, the Dummies 101 CD-ROM installation program starts up. Follow the instructions you see on-screen to get icons installed in your Start menu.

   If, after a minute or so, you see no messages regarding the CD, your PC does not have AutoPlay enabled, and you must perform Steps 3 and 4 to complete the CD installation.

3. **From your Windows 95 desktop, click the Start button and choose Run.**

4. **In the dialog box that appears, type** D:\ICONS **(substitute your CD-ROM's drive letter if different from D) and then click OK.**

The Installer program displays buttons that you can click to install any or all of the software on the *Dummies 101* CD-ROM. To install an item, click its button on the Installer. To learn more about setting up each program, refer to the unit where the specific program is covered (or see Appendix B).

If you have problems with the installation process, you can call IDG Books Worldwide, Inc., Customer Support: 1-800-762-2974 (outside the U.S.: 317-596-5261).

When you are done using the Dummies 101 CD-ROM, store it in a safe place.

IDG BOOKS WORLDWIDE REGISTRATION CARD

RETURN THIS REGISTRATION CARD FOR FREE CATALOG

Title of this book: **Dummies 101™: Internet Explorer 3 For Windows®**

My overall rating of this book: ❑ Very good [1] ❑ Good [2] ❑ Satisfactory [3] ❑ Fair [4] ❑ Poor [5]

How I first heard about this book:

❑ Found in bookstore; name: [6] ❑ Book review: [7]

❑ Advertisement: [8] ❑ Catalog: [9]

❑ Word of mouth; heard about book from friend, co-worker, etc.: [10] ❑ Other: [11]

What I liked most about this book:

_____

_____

What I would change, add, delete, etc., in future editions of this book:

_____

_____

Other comments:

_____

Number of computer books I purchase in a year: ❑ 1 [12] ❑ 2-5 [13] ❑ 6-10 [14] ❑ More than 10 [15]

I would characterize my computer skills as: ❑ Beginner [16] ❑ Intermediate [17] ❑ Advanced [18] ❑ Professional [19]

I use ❑ DOS [20] ❑ Windows [21] ❑ OS/2 [22] ❑ Unix [23] ❑ Macintosh [24] ❑ Other: [25]_____

(please specify)

I would be interested in new books on the following subjects:
(please check all that apply, and use the spaces provided to identify specific software)

❑ Word processing: [26] ❑ Spreadsheets: [27]

❑ Data bases: [28] ❑ Desktop publishing: [29]

❑ File Utilities: [30] ❑ Money management: [31]

❑ Networking: [32] ❑ Programming languages: [33]

❑ Other: [34]

I use a PC at (please check all that apply): ❑ home [35] ❑ work [36] ❑ school [37] ❑ other: [38] _____

The disks I prefer to use are ❑ 5.25 [39] ❑ 3.5 [40] ❑ other: [41]_____

I have a CD ROM: ❑ yes [42] ❑ no [43]

I plan to buy or upgrade computer hardware this year: ❑ yes [44] ❑ no [45]

I plan to buy or upgrade computer software this year: ❑ yes [46] ❑ no [47]

Name: _____ Business title: [48] _____ Type of Business: [49] _____

Address (❑ home [50] ❑ work [51]/Company name: _____)

Street/Suite# _____

City [52]/State [53]/Zipcode [54]: _____ Country [55] _____

❑ **I liked this book!** You may quote me by name in future
IDG Books Worldwide promotional materials.

My daytime phone number is _____

IDG BOOKS

THE WORLD OF
COMPUTER
KNOWLEDGE

☐ YES!

Please keep me informed about IDG's World of Computer Knowledge.
Send me the latest IDG Books catalog.